D1715698

SURVIVAL
AND PROGRESS

SURVIVAL
AND PROGRESS
THE AFRO-AMERICAN
EXPERIENCE

L. Alex Swan

Contributions in Afro-American and African Studies, Number 58

GREENWOOD PRESS

Westport, Connecticut . London, England

E
185.86
.S96

Library of Congress Cataloging in Publication Data

Swan, Llewellyn Alex, 1938-
    Survival and progress.

    (Contributions in Afro-American and African studies;
no. 58 ISSN 0069-9624)
    Bibliography: p.
    Includes index.
    1.   Afro-Americans—Social conditions—1975-   —Ad-
desses, essays, lectures.   2.   United States—Race
relations—Addresses, essays, lectures.   I.   Title.
II.   Series.
E185.86.S96   305.8'96073   80-1197
ISBN 0-313-22480-3 (lib. bdg.)

Library of Congress Catalog Card Number: 80-1197
ISBN: 0-313-22480-3
ISSN: 0069-9624

First published in 1981

Greenwood Press
A division of Congressional Information Service, Inc.
88 Post Road West, Westport, Connecticut 06881

Printed in the United States of America

10   9   8   7   6   5   4   3   2   1

Copyright Acknowledgments

Permission to quote passages or use extracts from the following publishers is gratefully acknowledged.

Passage from pages 155-56 of John Irwin, *The Felon*, Prentice-Hall, Inc., Englewood Cliffs, N.J. Copyright © 1970. Reprinted by permission of the publisher.

Passages from pages 21, 32, and 40 of Geoffrey Parrinder, *Religion in Africa*, Penguin Books Ltd., London. Copyright © 1969 Geoffrey Parrinder. Reprinted by permission of the publisher.

Passage from pages 148-49 of James Cone, "Black Theology and the Black Church" in *Cross Current*. Reprinted by permission of the publisher.

Every reasonable effort has been made to trace the owners of copyright materials in this book, but in some instances this has proven impossible. The publishers will be glad to receive information leading to more complete acknowledgments in subsequent printings of the book, and in the meantime extend their apologies for any omissions.

To the Swan Collective
Karla, James and Karlecia
and
Frances, Cornelia and John, Sr.

Contents

Illustrations

Tables

Preface

In this book I have tried to capture the essential issues facing Afro-Americans today. No doubt the discussion, analysis and conclusions will cause some of us to take appropriate action, and some will continue to believe that organized, collective, and consistent effort to achieve equality and liberation is fruitless. It is true that the nature and character of the American social order serve to prevent black liberation and equality. It simply means therefore that it is that nature and character that must be changed in order to achieve the goal of liberation. Many Afro-Americans are content to merely survive in America. Survival is a concept that suggests stagnation: One or a group merely exists and struggles against great odds to do so. It is time that Afro-Americans make progress that suggests a forward and onward movement, advancing to a state of progressive betterment with pomp and pageantry.

This work has taken several years. My experiences in "the struggle" and my many conversations with several people have been invaluable. I have received valuable feedback from many of my friends, students and colleagues on several of the issues raised in the book. At conferences a few took me to task while others shouted "right-on." I want to thank the few and the many whose comments stimulated my thoughts. Some of their comments are incorporated in the work and the rest were buried in the depths of the sea hopefully never to surface again.

I am grateful to Mrs. Hilda Gooch, Ms. Brenda Harris and Mrs. Jean Henderson, who typed various chapters of the book and provided very helpful suggestions. I extend thanks to Levy Jones, Andrew Jackson, and LaFrances Rodgers-Rose, the students who took my course, "Blacks in the New World," at Fisk University; to Ronald Parris, Ray Richardson, Roger Hicks, and Joe Towner for engaging me in conversation that fostered clarification of thought and analysis.

Very special thanks is extended to Margaret M. Brezicki, Lynn Taylor, Luanne Tucciarone and the other members of the staff of Greenwood Press.

I appreciate the many sacrifices Karla, James, and Karlecia made to allow this book to be completed. I hope James and Karlecia read this book during their school life and measure the progress Afro-Americans have made over the years. It is my desire that they dedicate themselves to the struggle for liberation, justice and equality.

Finally, I wish to thank my grandmother, Frances Swan, who walked me to school many days and stayed up with me many nights encouraging me to learn how to read, write, spell and work math problems. In the process, we would engage in conversation and I began to think. Even though she fell asleep at the table on numerous occasions, she never allowed me to go to bed without completing my homework. She made the task enjoyable with the short and funny stories she told. Then she would say, "Finish your work, son."

Introduction

This book is organized around critical issues that have been of concern to black society for hundreds of years. Several of my students and professional colleagues who have heard me discuss several of these issues in the classroom and at conferences urged me to develop and organize my ideas into a single volume. This book is also the response to their requests that material in several of my articles be made available for classroom purposes and general discussion among those concerned with justice and the removal of inequality, racism, and oppression from the society of America.

I have selected papers that deal with critical issues, a few of which we have avoided discussing in the 1970s. Nonetheless, they have not been resolved. The context for understanding the issues is provided in the first chapter. The nature and character of the arrangements of American society dictate against the liberation and freedom of Afro-Americans. American society is not simply capitalistic or colonial (racist), it is both; it is out of this dual nature that come arrangements that dominate, control, and oppress Afro-American society. The mask that this combination provides Afro-Americans must be rejected if they are to experience legitimation and liberation.

With whom Afro-Americans should form alliances is the critical issue dealt with in the third chapter of the book. Given the dual nature of the social order of America, Afro-Americans should form alliances only with groups affected by this dual nature. It would be a mistake, therefore, to ally with those who are affected only by the capitalist nature of the social order or simply by the colonial or racist nature of its arrangements. Increasingly, Afro-Americans are adapting the European philosophical/behavioral principle of individualism and abandoning their African philosophical/behavioral principle of collectivism. The danger of this, of course, is that an oppressed group cannot achieve liberation as individuals. Liberation is a group concept. The result of this shift, which is forced upon Afro-Americans to weaken their efforts towards liberation, is that crime increases among the group, suicide becomes more prevalent, and conflict among members intensifies, leading to a lack of tolerance and collective assistance to struggle.

It is imperative that blacks focus upon their youth, who are processed through the juvenile justice system in a way that results from arbitrary and selective identification and the misuse of discretionary power by police. The decisions of the judges are often discriminatory, allowing black youth to be branded for life as they are detained for behavior for which white youth are remanded to sociologists, criminologists, and psychiatrists. Community development centers should be established in black communities where they are needed to assist black youth to interpret their situation and make positive decisions.

Blacks, especially black men, are in prisons primarily for committing survival crimes. Muggings, robbery, burglary, aggravated assaults, and auto theft are *survival crimes* committed to enhance the economic and political power-position of the perpetrators and to facilitate the survival of those who perceive the social order as having few alternatives to address their powerlessness. Homicide committed by the majority of those involved in survival crimes is committed after the fact to the common design of survival crimes. The completion of the common design in a robbery or in any other survival crime is just as important to the perpetrator as the assertion of self, the display of self-worth, and the solicitation of recognition or enhancement of self-esteem in family conflicts or in conflicts with friends, or in the politics (exercise of power over the perceived status of the subject) of rape.

Institutional treatment does not enhance the likelihood of success of those who reenter society. Prisons are good at confining and punishing inmates. As a means of rehabilitation, institutional treatment (imprisonment) has had little success, primarily because treatment programs within the prison tend to be dehumanizing. In such an environment, there is little preparation for reentry into society.

The network of support systems that provides the basis for successful reentry constitutes an environment into which the ex-inmate enters. The environment consists of four subsystems (the family, work, school, church) that interact with each other to produce environmental circumstances conducive to successful reentry.

The support to black ex-convicts found within the community context of the family, the church, work experience, and college can allow successful circumstances that can challenge the negative circumstances created by the prison experience. The negative forces derive from the need of the state for prison labor and the need of the police and the other subsystems of the criminal justice system to be legitimated.

As political and economic arrangements become more disruptive and the social problems resulting from such disruptions multiply, the patterns of relationship among and within families will become disordered. This situation will intensify as blacks shift their philosophical/behavioral orientation from collectivism to individualism. Certain black professionals must be prepared in clinical sociology, family therapy, and the like to assist black families, using the facilities of the churches, to survive and make progress.

Society is becoming more complex and the arrangements of the social order more oppressive. Racism is more covert today; its expression is not so blatant as in the 1940s, 1950s, and 1960s. Black families in the urban areas and those that have experienced some degree of success during and soon after the civil rights era will suffer the greatest impact from such conditions in the social order. The church and the family, the two institutions most likely to survive in one form or another as black institutions, must be helped to assure black people their survival and progress. If this is achieved, a higher form of struggle for liberation and freedom might be realized.

Given the difficulties that blacks must cope with on an ongoing basis, the religious experience of Afro-Americans will intensify and again suffering will be perceived as redemptive. The role of the religious leader will re-establish its importance in the affairs of black people and their communites, as is beginning to be the case.

The church as a collective experience and as an institution and its leadership have been the single most important influence in the struggle for survival and progress among black people. At every point in the struggle, the presence of the church has been felt. There are those who argue that the church has shifted its basic position from the argument that oppression must be fought by the oppressed to the argument that oppression must be coped with, endured until the liberator—Jesus—liberates blacks from their oppression. Many Afro-Americans have even come to believe and accept that suffering is redemptive—that is, that suffering is related to ultimate redemption and that to some extent, the degree to which one suffers in this life is the degree to which one is eventually redeemed. For most blacks, however, one of the most difficult religious experiences to come to grips with is a distinction between the oppressor as the object of Christian love and the oppression as the object of hatred and resistance. Most Christians are confused on this matter and are reluctant to take action against racism and oppression for fear their behavior would be mistaken as an attack against oppressors whom they must love. Any apparent militant statements are judged to come from non-Christians because Christians leave such matters to Christ who will avenge oppressors in His own time and in His own way. What is crippling in the religious experience of black people is the false teaching and beliefs concerning such essential doctrines as "the state of the dead," "health laws," "the moral law," "the ceremonial laws," "the Sanctuary," "the Judgment," and "the holy day of worship."

Afro-Americans and their communities are presently powerless in redressing oppressive issues. Their participation in the political arena has not changed their relatively powerless position. Afro-Americans tended to believe that once they achieved or obtained some degree of political power in the American social order, their social position and their economic circumstances would change. Today, however, black leaders are raising serious questions regarding the benefits received by the black community as a result of political participation.

Gilliam's thesis of the political development of blacks is that "as long as the central fact of black life in America is racism, black politics cannot follow the pattern of white with its right, left and center. It must be an effort on every level to gain the share of power still denied blacks."[1] It is to the economic advantage of white America to deny political power to black America. If allowed such power, it is felt, black America could move to a level of equality never before experienced in the social order. One controlling concept is the sacredness of the right to vote, which has produced a degree of satisfaction in and of itself, with little or no emphasis on how effective is the organization and use of such a right. Power is not achieved simply in the exercise of the right to vote. When the vote is used primarily to elect individuals to political offices and not to advocate and influence political issues that affect a group's relative position in the social order or to assure a political agenda based on the needs and economic situation of the oppressed group, the right to vote is insignificant.

Since 1865 black people have lost in economic value. Unemployment has steadily increased. The majority of blacks who had slaved for their masters were released with no real economic hope. The "free" blacks struggled consistently to keep the little they had accumulated. The real struggle came, however, after 1890, when all southern states revised their state constitution to exclude blacks from political participation. The rules and regulations established regarding political participation were based on the consideration of race, for the purpose of domination and control of one racial group by another. The literacy tests were racist and were administered in discriminatory ways. Poll taxes imposed economic difficulties on poor people, but especially on blacks. Grandfather clauses were instituted, and the primaries were closed to blacks. One provision of the grandfather clause stated that if one's forebears voted prior to 1863 or 1870, one could register. Blacks found no relief in this provision because their parents and grandparents were slaves prior to the stipulated dates.

The Irish, Jewish, Italian, and Eastern European immigrants who flocked to the northern urban centers of America were encouraged to vote. These immigrants were rendered special services upon their entry. They were politically mobilized and given assistance in finding jobs, in securing licenses to operate pushcarts, and in obtaining citizenship papers. During this same period, Afro-Americans were systematically denied participation in the political process. Consequently, these immigrants who voluntarily came to America seeking political freedom and economic opportunity, who had not at this point invested blood, sweat, and tears in the development of the social order, stood to benefit more politically and economically than Afro-Americans who had slaved, without pay, to develop the resources of America.

The struggle to reestablish the legal right to vote took seventy years (1890-1965) after blacks had used the vote successfully to obtain educational and social benefits a short period earlier. This pattern of voting, to increase the group's educational and socioeconomic position, has now shifted to defining success in terms of the number of elected black officials, the number of black police and black mayors, and the number of blacks in this job or that job. These positions of apparent power do not significantly change the relative position of blacks and their communities. Since 1965 there has been no accumulation of real power by blacks from political participation. The economic benefits that would improve the lives of blacks and their community have not been forthcoming.

The colleges and universities established between 1855 and 1921 primarily for the education of Afro-Americans have, for the most part, survived without any significant degree of progress. They may have increased their population over the years, but so has every other college and university. What about their credibility, accountability, impact, and position of power in the education community as the creators of knowlege and the defenders of the political, economic, social, and cultural liberation of black people? Many of these colleges and universities, especially those in close proximity to white colleges and universities, even though they were established in many instances before the white colleges and universities, are under attack because of the dual system in effect with the presence of two competing educational systems. Some are being closed by deliberate acts, and others are struggling to continue despite more subtle attacks. Several are presently under court action to merge with the white institution next door or across the street. On the present course, no doubt, by the year 2000 black colleges will have disappeared from the American social order, or the few that remain will still be attempting to justify their existence, having had no role in creating knowledge, developing model curricula with liberating dimensions, developing new programs, advancing their offerings, and the like. They will still be struggling to survive, sending their graduates to white colleges and universities to complete graduate or professional training.

Progress, not survival, must be the goal of black colleges and universities. The role of black faculty must change to include the creation of knowledge, and their approach to teaching should be enhanced.

What would be the political, economic, and social position of Afro-Americans today were their ancestors paid appropriate and fair wages for their slave labor? What would be their relative degree of power in the American social order were they allowed material gain in terms of land and land resources to be willed to their children and their children's children? What would be the economic strength of Afro-Americans today if they were not victims of racism and oppression for over 350 years? What would be the social and economic condition of Afro-Americans and their community if 13 billion dollars per year were not denied them through acts of discrimination in employment? What would be the relative political position of Afro-Americans had they not been denied the legal right to register and vote for over seventy years (1890-1965)?

Blacks turned to the courts seeking legislation to establish their legal rights as citizens of the United States. The Fifteenth Amendment to the U.S. Constitution reads: "The rights of citizens of the United States to vote shall not be denied or abridged by the United States or by any State on account of race, color, or previous condition of servitude. The Congress shall have power to enforce this article by appropriate legislation" (1870). Court action through social legislation has not significantly changed the relative economic, political, and social position of Afro-Americans. Legislation is unable to redress the condition of oppression, especially racial oppression, because racism has an independence in the American social order that transcends legislation. Legislation addressed the policy but did very little regarding the practice of racism. Afro-Americans have been disappointed because racism continues in subtle and covert ways that give the appearance that it has been controlled and in some instances eliminated from the arrangements of the society. But those who are its victims know through experience that racism is alive and even stronger today in the face of corrective legislation. Racial equality in economics, politics, education, and other matters has not been achieved by the civil rights bills and other such legislation.

America has practiced restitution in regards to Germany, Korea, and Vietnam. Billions of dollars have been given to countries that have been war victims at the hands of America to restore themselves. However, as victims of racism and economic oppression, Afro-Americans have never been compensated for such crimes. How would their situation change if monetary restitution were to be legislated and obtained? If the debt were calculated for the descendants of black American slaves, say, based on fifteen-hour work days, six days per week for twenty years at one dollar per hour for one great-great-great grandparent of every black in America, each black who could make such a claim might be entitled to $86,000. What a change in the economic and social position of twenty-five million Afro-Americans if this were achieved by 1985! It could be that the black social movement that has attempted to change the relative position of black Americans should organize itself around the issue of restitution.

As a collectivity of individuals acting with some degree of continuity, the black social movement has organized itself around three ideologies in response to the racist-capitalist nature and character of the American social order. Even though some degree of success is identifiable, this small degree, primarily individual in nature, has not significantly affected a majority of the people. However, the failure of the black social movement to bring liberation to black people and their community is not a function of the leadership or the lack thereof. Rather, it is a function of the very nature and character of the social order, which is in opposition to the liberation of oppressed blacks by definition and operation.

Given the decline in progressive action, there is a silence among oppressed blacks regarding their next move. The burden to take action is operative, but blacks are assessing more carefully the possible outcome of such action.

Whether it's 1980 or the year 2000, collective action will again be waged with the hope of changing the nature and character of a racist-capitalist arrangement for the benefit not only of oppressed peoples but also of the oppressor.

The twelve chapters that comprise this work address the critical issues in Afro-American society. No doubt, the debate will continue regarding the nature and extent of the survival and progress of Afro-Americans. The issues will become more complex and intense as the economic and political situation worsens. In such an event, the struggle for liberation will continue. But the preacher could be correct in saying that justice and liberation will come to oppressed people only when they finally "lay their burdens down" or when "King Jesus comes to destroy this world" and secure the faithful for the new earth wherein dwelleth righteousness, justice, peace, love, and freedom. However, black people cannot take advantage of this ultimate act of liberation and freedom while they are believing and practicing individualism and false teachings, and destroying their bodies as if they have no sense of accountability and understanding of their destiny. A rejection of the mask is essential to present and future liberation, lest Afro-Americans continue to be "Stuck in the Mud," surviving, but not making any real progress.

Notes

1. Reginald E. Gilliam, Jr., *Black Political Development: An Advocacy Analysis* (New York: Dunellen Publishing Co., 1975).

CONTEXT FOR CRITICAL UNDERSTANDING

1

Nacirema Society: Capitalist and Colonial

This chapter will address itself to an analysis of the nature of American society, the power tools and main institutions that maintain and support it, and the kinds of changes that are possible and necessary if oppressed people are to be liberated and, at the same time, achieve a just society for all groups. Although it is not proposed to wage a full-scale critical analysis of all the assumptions and theoretical contentions that bear on slavery and racism, it does seem necessary to discuss a few conceptual assertions fundamental to any examination of oppressive systems that will serve as a foundation for all subsequent analytical comment.

The first conceptual assertion emerges from the role of Europe in the New World. European entry into the New World created a need for an abundant labor force to develop the mines, forests, and fertile fields to exploit the natural resources of the region. In Africa, Europeans found a people familiar with agriculture and conditioned to the kind of physical work required—a hardworking people who could turn these vast virgin resources into staggering profits. Black slaves were chosen on the basis of their strength, endurance, and experience in order to satisfy this greed-based economy with its unlimited need for unpaid labor and raw materials. It would be developed by the misfits and outcasts of Europe who sought redress by promulgating a belief in an inherently superior white race, created to rule the world. Whether or not this rationale justifies the economic and political greed of Europeans, one can assert that the practice of slavery and the superiority complex combination has produced the capitalist-colonial society operating in the United States today, with all its complexities and oppressive components.

A second assertion is derived from the relationship between the politico-economic structure and color. Though slavery was mainly a consequence of economic greed, color (blackness and whiteness) became, both during and after the period of slavery, a significant quality within a political and economic context. Consequently, in the American social order, blacks have been defined as an "underclass" and as such have been economically, socially, and politically oppressed by all other segments of the society. Lerone Bennett, Jr., argues that:

Black people in America are oppressed by all white social groups in America—by capital as well as labor, by white poor as well as the white well-to-do, by white illiterates as well as white intelligentsia. Every white social group has been conditioned to fear in some way or another our liberation.[1]

James Boggs expands Bennett's argument with the contention that:

After the Negroes were set aside to be systematically exploited, every white immigrant who walked off the gangplank to make his way in America was walking onto the Negroes' backs. The classless society of which Americans are so proud is the society in which white workers have been able to climb on the backs of others out of the working-class into the middle-class. This back-climbing has only been possible because there has always been a Negro underclass at the bottom of society to take the leavings of the jobs, homes, schools, public buildings, etc., as technological development and economic expansion created better opportunities for whites and made no difference how much education or ability a Negro had compared to a white man.[2]

This situation has persisted throughout American history, and the pattern has undergone no significant change. This fact gives credence to the second assertion that color has been a political and economic stigma and an obstacle to the upward mobility of blacks in the United States. The questions arising at this point are: How has this situation persisted? What power tools operated to maintain such a situation? What kinds of changes are necessary for oppressed people to be liberated?

Historical accounts of slavery accept the idea that "economic necessity rather than racial prejudice dictated the beginning of black slavery in North America."[3] This conceptualization insists that the imported Africans were exploited because of the dictates of the plantation economy for unpaid labor. Blauner suggests that, in contrast,

. . . plantation slavery and colonial subjugation were fundamental economic phenomena in that labor exploitation and profit were the overriding purpose of these social arrangements. But there were features in the slavery system and in classical colonialism which were not present in the class relations of western capitalism. These additional realities engendered a dynamic within racial labor systems and the societies in which they were embedded which in times made race relations and white domination considerably more than a matter of class forces and economic motives.[4]

The validity of this statement is evident in the sense that American society is not only capitalistic but also colonial, a combination that produces a unique national social order. The truth of Blauner's comments is further substantiated by historical evidence that reveals that loopholes in the economic and political arrangements, justified by legal arrangements, provided for the escape of poor whites. The fact that Richard Nixon and Harry S. Truman were poor when young is significant and sufficient to illustrate this point. Therefore, it is feasible to suggest that political and economic power is bequeathed to whites by whites in the American society. Moreover, the social order provides for the mobility of whites (poor whites and white workers) at the expense of blacks. Black people not only have been politically dominated and economically exploited but also have suffered systematic cultural and social repression. The economic decisions and political policies put into operation by the "establishment" were, over the years, predicated on the consideration of blackness and whiteness for the implicit purpose of subordinating and maintaining control over black people, the communities in which they live, and the institutions that attempt to serve them.

Between 1895 and 1921, institutional racism achieved acceptance by a majority of Americans, North and South, as the American way. In the vanguard of this philosophical movement and leading the people astray were their presidents and the Supreme Court. Racist doctrines throughout the eighteenth and nineteenth centuries were grounded in a concern for poltical and economic progress. Moreover, this preoccupation with progress—and its resultant exploitation of the dark peoples of Colonial Asia and Africa—supposedly explained why some nations advanced and achieved high levels of "civilization" and why others did not. This belief represents only one of the many disseminated by European peoples during the colonial expansion to develop convenient rationalizations for the exploitation of the black colonial labor force.

The practice of rationalization had become so widespread and accepted that, by the beginning of the nineteenth century, the terms "slave" and "Negro" had become interchangeable. The terms, in fact, designated the same position of servitude. In 1819, the South Carolina Supreme Court ruled that "a black was a slave and a slave was black;" the terms thus became legally synonymous.[5] Several states accepted this position, and the law again justified, legalized, and legitimized oppression that meant political, social, and economic limitations for black people.

Color and race have become significantly influential designations within the social order of the American society to such an extent that their exclusion from a discussion of politico-economic competition and oppression from a class perspective renders such discussion a theoretical and practical failure. In addition to illuminating the politico-economic spectrum, the class perspective has provided an understanding of conflict and change in human contemporary society. However, the class perspective variable, like others, is not all-inclusive. It tends to ignore the significance and dynamics of other operative social (racial) distinctions evident in a colonial society, but it remains important because it is a valid fundamental concept for the concerns of this paper.

An analysis from the capitalist class perspective suggests that the fundamental cleavage within a capitalist society is that between the working and the owning classes. Within this context, the capitalism realities of race seem to be illusive and operating as an undercurrent rather than an observable phenomenon. On the other hand, the colonial perspective addresses itself to a situation in which one race not only exploits and dominates another race economically and politically but also attempts to destroy its culture, values, language, history, and virtually all else in the process of dehumanization. It seems important, therefore, that any theoretical conceptual assertions from a black perspective must incorporate certain racial phenomena in attempting to explain racial oppression in a capitalist-colonial society.

The crucial role of racial phenomena in a capitalist-colonial society is further elucidated by Fanon (1963; 1967). It becomes clear from his discussion that black people are not struggling merely to improve their economic situation or to acquire better jobs or even greater political power. They are, in addition, struggling for their humanity. In the process, they have found themselves fighting poor whites who were merely striving for better jobs, more money, and more property. The poor white would-be capitalists who have become capitalists thus have also become the oppressors of black people. Given the fact that American society is racist, one of the fundamental mistakes in seeking ways to end racial oppression of blacks is to suggest that black and white workers form a coalition to fight their common oppressor.

What seems to be forgotten is the fact that the dominant society also has established colonial relationships with black people and their communities. Although black and white workers struggle essentially against the same force, it is for different reasons, and they also struggle against each other. Moreover, the society responds to these groups differently, providing for the escape of the one and continued control and domination of the other.

A Synthesis

The concept of colonialism refers to a system of relationships between the colonizer and the colonized in which the colonizer establishes external control over the territory of the colonized. This control may be operationalized by members of the colonizer's community who are external to the colonized community, or by representatives of the colonizer who are members of the colonized community. Whatever political, economic, and legal status the colonized community enjoys, it is determined by the colonizers, the consequence being subordination and domination of the colonized community. Furthermore, certain institutions and agencies are set up to maintain, control, and subordinate the colonized.

Power domination is essential to the understanding of the system of colonization of blacks because it denotes the involuntary nature of their initial entry into the American social order. It further speaks to the impact of power domination on the social organizations and cultural institutions of the colonized. This impact goes beyond the mere process of socialization and acculturation to an attempt at the restraint and destruction of indigenous values that will create cultural dependency and the social allegiance of the colonized to the colonizer. Institutional racism begins to set in when the superordinate group (the colonizers) establishes cultural cookie-cutter institutions to coerce and brainwash the subordinate group (the colonized).

There is also an essential working-class capitalist relationship that describes the two interrelated systems and processes in America. Those who are colonized work (experiencing little or no vertical mobility) on behalf of the colonizer, who is also the capitalist. The major thrust is that the mode of production in the colonized community is the exploitation of the working people in industries and other enterprises owned by and operated for the profit motives and social well-being of capitalists. The process of colonization is essential to colonialism and capitalism. Both systems and their related processes must be discontinued if oppressed people are to be liberated. A beginning would be to establish a balance between (1) technological, cultural, and power relations, (2) the authority or right to determine political and economic mobility, and (3) the establishment of social practices supporting formal and informal cultural institutions. A capitalist-colonial society is characterized by a system of relationships based on political domination, economic exploitation, and cultural repression. The process of domination, exploitation, and repression is characterized by brainwashing, coercion, force, and violence. One additional factor is that these arrangements, once institutionalized, stabilize and perpetuate themselves. Although the system was established initially by laws and reinforced by explicit acts, it has now become an autonomous entity propelled by its own internal dynamics.[6] Therefore, it is eventually realized, the law has been rendered unimportant in regard to making or effecting just and equitable changes in society. It has become neutralized as a viable force for justice.

The individual acts of the colonizers, combined with the institutionalized practices and policies of a capitalist system, breed a situation wherein politico-economic domination gives rise to cultural domination which in turn reinforces the politico-economic domination.

The subjugation, control, and exploitation of blacks and their community were willed, designed, and constructed as an integral part of the institutional infrastructure of the American social order. Within the context of control, the colonized community is made a target for administration of policemen, politicians, social workers, and other such public service agencies, which are forced to justify their very existence and protect their sanctity by establishing parasitical relationships with the community. This situation is maintained by every available power tool, even by violence.

Power Tools of the Nacirema Society

One way of understanding the history of a society and how its arrangements (practices and policies) are maintained is to look at the basic concepts used to motivate the people and the power tools that undergird that society.

It is important to note the role that oppressed people play in a capitalist-colonial society and to understand how, by their presence, their behavior, and sometimes by their nonbehavior, they have been instrumental in shaping concepts, attitudes, and international and national policies.

The questions at this point are: (1) What are the basic power concepts that undergird the American society—shaping it, structuring it, and sustaining it as a cohesive whole? and (2) How has the presence of oppressed people helped to shape these concepts and, indeed, to force Americans to reexamine them?

One of the basic power tools that keeps American functioning and has been its nationalistic bread and butter is the concept heard during the election campaign of 1968—the concept of "law and order." From the outset (the beginning of the Republic) Americans have been concerned about law and order. Historically, the question of law and order has been a fundamental power concept. It has been operative in keeping the nation solitary and maintaining oppressive arrangements for many. However, when the concept of law and order is examined along with the manner in which it has traditionally functioned in the American society and when it is projected against the present—the activities and the experiences of black people in America—the question to be raised is whose law and what order? Law and order for whom and to the benefit and well-being of what constituency, as it clearly does not serve all Americans?

When Richard Nixon campaigned in 1968 on the plank of law and order (manipulating this American power tool), what was he actually saying? One finds it difficult to believe that Richard Nixon was suggesting that if he were elected president, he would put rapists, murderers, gangsters, and thieves in jail. The fact is that we all are against these forms of behavior. He was not suggesting that he would round up all prostitutes and bring politicians who steal large sums of money to trial and incarcerate them (especially with Watergate looming precariously over his head). What Nixon was not only suggesting but promising, along with other law-and-order politicians, was the continued utilization of irregular and illegitimate enforcement procedures to keep "minorities" (black especially) "in their place."

Fundamentally, the concept of law and order is an operative power tool in the American society that means that those in power are going to make the law and others are going to be kept in order. Consequently, they fashion the law in such a way that it provides freedom for them to live and function comfortably and repression for others in order that those others be kept in their "place." One of the things black people and other oppressed peoples have tried to accomplish is to force America into a basic reexamination of the concept of law and order.

Law without justice is tyranny. No one denies that Hitler had law, and there is little doubt that he kept order; however, in the process he killed sixteen million people. Black people have forced to the forefront the reexamination of the concept of law and order in order to insist that it now incorporate the concept of justice. The concern here is mainly classic lawbreaking, not common criminality.

Mankind has progressed not on the backs of the law-and-order crowd but on the backs of the lawbreakers; they have made man what he is today. If someone had not broken the law, most Americans would be Catholics and/or British subjects. If someone had not broken the law, women would not be able to vote. If someone had not broken the law, many blacks would not be able to sit on park benches in many cities built with their parents' taxes and labor. A thirty-three-year-old country preacher from Jerusalem one day walked into the temple and violated many of the laws; he got a bull-whip and beat a few people, then walked out of the temple and broke another law against miscegenation. He drank water with the woman of Samaria and staged the first "drink-in" in recorded history. Finally, someone confronted him with his apparent deviant behavior. "You are breaking the law, preacher." "I know," he replied, and the rest of the response is a classic: "Man was not made for the law, the law was made for man!" Black people in America have forced America in Socratic terms to raise the question—what must a good man morally do when faced with unjust laws that legalize oppressive arrangements?

A great moment in American history occurred when Henry David Thoreau was faced with an unjust tax law, and he disobeyed the law and was jailed for the violation. While in jail he was visited by his close friend, Ralph Waldo Emerson, who asked in apparent astonishment, "My word, Henry, what are you doing in there?" And Thoreau replied, "My word, Ralph, what are you doing out there?" Implicit in Thoreau's reply to Emerson is the notion that in evil times all good men belong in trouble and that in times of change the just man has no alternative but to break the law to bring about a just and good society. Black people have had to break the law because they have been victims of legalized injustices. For example, a law is passed to put blacks in slavery, and then they are jailed because they attempt to run away. Let us continue this point one step further. The earlier law of the American Constitution stated that women could not vote. Free black men had three-fifths of a vote. Women could not vote at all; they were the "niggers" then. These were legalized injustices; and until the women of America took to the streets and broke the law, they did not have the right to vote.

The preoccupation with law and order is disturbing at times. For why is it that white Americans are only now acutely "uptight" about law and order? All of those years when blacks and Indians were being killed and their bodies floated in the Mississippi River and black bodies were hanging from many trees in the South and the Midwest, very few whites said anything about law and order. In 1954, the Supreme Court ruled that school desegregation was the law of the land, but in 1974 only about 12 to 15 percent of black children are involved in an integrated education. Whites were not concerned about where black children went to school until the court decreed they should go to school with whites. This is not to suggest that blacks, in 1974, are that concerned about "integrated education" but rather to indicate the nature of a racist society and its implicit power to deny rights and control black initiative.

Returning to the questions posed at the outset of this section, one finds that the preceding discussion has necessarily evolved to the following conclusion, which responds to that second question: How has the presence of oppressed people helped to shape these concepts and force Americans to reexamine them? Oppressed black people, in their quest for a just society, have forced America to reexamine its basic tenets of law and order. Max Ways further substantiates that:

. . . the (black) crisis, by pressing hard upon the longstanding defects of the U.S. communities, can make us understand how much is unnecessarily faulty in American life, white as well as black. The protest has performed the service of awakening us to our society's weakness, and we cannot deal with (black) unrest without remedying social defects that extend far beyond the (black) problem.[7]

When we have a society with justice under the law—a society that remains fluid and admits the necessity of change—only then do we have what is called a just and valid society.

The Concept of Violence

Still dealing with the question of the basic power concepts of the American society, attention now turns to the concept of violence. During this time of the riots, initiated by blacks, white Americans grew very concerned about violence in America. Not much concern was demonstrated when blacks were being lynched; their churches bombed; their women raped; and their youth shot and killed at South Carolina State, Jackson State, and Southern University. White law-enforcement Americans became concerned only when white students were the victims of shootings at Berkeley, Columbia, and Kent State.

During the early 1960s, when black speakers were invited to speak on white college campuses the most frequent question asked them by administration representatives admitting these speakers was, "Are black students going to get violent?" The answer—more often than not—was "Yes." But black people got violent not because they were black but because they were oppressed people trying to survive in a system that breeds and employs violence to achieve its ends. In America, violence has been one of the power tools that has been manipulated, and black people have forced America to reexamine it. Let us clarify this notion somewhat. Those in America who are in power came to that power through violence, and they use violence to maintain their position of power. Mayor Daley made this point very clear to the demonstrators in Chicago in the summer of 1968. His position was that if they did not remain nonviolent, he would use violence to control them. It seems very difficult for white America to come to grips with this truth, namely, that Rap Brown is right when he says, "Violence is as American as apple pie." Everything white America has was obtained through and is maintained through protective violence. Violence is used here rather broadly to include such practices as trickery, bad-faith trading, shrewd business deals that include dishonesty with the Russians over Alaska, cajolery, and so on.

Which Republican conservative would dare suggest that America behaved nonviolently toward the Indians or toward the British? Not only was America violent, but she was a thief and a litterbug, stealing the British tea and dumping it into the harbor. Just imagine Paul Revere galloping through moonlit New England shouting, "The British are coming, the British are coming!" and some white Bircher raising his window saying "Slow down, boy, you are disturbing the peace." What would have happened had Stokely Carmichael gone to the top of the steps of the Capitol in Washington, D.C., in 1966 and lifted his black power fist exclaiming "Give me liberty or give me death!" But Patrick Henry was white, male, Protestant, middle-class; when he made such an exclamation, he was regarded as a hero. Stokely, however, would be labeled as a communist, militant, Black Power advocate and an outside agitator. Somehow, white America cannot come to the understanding that the same search for freedom and liberty that ran rampant within Patrick Henry also runs rampant within Stokely Carmichael and in all oppressed people.

One does not have to stay in the recesses of history to establish this point. The governor of California, Ronald Reagan, was ambitious enough to seek the Republican nomination for the presidency in 1968. *The Los Angeles*

Times presented a profile on him in which the following three issues were discussed: "Governor Reagan, what about Vietnam?" "Turn it into a parking lot," he replied. "What about the seizure of the U.S. ship Pueblo by the North Koreans?" "Give them a month, and if they don't give us our ship back, go in there and kick the devil out of them," he suggested. "What about San Francisco State College and the unrest there?" "Keep the school open even at the point of a bayonet," replied the governor. His proposition for solving the problems of the nation consisted of: (1) bomb Vietnam off the map, (2) kick the devil out of the Koreans, and (3) keep the schools open with guns. Now a black youth in his community, who understands the problems of his community, after watching television or reading of the approach Reagan proposed says, "Thank you, Brother Governor." The end result is that this youth can't wait to grow up to (1) fix his bayonet, (2) turn Sacramento into a parking lot, and (3) kick the devil out of Ronald Reagan.

Black people have tried to force white America to come to grips with the essential moral duplicity inherent in a nation that uses violence to solve its problems and condemns violence only when others resort to it. If you want me to remain nonviolent, then don't make me the target of violence and expect me to "turn the other cheek." Lord Acton said it almost a century ago: "Power yields only to power; and, even then, not without a struggle." The real question facing all Americans is how just and equitable changes will be achieved without resorting to violence. Will it be necessary to burn down a library to check out a book? Should it be necessary to hit someone on his head to get him to take his finger out of your eye? Following the riots in Detroit, the Ford Foundation and other billionnaire foundations got together and within a year (1968) they had found jobs for 45,000 so-called unemployables, with many involved in on-the-job training. Black people could have gone to Detroit and sung, shouted, cried, prayed, and staged sit-ins for ten years without achieving 45,000 jobs.

White Americans must be forced to examine culturally the function of violence in American history to determine whether or not they will respond to just and equitable change without forcing those seeking change to resort to violence. There is a need for a healthy examination of this power tool, used for years both nationally and internationally to maintain control over oppressed people.

The Concept of Church/School
Institutional Brainwashing (Pigeonholing)

The other power tool used in America to maintain control over black people concerns itself with the two major public institutions, the church and the school. These two institutions have been used as a sort of Xerox machine to produce middle-class, white, male, Protestant society as it is. As these institutions build their programs and doctrine around white middle-class culture and customs, they have tried to impose white culture and customs upon blacks rather than endeavoring to nurture and develop black life and the black point of view.

Traditionally, the college has operated as a cookie-cutter machine designed not to promote creative, earthshaking thoughts but to turn out people who were just like mother and father—replicas of the system—who were willing to go out into society and fit into their little round hole or their little square notch and keep the image of American society the same. This offering may be sustained by a few short examples. The content of IQ tests and the curricula of our schools affords us valuable data for analysis.

The school is a white, middle-class, male, Protestant, cultural cookie-cutter, designed to cut out more cookies just like those who are in power. The largest standardization group for IQ tests is white middle-class society; consequently, the tests are permeated with white middle-class subvalues. In 1968, a number of black and Chicano youth put together an IQ test that displayed a degree of cultural bias similar to that of the one in popular use. The test was administered to many members of the graduate faculty of USC, and these learned persons with advanced degrees all did poorly.

Many oppressed youth of "minority" groups do poorly on tests, not because they are inherently intellectually inferior. The cookie-cutter operation is done in psychology, sociology, literature, and anthropology. There is no account of the disruption of the black family or of black culture in the sociology books. The cookie-cutter is in operation, turning out middle-class white cookies out of chocolate fudge dough.

However, where this operation is most evident is in the way history is taught. An examination of any classic American history text will show the pictures of all the heroes who allegedly put together the Yankee colossus. With few exceptions, the pictures are white, Anglo-Saxon, Protestant, and male, as though no one else has done anything. There are few, if any, pictures of Jews, Catholics, or Mexicans, and most Indians one sees are the dead ones. There are only two pictures of women—Betsy Ross with the flag and the writer of *Uncle Tom's Cabin*, Harriet Beecher Stowe. If you are black, you are looking for black people because you know that black people came to America with the early Spanish explorers; a black man invented the first pendulum clock; another performed the first heart surgery, in 1893; another founded Washington; and another founded Chicago. Moreover, black people took part in the Revolutionary War, the Civil War, and the War of 1812; and they have played significant roles in protecting America in every war in which it was involved.

Beyond all this, Garrett A. Morgan in 1916 invented the gas mask and in 1923 invented the traffic light. Another black man, Hyram S. Thomas, invented potato chips; and Augustus Jackson invented ice cream. These facts are presented only to suggest that the traditional American history text inadequately treats or, better said, ignores the role of black people in American society. A typical example would show on page 312 a picture of a few slaves with chains around their legs and a caption reading: "Happy slaves relax eating watermelon after a day of work."

For the most part, this white middle-class white lie has served its purpose. It is rather sad that 90 percent of college students graduate without knowing the honest history of their own country. In the process of attempting to force the college as an institution to meet their own cultural needs, black students have contributed to the education of their white counterparts by demanding that they also receive an honest and complete education.

The same thing is true of the church as an institution. The church is another part of the cookie-cutter operation in its policies and practices. If we were to examine the big Bible—another classic—very evident are pictures representing biblical characters. This is also evident in the stained window-panes whose carved images are of whites with blond hair and blue eyes and middle-class in appearance.

In the Bible there are pictures of Adam and Eve and John, who wrote the books of Revelation. Now it must be remembered that the history of the Bible occurred between the Nile and the Euphrates, that is to say, in the valley of Mesopotamia. In the common editions of the New Testament, Jesus is pictured as white and middle-class, with blond hair, blue eyes, and a Gentile nose. Historians and geographers raise the question of how such men were engendered in the Valley of the Nile. Scholars who have traveled in the Holy Land and Bethlehem will agree that in this latitude no truly white thoroughbred with blue eyes and blond hair is produced. The pictures illustrate the extent to which the western white man has indulged in self-ingratiation; that is, he had tried to create God in his image. This step, once taken, leads to the other, of making God think like him. The cookie-cutter is now in operation.

The danger, of course, is that this practice becomes a cultural process that spreads throughout the body of the society and influences not only race relations but also international relationships. To illustrate, America views Russia as a devil and insists that the Russians remove their missiles from Cuba but defends the right of the United States to have missiles in Turkey pointing at Moscow. Given this philosophical inconsistency and situation reality, what are the options in terms of substantive change?

The Concept of Change

Social change, as defined by the *International Encyclopedia of Social Science*, is the significant alteration of social structures (that is, of patterns of social action and interaction, including consequences and manifestations of such structural arrangements embodied in rules of conduct, values, cultural products, and symbols). From a black perspective, change must be radical, substantial, and very significant to be meaningful to the entire black community.

One of the greatest controlling forces is the very appearance of change. Therefore, the power elite and their associates welcome such indications as predictors that serve to enable them to assert or maximize social control. They achieve this by making visible a few blacks who have moved a few steps higher when the masses are still hungry. This upward mobility of a few tempts the black masses into thinking that change is imminent. In this way, the system makes visible the promotion of certain blacks, even some of our leaders, to powerless positions, making them ineffective and destroying the viability of the struggle for substantive change. The leaders, in turn, lose all credibility in the struggle and in their community. In the same vein, to make visible to the world the arrest, trial, and release of a few political prisoners gives the appearance of change, when in effect the masses are still oppressed by the arrangements of the system.

In a society where status is stratified, progress is seen as a continuum and individuals who perceive the society as fluid develop a sense of hope, especially if such a society is arranged to make progressive gestures (giving those at the bottom of the society some indication of the possibility of vertical mobility). Often the oppressed will develop also a partial sense of identity with those gestures to the extent that they become legitimized and the arrangements that make the gestures possible are reaffirmed.

Change from the bottom up must have a black viewpoint, for the simple reason that ruthless control and domination by whites have forced the masses of blacks to the status of subproletariat. Very few blacks have not experienced physical or mental discomfort from the existing arrangements of the social order of America, which were established and maintained by whites—capitalists and would-be capitalists. The means and methods were inhuman, and the main concern was to establish order with limited power involvement of blacks and their community. Consequently, the struggle has been for relief from oppression, release from restraint, the avoidance of self-negation, redefinition of self, the opening of new conceptualizations of the Black Experience, and power itself. The ultimate goal, however, is change that facilitates the reduction of the liberation struggle with full control of institutions in the community.

Three Kinds of Changes

I would like to identify, at this point, three kinds of changes and to discuss their potential for the liberation of oppressed people. Many critics have suggested that the operative concepts of law and the legal-political institutions are inadequately responsive to the demands for change made by various groups. Although the operating principle of the society has been "survival is a consequence of the capacity to respond to pressures for change," this chapter argues that American society, though born in revolution and dedicated to economic and technological development, has become sluggish and insensitive to the social reforms dictated by its technologically based society—slow to perceive and slow to respond to changing conditions.

Some critics have urged patience and renewed dedication to "making the system work through established institutions" and by "accepted" means. They advocate gradual change or gradualism. Change I (see Figure 1) indicates the operation of gradual change. Gradual or marginal change takes place over a long period of time as power shifts from a few persons to another few persons within the same group. Core power is in the hands of a few whites and represents the level of political and economic power that determines the policy and regulates practices in the society which maintain the arrangements of the social order. The line of admissions to power is controlled by those who have core power. Individual and coalition pressure groups that are usually at the base of power struggle to gain admissions to level three, five, or even seven to influence those who have core power or to achieve positions of power themselves to change those policies and practices that oppress, exploit, and dominate their lives and control their life-chances.

The marriage of the present set of arrangements which can be expected of the future set of arrangements does not represent any hope for substantive change. The future can be expected to be the same with minimum changes controlled by those with core power. For the most part, oppressed groups will continue to occupy marginal power, experiencing a sense of the possibility of change with no real change affecting their lives for the better. Their representatives at power three, five or even seven will enjoy apparent power with no real power to establish policy and change practices that oppress, discriminate against and exploit their group members. Coalition and individual groups tend to share the belief that change is necessary and they share the same definition of the arrangements of the system as oppressive and racist, but their approaches to change are usually different.

Pressure groups may move nearer to the center of power, but never passing power five. However, one or two "representatives" of the pressure groups may move to power six or seven, again giving a false sense of accountability and progress. Core power is in the hands of a few whites who bequeath their power to a few within their racial group.

Representatives of the oppressed group (pressure group) are promoted to power four or five to create a sense of change. However, the system makes these gestures only to sustain its arrangements. In the process, the pressure groups tend to reduce their pressure on the system for change. Later their

Figure 1. CHANGE I

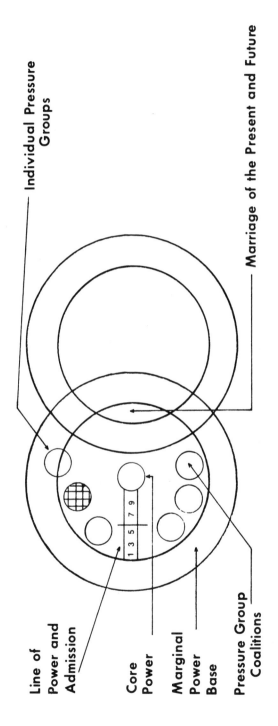

representatives are discredited and powerless and lose their credibility as representatives because the hope vested in their move to power four or five did not translate itself into any real change for those to whom the representatives are accountable. In many instances, these representatives switch their sense of accountability and seek legitimation as participating members of the social order. Once individualism is achieved, these individuals are used by the social order to regulate change. In some instances, the individuals may become frustrated and seek other avenues of endeavor, publicly or privately.

Various pressure groups do not commonly practice coalition protest. Usually, progress gestures are made to members of each group, either by government sources or by private sources, usually to the leadership of each group. By design, the end result is that competition is waged among the groups rather than between the oppressed groups and those with core power. The gestures are to distract the groups so that those who control the various arrangements of society (political, legal, educational, economic) may continue to organize their power for continued domination. It is true that certain obvious signs of oppression are removed and certain legal changes are achieved, but this is also intended to give the appearance of change. Over time, the essential character of power remains the same and the social order remains oppressive, oppression taking a different form, but the subjects of the oppression may change to another generation.

Some critics have urged far-reaching structural reforms as a means of streamlining the institutions and their arrangements to make them accountable to all people in the society. They advocate a build-up of pressure on the system through the increased use of extralegal but essentially nonviolent methods. These critics, all from the school of gradualism, speak in comprehensive terms. Most changes are small enough to be dismissed as trivial, yet they realize that they may add up to something substantial. They address themselves, therefore, to the numerical and time factors implicit in Change I. They see changes as being incremental and cumulative, consisting of many component elements that over time amount to change substantial enough to be identified.

Groups that advocate Change II (see Figure 2) comprise members who advocated confrontation politics but soon realized that such strategies do not induce change in the basic ideological foundations of the social order. Change II is an attempt to break away (culturally, socially, politically) from the original oppressive system of arrangements, yet it stays within the boundary of the system to influence rather than be influenced by it. The imagined cultural threat is too great for those who control to experience. It becomes acceptable for the groups, in frustration, to withdraw to safe communities where the members of the various groups practice their own brand of social, political, and economic life. In some instances, the groups

Figure 2. CHANGE II

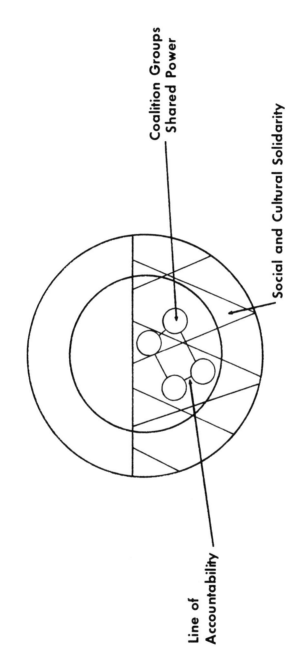

Line of
Accountability

Coalition Groups
Shared Power

Social and Cultural Solidarity

are assisted financially by their oppressors, who make public the terms, basis, and reasons for the aid to induce the compliance of any "deviant" group that seems difficult. Those groups that see compromise as a form of weakness usually hold out until they realize that their economic resources are not being replenished as they are used. These groups either dissolve or reluctantly join forces with other groups whose future is determined by the oppressor. In such events, these groups have no hope for independence. Political statements are carefully made, and any form of protest is controlled by imagined approval or disapproval of those who exercise economic control over the groups. Even where there are communities of the oppressed established without protest by the actions of the oppressor, the control of the institutions is influenced by the control of the means of production, which are owned by those outside the community of the oppressed. Whatever power is exercised in these communities is exercised on behalf of the powerful outsiders. The result is that the political and economic orders dominate the social and cultural orders of the coalition and the cultural solidarity of the groups. If the strain is not adequately dealt with, leaders of the community find it rather difficult to achieve accountability to members of the community, and the temptation arises to destroy the coalition because no real progress can be achieved. The hope for shared power with regard to political and economic matters is also destroyed.

The hope is for a possible breakthrough through confrontation. The dominant group will tend to exercise control, tolerance, and ultimate power because of the boundary relationship. However, change of this nature does not guarantee nonrepetitive alterations in the established modes of behavior in the former social order. Mere changes in political well-being, in technological advances, or in basic attitudes constitute social motion. Social change occurs when actual behavior changes happen, bringing about shifts in interaction patterns of person-to-person and group-to-group or when new relationships emerge and take hold.

Change in social, political, legal, economic, and cultural structures that allows for the freedom and liberation of all is addressed by Change III (see Figure 3), which offer that possibility. The arrangements to be changed are the political ones that render the oppressed powerless and the economic arrangements that exploit and define conditions systematically restricting the economic position of those whose labor creates surplus profits for those who own the land, wealth, and technology. The legal arrangements and the educational arrangements must also be changed. The combination of these arrangements is what has come to be referred to as the system or the social order. No other form of change can adequately alter the underclass and marginal working-class status of the oppressed, who are dominated and exploited for the benefit of the ruling elite colonizer. Exploitative capitalists perpetuate these exploitative conditions, which emerged during the capitalism of slavery. No other attempt has the potential for bringing about the necessary changes. Coalition efforts could be effective here if the working whites had not come to fear the economic and political mobility of blacks.

Sidney Willhelm argues that:

Some writers attribute the perpetuation of racism directly to the ruling stratum seeking to restrain wages, by instilling in white workers a racial prejudice against Negroes. The latter remain vulnerable to brutal exploitation while the former are rendered less competitive because they strive against the slave wages of blacks. In this manner, the ruling elite derives cheap labor from both black and white.[8]

In a complex capitalist-colonial society, the chances of a cohesive, united front against exploitation, racial oppression, and domination are hindered by special secondary interests and intragroup cleavages. Furthermore, the employment of a sense of change reduces progressive activities and undermines collective effort at substantial change. The result is the acceptance of the notion that continuous change will occur through normal channels and orderly procedures. In such a climate, a society as defined above returns to business as usual and the oppressed tend to lose their will to struggle. In such an event, the acceptance of gradual and cumulative changes is assured, and oppression becomes less apparent but more real. Those who once struggled for change become part of their own oppression and develop techniques to neutralize their sense of failure.

Those who advocate Change III (see Figure 3) realize that the society has prepared to deal with their actions in a military fashion. Therefore, underground efforts characterize the initial action of the advocates. Change III is radical or revolutionary; a complete change with new definitions, new goals, and a different interaction perspective.

Once the conventional arrangements are destroyed, because they have no further usefulness, a new set of arrangements comes to the forefront with power in the hands of the masses operationalized on their behalf by a few. These new arrangements will be defined by and be accountable to the masses of people. Such arrangements must have, however, the ability and capacity to meet the relative and the absolute needs of those being served.

The present arrangements allow power to be controlled by a few who have no sense of accountability to the masses. Whether it is the school board, the city council, the political conventions, the police review board, the adult authority, or whatever, power to define and power to make vital long-term and short-term decisions is still controlled by a few whites who make sure that this power stays within the white family. Explicit and implicit in these arrangements is the notion of compliance. Violation of these arrangements is met with severe sanctions. Therefore, those who advocate Change III realize that there will be bloodshed, for the few must die to save the many. The scope of Change III is capable of effecting significant and substantial alterations for the purpose of the liberation of oppressed people in the American society.

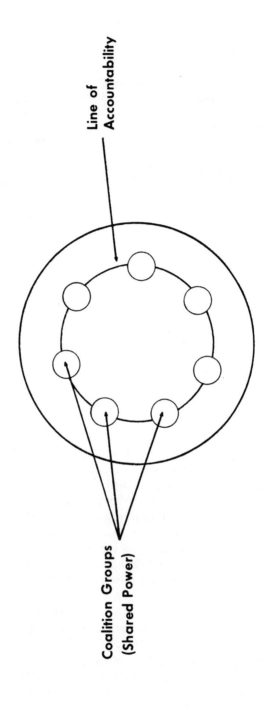

Figure 3. CHANGE III

Line of Accountability

Coalition Groups (Shared Power)

Conclusion

The issue of change requires the commitment of all oppressed peoples. The individual must be submerged into the collectiveness of those efforts for substantive change. As it may be difficult to explain to others the ideology of change, it should be easier and more fruitful to demonstrate change if we put aside our attempts at comprehensive and extensive explanations. Examples through demonstrations are not easily eradicated from the mind. However, change is influenced by an intimate interplay between explanation and demonstration.

The American social order requires change. The process of change, from the alteration of the institutional arrangements to the operation of new arrangements that redefine the social order, necessitates a variety of techniques to guarantee action among and between those advocating change. However, the objectives must be the qualitative elements that unite the forces, not the techniques employed. Each oppressed group must maximize the techniques of other such groups to enhance the objective concerns of all oppressed people.

The problem of unity on the basis of objectives, when different techniques are employed by different oppressed groups, is the implicit notion that the decided techniques of each group are adequate and appropriate. To struggle over techniques is to facilitate conflict that will enhance continued control by oppressors through financial support for the one or the other. What should be finally kept in mind is that to the extent that one sees oneself as a part of change, to that extent will one resist or assist it. A sense of being a part of change must be the experience of all oppressed people.

Notes

1. Lerone Bennett, Jr., "Clarity and Black Base," *Ebony*, October, 1971.

2. James Boggs, *Racism and the Class Struggle*. New York: Monthly Review Press, 1970, pp. 10-11.

3. Rayford W. Logan, *The Negro in the United States*. New York: Van Nostrand Reinhold Co., 1951.

4. Robert Blauner, "Marxian Theory and Race Relations," unpublished paper, 1971, p. 20.

5. Bennett, "Clarity and Black Base."

6. Ibid.

7. Max Ways, "The Deeper Shame of the Cities," in Gerald Leinwand, ed., *The Negro and the City* (New York: Time-Life Books, 1968), pp. 14,16.

8. Sidney Willhelm, *Who Needs the Negro* (Cambridge, Mass.: Schenkman Publishing Co., Inc., 1970), p. 170.

2

Black Liberation and Legitimation: A Rejection of the Mask

Introduction

> *We wear the mask that grins and lies*
> *It holds our cheeks and shades our eyes,*
> *This debt we pay to human guile;*
> *With torn and bleeding hearts we smile,*
> *And mouth with myriad subtleties.*
>
> *Why should the world be overwise*
> *In counting all our tears and sighs?*
> *Nay, let them only see us, while we*
> *Wear the mask.*
>
> *We smile, but O great Christ, our cries*
> *To thee from tortured souls arise.*
> *We sing, but oh, the clay is vile*
> *Beneath our feet, and long the Nile;*
> *We wear the mask.*
>
> *"We Wear the Mask," by Paul Lawrence Dunbar*[1]

This perceptive description by Dunbar reflects the painful restraints with which the black man in America found himself encumbered at the turn of the twentieth century. Daily living in fear of his life in a system whose justice code consciously excluded him, whose politics and social norms debased him, and whose racism imposed an artificial but self-serving identity to the cause of white oppression, the black American of this period lived within an irrational dichotomy—separate but equal segregation. This incongruous situation wrought frustration, fear, and pain, both physically and emotionally. As a matter of survival, the black assumed a "mask" and played a role he disdained. The "mask" he wore as protection by day and the reality of remorse and aggravation he wore by night as he prayed for this "bitter cup to be removed" and for the heralding of a better day.

Now in the last half of the twentieth century there is in one sense the reality of a better day. Although oppression still operates in American society today, blacks can and must reject the "mask." Blacks no longer must hide their grievances and their wrath. The perceptive black at this time realizes that life without freedom of speech, redress, and representation is not worth the energy of pretense. However, this view is not shared collectively, because this "good news" has not reached all black people. Therefore, this chapter is written for all black people, internationally, but specifically those who have somehow internalized a white value system; those who seek to exploit other blacks—the hustlers, the pimps, the vice lords, and those of the "middle-class" who seek to escape the "dominant values of the Black Culture."[2] These blacks perceive whites as the personification of "success;" therefore, to be successful they feel they must behave as whites behave. The very progress toward liberation for blacks dictates, indeed demands, *rejection of the "mask."*

The quest for liberation by black people has taken many forms and has demonstrated itself in certain defeating and contradictory trends. Many blacks have sought to be free by accepting, for the most part, the values and definitions of whites and by attempting to associate in intimate ways— emotionally and intellectually—with their oppressors, somehow believing that in so doing their oppression would be eradicated. In such a process the independence of freedom and liberation is lost to cooperation, compromise, and the acceptance of a mild—sometimes defined as friendly—white assertion.

It seems impossible for black people to find freedom and liberation in America or anywhere else where white people systematically dominate and oppress them, especially if they continue to seek or sense a need to be legitimized by white people. The first step to liberation for black people is the realization that their existence and worth are not, and should never be, a function of the approval of white people.

Many black people still tend to feel enhanced when they share the company of white people, especially those whites who smile as they timidly say, "I don't see you as black." No answer is heard, however, to explain why blacks are not concerned as much with whites' concept of their blackness, as in many cases this is obvious. But more importantly blacks voice a concern that they not be viewed as street sweepers, waiters, and generally as menial laborers selected to do the dirty work of white America.

Those blacks who view association with whites as a goal are observed to be gentle, softspoken, accommodating, overly protective, considerate, and acutely concerned for the comfort of whites. "Right" behavior is of the utmost importance. To say anything which might hurt the feelings of their white companions, or for others to do so, is disapproving and makes them uneasy. In the process of such experiences these blacks yearn for the approval of their white companions from whom their legitimation comes.

Whites as Agents of Legitimation

During the era when integration was sought as a goal and thought to be an end in itself, blacks, along with white "liberals," seemed satisfied to achieve an integrated lunch counter or an integrated toilet. Many blacks seemed to be content to end the struggle once achieving mutual toilet space. But enlightened, perceptive blacks realized that an integrated society was not a sufficient goal for which a people should strive—a people who have been systematically kept powerless and denied any meaningful input and participation in the political, social, economic, and educational order of a society. Striving for an integrated order has forced black people since the 1960s into frozen inactivity and a low level of initiative. The realization that must come to all blacks is that "integration" was a means to an end and not an end in itself. It constituted only the first plateau.

Within the interactional context of integration, blacks hesitated to take the initiative. This seems to be a preferential hangover that stifles the covert and overt struggle for total liberation and freedom. It is astounding to observe blacks still giving way to white people who still operate on the assumption that the "nigger" will move out of the way, even when blacks have the right-of-way; to observe blacks going to restaurants with whites and displaying that "backseat" psychology as they walk in "humble deference" a few paces behind the white person; and further, to note blacks permitting whites to exercise all decision making even with the simple matter of selecting a table. In seeking to be legitimized, they have lost the power of independent initiative. Instead of taking the initiative, they passively acquiesce. No preference is stated, and no independent input is attempted. A critical look at efforts in the civil rights struggle indicates that all blacks seemed concerned with was that white people treated them well. There was little concern as to who took the initiative, who owned the restaurant, who controlled the social situation, who talked about his family and personal problems, or who determined the topic of conversation. This situation is no simple matter in light of the historical nature of black-white interaction in the society. Even now some blacks frequently talk to others about their social experiences with whites as though such experiences "make their day." Some blacks boast that they hobnob with whites from the outlying suburbs and even go so far as to have the children adopt them as "dutch uncles."

Traditionally, blacks have interacted with whites on the basis of their concept of white people's concept of them. But today it is important and vital to the progress of liberation and freedom that blacks interact with whites on the basis of blacks' concept of themselves, thus forcing whites to confront their distorted concept of black people. (Even during slavery and segregation blacks never really lost a true positive self-concept; however, the free exercise of their self-concept was restricted by the realities of the times and the survival behavior dictated thereby).

In Huntsville, Alabama, in 1967 an exploratory research project was initiated to determine the extent to which white racial attitudes had changed since the removal of the phrase "white only need apply" from the job advertisements in the newspapers. The manager of a burger joint had advertised for an assistant manager and also for a boy to sweep the floor and clean the tables. As the project applicant entered the door (well-dressed), he informed the manager that he come for the job, not really specifying which one he sought. This applicant had a degree in business administration and a degree in legal aspects of business, but the white manager asked him if he had ever *swept* before. The manager had dismissed the possibility of this applicant being interested in or even qualified for the assistant manager's position, despite the applicant's credentials.

Another similar incident was reported by a project member, a junior college teacher, who went to a bank and found himself at the end of a line of three persons waiting to be served. The one immediately in front of him was an older white woman who was evidently having problems spelling the word "eight." She tried several times without any success. After she had erased several of her efforts, he made the mistake of attempting to assist her. She refused in no uncertain terms. However, her refusal was not fully understood until she permitted the white clerk to spell it for her. It was not that the white woman did not want assistance in spelling the word "eight;" it was that she did not want assistance from a black man. She resisted changing her concept of black people. She wanted to continue to see blacks as "stupid," "illiterate," and so on, despite any evidence to the contrary.

Senator Edmund Muskie, who ran in the 1972 presidential primary, was correct in his statement that a black man running on a national ticket as a vice-presidential candidate would be defeating and negative; not because a black person is not capable, but because this white racist society does not view blacks in this light. Muskie may have implied racist overtones, but black people's interpretation of the statement must reflect the racist and colonial nature of this society. Tap any person on the street, and one can get, in short order, three or more names of black persons capable of functioning as vice president of the United States.

In retrospect it becomes clear that the civil rights struggle has only yielded an artificial and precarious posture for blacks—integration. Integration has not yet been realized, yet many blacks operate under the great misconception that it has. As a result, the progress toward full equality for blacks in this society has been abated as they become entranced and entrapped by mere tokenism. This will continue to be the case until blacks see integration in its true powerless perspective and reject the mask as they become the source of their own legitimation.

Black Professionals: Misplaced Efforts

In 1971, two black women wrote a book entitled *How to Get Along with Black People.*[3] There are numerous questionable assumptions implicit in the topic. The one that is most mysterious is the assumption that black people are desirous of getting along with white people and of white people getting along with them. These Harvard and Yale law school graduates seem to express an uneasiness as they describe being asked by their white friends about the "black experience." At this point, the question arises, if blacks don't articulate their experiences, who will? They suggest that there are other things to talk about, and maybe they are better off, and so are blacks, if they would water down the subject. For the most part, blacks talk about experiences in a very assertive manner these days, which does seem to place whites on the spot and make them uncomfortable. This is especially true of the white liberals who will invite black professionals to their homes for dinner or go out to lunch with them. Naked black rhetoric speaks candidly, with no apology. It does not exclude the white liberal as it identifies the culprits of racism and the failing national institutions.

This book is written in an escapist tone with a distorted perspective of the masses of black people, especially grass-root blacks. There are so many legal matters in the black community to which these able lawyers should address themselves that it is difficult to see how they could permit their social insights to be clouded with such a strong desire to write a book for white folks. It is understood that the authors have educated themselves into a distorted social posture from which they articulate their perspective. However, there are thousands of black people who have never, will never, and do not desire to sit down to dine with white people. As a matter of fact, a great majority of blacks do not find themselves in the social milieu to be invited to dinner by white middle-class liberals, thus diminishing table talk on the black experience as a legitimate concern.

The sad thing about the authors is their inability to understand the need for a coalition of the black middle-class and the grass-root blacks. If liberation is to be achieved, these two groups must agree upon a common purpose. Several questions come to mind: (1) Why have they not sensed such a need? (2) Is it possible for these black groups to unite? (3) Is the approach they offer the only possible way for whites and blacks to get along? and (4) Which blacks are they really talking about? Until the authors can crystallize concrete statements to these questions, they cannot hope to speak authoritatively on black/white relations. This book is, therefore, a waste of time and effort. It is invalid and its assumptions absurd. If the authors and those blacks sharing this point of view do not want their white "liberal" friends (who now feel alienated from the movement) to use them as clearinghouses for information concerning the "black experience," then they should express this concern. When these authors and other blacks sharing their point can desist from external legitimation by whites, then they too will have moved toward true liberation and self-legitimation by rejecting the mask.

Some time ago, a black neurosurgeon appeared on the "Today Show" to discuss the activities of his organization, NEGRO. Its primary and most extensive project—utilizing all the time and effort of its leading members—was a trip to Russia to study the problems of Russian Jews. It is beyond comprehension that a group of such talented blacks could invest their energies in a pursuit so far afield from their own ethnic connections. What justifiable reason could they give for expending black energy and expertise to the amelioration of those so far removed from the black man's exigency, so that their efforts are rendered fruitless in the service of their own people? What is even more inflammatory is the matter of the thousands of dollars spent in this project which should rightfully be channeled into constructive programs to undergird and elevate the black community. The entire effort is highly problematical. In the first place, Russia makes no pretense about its basic ideological principles. Second, Jews are one of the most powerful groups in American society. They control the educational institutions, television, much of the tourism, and many other institutions with international impact. Third, as blacks have not achieved sufficient economic power, philanthropy is a luxury they can ill afford. Consequently, to misappropriate funds localized within their sphere of control in light of the many socioeconomic and political problems facing black Americans is a travesty bordering on sacrilege. Jews were once allies, but today there are signs of dissociation. If the DeFunis[4] case is illustrative of the general Jewish attitude, then indeed, they can be viewed among the ranks of our oppressors. The schism is evidenced by a 1974 article in *Ebony* magazine in which Alvin Poussaint appeals for unity among blacks and Jews. Poussaint points out that "There has been steadily growing contention between Jews and blacks since the late 1950s, particularly around educational issues. Many Jews revealed their latent prejudice with respect to school desegregation."[5] Lenora Berson, author of *The Negroes and the Jews*, perceptively admonishes that: "As allies, they (blacks and Jews) are at the core of the liberal movement in the United States. As antagonists, they may well hasten the nation down the bloody road of racism."[6]

This neurosurgeon projected a great feeling of pride that his organization could undertake such an endeavor, while the needs of blacks in this country and the acute medical needs of black Africans and West Indians go unnoticed by his group. This doctor is typical of the many blacks who still seek the approval of whites from whom they gain legitimation. In the process, they remain blind to the fact that the contradiction in their efforts is blatantly apparent. If they are to be of any benefit in furthering the cause of the black community, they must reject the mask.

Africans and Afro-Caribbeans

There are two disturbing factors with regard to efforts for the liberation of black people. The first is that black people sought integration with white people as a goal; and second, that West Indians and Africans, for the most part, moved toward the white world because they were not treated as subservient and set apart from their fellow blacks by whites. One West Indian black reports that he had to come to grips with these concerns. He relates that:

Many nights I stayed awake trying to conceptualize and articulate a position on these issues. In the meantime, more questions haunted my mind complicating the entire situation—why did West Indians and Africans in certain social settings make sure that whites knew, without a doubt, that they were from the West Indies or Africa?; Why is it that most of them date white women or white men?; Why is it that certain whites made attempts at associating with the civil rights movement—some of them even establishing intimate relationships with blacks?; and finally, why was it that many blacks seemed more protective of their intimate white companions. I arrived at several positions which seemed to provide answers; yet these answers did not completely satisfy me. At social affairs with their intimate white friends many of my West Indian friends behaved as though they had reached the pinnacle; they had finally "made it"—"Liberation at last!" The behavior of many black Americans was no different.

My search for an answer led me to conclude that black people, depending on the degree to which they sense oppression, believe that the basis of their liberation and identity was dependent upon the approbation and legitimation of white people. This is ironic because, at the same time, they believe that whites are also the function of their oppression. With this realization I began to understand why blacks (American, West Indian and African) seek approval and legitimation of white people.[7]

Many black Americans feel victimized, and their white associates sense this feeling of victimization. Africans and West Indians also sense this situation and attempt to define their associates in terms of the avoidance of the victim. The defined and perceived victim attempts to identify with representatives of the perpetrators of his victimization, hoping it will free him. He defends his association on the basis of his freedom of choice, not understanding that in a liberation struggle one cannot afford to do what he wants to do; rather, he has to do what must be done.

Somehow, it is a psychological shot in the arm for many blacks to associate with whites. Many white associates of blacks, on the other hand, feel that somehow by their association with blacks, they are removed from being the objects of the oppression and victimization of blacks. Often they exclaim, "Some of my best friends are blacks," or, "I went to school with blacks, and one was my good friend." What they don't realize is that this has always been the case—whites have always been protective of blacks in their employ. However, they suffered no qualms in shooting or lynching another member of that person's family. It was always the warped belief that those blacks who waited for them personally were somehow "better than blacks in general."

Africans and West Indians, in an attempt at not identifying with the victim (trying to escape being victimized), see to it that white and black Americans understand that they are from some place other than America and that this somehow sets them apart from the black American. Somehow they believe that this attempt will remove from them the stigma of being the victim which comes automatically with the color of their skin, notwith-standing that wherever African people live they are victimized. The very sense of the necessity for their action of avoidance speaks to their victimization. Consequently, it must be believed, understood, and operationalized that the freedom and liberation of African people must not and cannot be the function of the approval and legitimation of white people. Rather, they are the function of the initiative, approval, and legitimation of black people by black people.

This avoidance behavior on the part of non-American blacks is an attempt to reject the mask. The approach, however, is illusory and deceptive because it does not permit these West Indian and African blacks to define themselves and select their associates. They are pressured to behave in a certain manner in order not to suffer the problems of other black victims of this system. But in so doing they find they must restrict their movements and consciously seek to prove themselves different or better than their African brothers born in America. They find they too are victimized by this system and manipulated by the white majority, which succeeds through them in creating divisions among black people. What the West Indians and Africans seem to overlook is that they will never be fully accepted by whites and will always be kept on the periphery. Overlooked as well is the fact that their attempts to seek entry into another ethnocultural milieu only serve to alienate their fellow blacks. Hence, when "the chips are down," so to speak, they will have nowhere to turn for true brotherhood and will become the targets of both sides, since they have straddled the fence.

The haunting realization that emerges vividly is the old truth of "no man is an island." It is impossible for any individual black person in America (or the world), be he native or immigrant, to experience free mobility in this society until *all* blacks in America are antecedents. We share in the plight of blacks and cohesively in the elevation of the black race to human dignity everywhere. When this is accomplished, then, and only then, will we have rejected the mask.

Collective Blackness

We have been led into legitimizing our existence on the basis of "white" as the norm and "black" as the deviant; therefore, to be equal meant the denial of self. Once we begin to understand this, we may be in a position to correct our socialized preference for whites. Our struggle for relative liberation is stifled in the presence of this subtle white preference syndrome, which must be dealt with if black people are to experience true individual freedom and group liberation. Somehow, our efforts for freedom and equality express themselves in individualistic terms without our fully understanding the liberating significance of the immersion of that individuality into a collective blackness.

Stokely Carmichael, in the 1968 November-December issue of *Shrewd*, attempted to explain the notion that black people should fight for liberation, not freedom, a distinction which speaks to a group effort rather than an individual one. He argued that:

The concept of freedom is vague. Everybody strives for it, but it's an individual concept. Liberation is a concept of a group, a community, a nation. Black people cannot reach liberation as individuals. We have to reach it as a group of people, as a community. It is very important that we understand that with the concept of liberation, you must have a concept of nationalism.[8]

With respect to the question of white preference, many blacks tend to deny its existence, not only because it is difficult to deal with but also because its correction will impede their short-term goals and personal desires. A community of liberated people with an effective operationalized perspective of nationalism must be purged of such preferences, especially in Africa and the West Indies, where such preferences are so subtle.

Many blacks attempted to hide their white preference—the product of the consequences of dehumanization and a long historical process of partial acculturation into the white society. The fact is that the economic, legal, political, social, and cultural arrangements of this society were established and maintained on the basis of what blackness and whiteness had come to mean in relation to each other as operationalized and defined by whites in political, economic, social and educational terms. Consequently, traditional interaction between blacks and whites was within the context of the power of whites to operationalize distorted definitions of black people. Systematically, laws were constructed whereby whites who controlled the system defined blacks out of it by legalizing injustices and by indicating the inter-racial interactional relationships.

Although many blacks never lost the positive image they had of them-selves, out of necessity they appeared to have accepted the distorted con-cepts of whites to make interaction less frictional. There is no question as to the power of whites to operationalize distorted definitions of black people. The times suggest and the liberating struggle demands that black people everywhere establish and operationalize a common perspective of their Africanness; this applies also to definitions of their existence that must be projected to the world through a collective black effort. This collective effort will constitute a rejection of the mask.

The Question of Allies

All too often black people have had to modify and compromise their positions to include poor whites; today, this includes white women, who suggest that they are oppressed. Evidently, if they are oppressed, it is an oppression brought on them by their own brothers and sisters, thus making their struggle a "family quarrel." Black people know all too well that one should not interfere or involve oneself in family disputes, for the intruder eventually becomes the victim.

Although poor whites may have suffered as a result of the economic and political arrangements of a white capitalistic society, a historical investiga-tion of the implications reveal that there were loopholes in the arrangements that provided for the escape of poor whites. Political and economic power is bequeathed to whites by whites. With regards to the white worker, James Boggs observes that "the fact is that the white workers have been gaining at the expense of the Negroes for so long that for them to unite with Negroes would be like cutting their own throats."[9] What blackness had come to mean in relation to whiteness restricted and controlled the vertical mobility of the black in economic matters. Boggs further notes that:

All he [the black man] could get was the menial job of porter or elevator operator. All he could live in were the buildings which had been abandoned as too old and too dilapidated for the white man. Meanwhile, the white man was moving on to the better jobs, the better schools, the newer homes, that represent progress and the American "way of life." He could only do so because there was a Negro underclass to whom he could bequeath the jobs, the schools, the homes, that the white man considered beneath him.[10]

This situation has persisted throughout American history, and the pattern has not significantly changed. Young whites try to escape it by suggesting that they never owned slaves. The fact is that they are the benefactors of the racist arrangements of this society, and power through such arrangements is bequeathed to them.

It is often assumed that because this society is capitalistic in nature, blacks and poor whites, including white women, should form a coalition to fight their common oppressor. The fact is that they are oppressed in different ways, and for blacks, the oppression is more intense—so much more so that even to white workers blacks are the underclass, and the social order provides for the mobility of poor whites and white workers at the expense of blacks. Therefore, although they struggle against the same force, it is for different reasons in this unique social structure of the American society. This uniqueness is demonstrated in the fact that the American society is not only capitalistic but is combined with a colonial model to produce a peculiar national product.

With respect to the question of allies in the struggle of black people against their oppressor, Carmichael makes the following point:

The only people we can ally with are people who have been colonized. There are two types of oppression. There is exploitation which just speaks to being oppressed economically. For example, there are poor white people in this country. They are economically exploited. But colonization is when a race oppresses another race. Because they do not only exploit you financially, but they destroy your culture, your value system, your religion, your language, your history—everything is totally destroyed. So then when people who are colonized are fighting, they're not just fighting for more money. They are fighting for a process to humanize themselves. I think Fanon speaks about this very clearly in *The Wretched of the Earth*, but especially in *Towards African Liberation*. For us to ally with people who are just fighting for money would be for us to completely miss our goal in the liberation struggle. White folks say after a rebellion that it was because "they (we) don't have jobs—unemployment, bad housing." They miss entirely what the fight is about. It is a fight for humanizing because we have been dehumanized, . . .[11]

James Boggs complements Carmichael's perspective as he argues that:

The Negro revolt is therefore not just the struggle over material necessities. It does not belong to the struggle over goods and for the development of the productive forces which we call the era of "Dialectical Materialism." Rather it ushers in the order of "Dialectical Humanism," when the burning question is how to create the kind of human responsibility in the distribution of material abundance that will allow everyone to enjoy and create the values of humanity.[12]

In this country, for example, "poor whites have passed on their homes to blacks at prices far higher than they had originally paid and at higher interest rates, using the proceeds to buy or build themselves new, up-to-date homes and schools in the suburbs." The American system has systematically operated in this way toward blacks.

While the American dream is a reality for whites, it has been a nightmare for blacks. Somehow, the black integrationist believes that the farther away one gets from the victim and the closer he gets to the source of his victimization the less victimized he will be. The realization is that the opposite is true. Many West Indians and Africans have come to realize that implicit in their sense of the necessity not to identify with "the victim" is subtle victimization.

If a group of people have no history and culture worth saving or mentioning, then it follows that they have no humanity to defend. Black people have not only been economically exploited and politically dominated, but they have been systematically culturally and socially depressed. The system's arrangements simply defined whites *in* and defined blacks *out*. If this were not the case, then somewhere in time, other than a few years of political power during reconstruction in a few Southern states, blacks would have experienced political and economic control of some of the basic institutions in the American society; at least, they would have had significant influence and input within them. In the light of this fact, the questions before black people today are: (1) How are we to define the struggle for liberation? and (2) How do we rid ourselves of white preference or the residue of this socially acquired disease? The first step is the realization that the freedom and liberation of black people is not a function of the approval and legitimation of white people. The next step is to evaluate and operationalize the significance of a political, economic, social, and cultural collectiveness, not only in national terms but also in international terms.

This will lead to the freedom and liberation of black people by the approval and legitimation of black people by black people. Every black person, whether he has experienced internal colonization or classical colonization (the consequences being the same), has to come to grips with these issues—Who is to legitimize black people? How should a group seek and gain liberation?

Somehow the arrangements of the system allow for the movement of an individual black who escapes into a racist situation, thereby losing all sense of accountability to black people and at the same time giving other blacks the impression that the black person can make progress if he tries hard enough. This gesture of the white power structure (in an attempt to survive) tends to weaken the group struggle, for in the process black people are tempted to define their struggle in individual terms, which forces them to include others (poor whites, white women, and so on) who suggest that they are also oppressed and are fighting the same oppressor. The fact is that the promotion of a few blacks cannot liberate black people. Nor are the reasons and interests of blacks the same as those of poor whites or white women, hippies, yippies, and homosexuals. The danger which presents itself here is that, in accepting the definition of success as whiteness with all its attendant favors, and to some degree its norms as standards to which all must strive (sometimes called being American), black people have sought to be successful within this context, thus legitimizing white culture, its norms and values, its belief systems, and its repressive institutions. In their quest for equality, this is what most of the civil rights movements accomplished—they legitimized whiteness as a success goal.

This process is clearly understood by whites, and so they permit limited progress of powerless individuals. Black people must come to realize that white people will embrace every opportunity to neutralize and minimize the struggle for liberation and freedom, including shrouding us with the mask. The task is clear—blacks must reject the mask.

Blacks at White Cookie-Cutter Institutions

From 1960 through 1969 black students at white institutions made specific and general demands, which, in effect, forced the universities to consider the question of accountability. For the most part, the demands spoke to the interest of the black community, but they were also on behalf of white students who were being miseducated. The cry was that the universities were not relevant and accountable to their black population. Demands were made for more black students; more black faculty members; more blacks on policy-making committees and in policy-making positions; more blacks in clerical and middle management jobs; and more facilities where the black experience could be put into proper perspective. Soon after these demands were made, black schools began to talk about "brain drain" —the decrease of brilliant black students and faculty on their campuses. Many blacks who accepted positions at white institutions were glad for the *break*. Many of them paid little attention to the "house nigger syndrome" or to the notion of the "black militant in residence." They soon found themselves defensive and in open and subtle opposition to those blacks whose protest was a function of their presence on the campuses. Not only had they confused the issues, but they had formed an alliance with the oppressor on whom they relied for approval and legitimation. Consequently, they were controlled and those to whom they were to be accountable were also controlled. Such faculty members fell into the trap of fighting individual battles for which there was no group support. Here again a segment of the black society had been lured into wearing the mask imposed by the white society.

The operation is so subtle that even great minds cannot always detect it. The solution, however, remains the same—wrench free of this cumbersome pose.

The role of white women must be understood from a historical perspective. Society has always protected them by institutionalizing subjective and restrictive policies to regulate the behavior of black people who interacted with whites. Many of the restrictive arrangements to which they address their freedom efforts were established and maintained on their behalf. When certain laws talked about protecting society, their authors meant protecting white women and the economic, social, and political interests of white men. Apart from the lynching of black men on their behalf, there were many black men who experienced "street justice" at the hands of white men for the "reckless eyeballing" of white women. Moreover, white women who lusted after black men screamed rape when caught in the act of sex with black men by their white men; the end result was black death. White women knew that society had arrangements to protect their image and pride, and white men demonstrated their insecurity by resorting to any means to assure that protection. Resorting to violence indicated their inability to relate to the interaction in any other way. Today, if they thought black men would not retaliate, they would continue to respond in a violent manner. One of the mistakes white men made was to believe that all black men wanted was their white women, not realizing that, for the most part, white women hungered and thirsted after the black man. If, according to their saying, "A white man is not a man until he goes to bed with a 'nigger,' " then it is equally true that "a white woman is not a woman until she goes to bed with a black man."

Some black men believe that the most powerful protest is their intimate association with white women, since white men, regardless of their outrage, cannot as readily lynch them anymore. The subtle counterproductive aspect of this position is that these men do not realize that, in effect, they inadvertently feed the ego of their white preference. Moreover, in the process they attempt to neutralize any form of guilt and shame associated with their interaction. The liberation of black people does not necessitate intimacy with white women or white men. In fact, such relationships often suggest continued bondage. It is believed that this white preference syndrome is diminishing in the light of the movement toward blackness.

Many blacks suggest that those blacks whose goal it is to associate intimately with white men and women are irrelevant to the struggle for the liberation of black people. Furthermore, those blacks who have not come to grips with their blackness as it relates to the liberation of black people are also irrelevant to the black struggle. It is ironic to say that we love ourselves and serve and worship whiteness as a preference. The danger of contrary reasoning is that the implicit individualism becomes so great that it prevents collective solutions to the liberation struggle; in fact, it further sustains the associated difficulties.

Distracting Movements

The struggle of black women is inextricably bound up with the struggle of black men. It is defeating to discuss their problems outside of the context of black men and the definition of blackness operating within the larger society. An exploratory study of black women compared to white women will indicate that the preferential treatment of white women in this society is not based on the fact that they are women, but rather that they are white women. Blackness and whiteness have significant operative definitions, for women as well as men. Therefore, to think that the liberation and freedom of blacks are implicit in the composition and integration of various coalitions with white groups is defeating.

Many, if not all, of the recent white movements are distracting to the black struggle. Many members of these groups seek to define themselves as oppressed, rejecting arrangements that cater to them to neutralize the guilt feelings they experience in their role as oppressors of black people. In the process, they seek to justify their efforts as oppressed people by legitimizing their struggle and relating it to the black experience, trying to establish a common bond of oppression.

As one listens to their arguments, one senses a subtle conspiracy that has operated to weaken the efforts of black people in their attempts at liberation and legitimation. These white groups have not been colonized and as such have been, by their very presence, part and parcel of the oppression of black people. They may have slight disagreements with their white brothers and sisters, but this disagreement may easily be solved to the disadvantage of black people. Indeed the contention is a "family affair" and although there is a partial separation, the hippie will return home as soon as his parents grow long hair, or whenever he cuts his long hair, or as soon as his parents change their attitude toward his behavior.

Conclusion

When blacks permit whites to define and legitimize them, they are accepting a grave encumbrance to the progress of black freedom and liberation. Blacks must recognize this and assert their own identity and culture. It is imperative that black people legitimize themselves and exclude from their definition of liberation the sense of a necessity for the approval and legitimation of white people. When this becomes a collective and mobilizing effort, then and only then can the black man ensure for future generations a legacy of truth, wisdom, and beauty of self. Then can we move as a collective to lead the oppressed peoples of the world to freedom and liberation. Blacks of the present generation must achieve *rejection of the mask*!

Notes

1. Jay Martin and Gossie H. Hudson, *The Paul Lawrence Dunbar Reader* (New York: Dodd, Mead and Co., 1975), p. 306.

2. La Frances R. Rose, "The Dominant Value of Black Culture," unpublished manuscript, 1972.

3. Shelia Rush and Christ Clark, *How to Get Along with Black People: A Handbook for White Folks and Some Black Folks, Too* (New York: Third Press, 1971).

4. DeFunis v. Odegaard, No. 741727, Oral Decision 2 (Washington Superior Ct., King County, 1971). See also Walter J. Leonard, "DeFunis v. Odegaard: An Invitation to Look Backward," *The Black Law Journal* 3 (2): pp. 224-231, and Jack Greenberg, "DeFunis: A Non-Decision of Great Controversy," *Contact*, 1971, pp. 68-70.

5. Alvin Poussaint, "Blacks and Jews: An Appeal for Unity," *Ebony*, 29 (91) (July 1974): 120-28.

6. Lenora E. Benson, *The Negroes and the Jews* (New York: Random House, 1971).

7. Interview with a West Indian living in Berkeley, California.

8. Stokely Carmichael, "Stokely Carmichael Talks Openly To *Shrewd*," *Shrewd*. (November-December, 1968).

9. James Boggs, *Racism and the Class Struggle* (New York: Monthly Review Press, 1970), p. 10.

10. Ibid., p. 11.

11. Carmichael, *Shrewd*, p. 16,17.

12. Boggs, *Racism and the Class Struggle*, p. 18.

CRITICAL
ISSUES

3

Alienation: The Case of the White Liberal

Many blacks have blamed the white liberal for the setbacks or what some prefer to call slow progress that blacks have made during the 1960s. The notion of expulsion of all whites from many of the militant civil rights groups suggested that the white liberal was not really needed. Another notion was that those gains made were permitted and controlled by the white elements as rewards for the blacks remaining relatively passive.

The passive word and the nonviolent appeals were safe, appropriate, and approved. Any other tactics would not have gained the support of many whites who were regarded as essential to the struggle in conveying and representing the verbal utterances of black people. Many black leaders were locked into the nonviolent perspective, yet they realized that nonviolence was not the language of America, that came to power through violence and maintains her position of power through violence.

What took white liberals by surprise is that the white power structure responded to violence. The Detroit experience is proof enough. After the riots, 45,00 jobs were found for so-called hard-core unemployables. However, the questions to which we will address ourselves here are: Did the white liberal have a role in the black man's struggle? Has he been alienated? If so, by whom and why?

Black people have always resisted, protested, and rebelled against the oppressive system imposed upon them. There were hundreds of insurrections. One of the three major insurrections, that started in 1800 by Gabriel Prosser, has significance for a basic understanding of why the white liberal might have been alienated from the civil rights movement.

Prosser began to organize slaves by making them aware of their conditions and the necessity of fighting for their liberation. At first blacks were the only persons involved, but as the plan developed landless whites joined. It is important to make precise distinctions between the reasons for the black man's involvement and the reasons for the white man's.

Figure 4.   POWER-STATUS MOBILITY DIFFERENTIATION

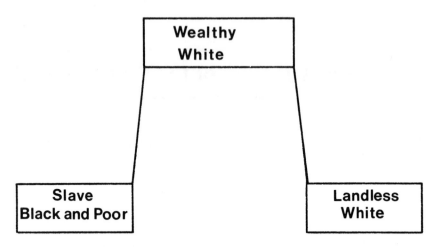

First, we must understand that they were both fighting a common enemy who had denied them both an opportunity to make progress. The wealthy white slaveholders were doing and had done much more than withholding wealth from black people; they attempted to deny them their humanity. Not only did they force black people to severely alter their culture and accept and speak the English language, but they owned them as they owned property.

Figure 4 highlights the distinction between the wealthy white or slave-holder, the landless white, and the black slave. The slave was not only land-less, thus sharing a common economic condition with the landless white, but he was also owned by the white slaveholder.

The landless whites were fighting for more money and property. They were not owned by the wealthy whites. The men they fought were the wealthy landholders whose wealth they wanted to share. The landless whites had no experience of how it felt to be owned and denied humanity. Their culture and the culture of their wealthy white brothers was the same. They had much in common; the only difference was that one was poor and the other rich. Although the landless white did not live in the "big house" of the master, he did not live in the huts with the slaves.

The black man was not merely fighting for land and money, he was fighting for his humanity. All efforts were made to strip him of his identity kit, and strenuously he had to struggle to maintain family and kinship ties. His battle against the wealthy white was a battle also against a slave-holder, all in the same body. In the final analysis, he has always had to fight the once-landless poor whites who finally become a part of or who were being used by the power structure they once fought.

A distinction of status also developed among blacks, and the house slaves jealously guarded their "superior positions." Slaveholders and their families usually preferred mulatto house servants and encouraged this social division between the slaves. This game is still played on "Negroes" to a great extent, although many, seeing through the game, are becoming aware of the significance of their heritage.

James Farmer was one of the most vociferous men in the civil rights movement. In fact, in 1963 during the march to Washington, unable to participate because he was in prison, he sent a message by Floyd McKissick. He became a part of the Nixon administration, and blacks raised questions about his accountability to the black community because of this association and his support of an administration that was not responsive to blacks. His resignation from the position in the Nixon administration did not correct his low credibility in the Black community. It is most interesting to note that when Farmer came to the campus of Miami-Dade Junior College-South in the 1969/70 school year (where the author was teaching), he defended the Nixon administration on many issues, which astonished black people. This is what happens when people are fighting as individuals and not as a group; the reasons for the struggle do not correlate. The real danger is the degree of individualism in a culture, which may become so great as to prevent social or collective solutions to racial problems and actually create and sustain problems.

Malcolm X maintained that the so-called black leaders were used by white liberals against the black revolution. He used as an example the large civil rights organizations, which were experiencing financial difficulties because of their failures with respect to desegregation. The national leaders, Malcolm felt, lost prestige and influence, and local leaders began to gain influence at the grass-roots level by stirring up these people, an accomplishment that the national leaders had not realized. Malcolm contended that the national leaders were indirectly used by the white liberal establishments to control and contain the masses. Failure on the part of civil rights leaders to ameliorate the condition of black people sent these blacks to the streets, and the various leaders began to blame each other. The white liberal liked the struggle because he felt legitimized, but did not realize that the revolution was in the hands of the black grass-root masses who viewed these black leaders and their liberal white associates as "cut-throats and thieves." The final realization of this fact disturbed the power structure. They called the leaders together, seeking their help in controlling the situation. According to Malcolm, the leaders informed the power structure that they had not started the new move and that they could not stop it. They declared that they were not even a part of the masses that had exploded.

Realizing that the black revolution had to be checked, the power structure endorsed the 1963 march on Washington. The national "Negro" leaders were placed in charge along with the white liberals and given media coverage. Milk was placed into the black coffee, and the strong black coffee became weak.

The march was powerless, just like all the other marches. However, America made a grave mistake by not responding to a peaceful protest by her people. The end result is violent protest, which is responded to in ways of destruction. The leaders and marchers were welcomed to Washington, where their pleas were listened to, but they finally left without gaining any significant change. For the most part, conditions for poor people remained the same. Soon after 1963, white liberals realized that they were fighting in vain. There was additional white backlash. In Mississippi whites were killing white civil rights workers. Black and white civil rights workers were being jailed; white civil rights lawyers were being insulted and threatened for representing black civil rights causes. Many of the whites who were involved fought consistently with the establishment and their white brothers and sisters for the rights of black people. As the establishment developed a degree of reluctance, white liberals became despondent and less active. At the same time the young blacks became impatient—rightly so, for nothing was about to change. Young blacks felt their movements and activities were overly influenced and controlled by whites—from within and from without. This feeling evoked a radical reaction. Many of them sought total control of their black organization. This desire did not bring about the alienation of many white liberals, but the talk about "any means necessary" caused them to drop back to the rear of the struggle.

Rap Brown, Stokely Carmichael, and other young black leaders were students of history. They had studied the insurrections of Gabriel Prosser, Denmark Vesey, and Nat Turner. They understood what it took to bring about real change.

John Brown's attack on Harper's Ferry was an important uprising that played a major role in the abolition of slavery. Although not many slaves joined the final action, John Brown devoted his entire life to the elimination of slavery. An important realization came to John Brown; he saw that moral appeals to the white slaveholders were of no avail and that the concerned white liberals and slaves had to concentrate on armed revolts. In 1859 this white man was not really fighting for his freedom or his liberation, yet he knew that the only language his white brothers understood was the language they spoke—violence. This realization the white liberal in the 1960s was afraid to admit. So frightening was this truth that it slowed up the white liberal's drive and retarded his efforts. He found himself in a state of ambiguity and conflict, which was sensed by the young blacks who were talking about "any means necessary." They did not want anyone (not even the Uncle Toms) holding them back with the rhetoric of nonviolence.

The white liberal's position is understandable in that one needs an emotional identification to make determination constant. Moreover, the white liberal had not defined the civil rights situation as his fight. He did not see the "cause" as his own; he was merely fighting for someone else's freedom and survival. Until he had a cause of his own to fight for would he really understand the attitude of young black militants and radicals? The white civil rights worker was supposedly the "sensible," "intelligent," "sane," "rational" human whose conscience was functioning. Although he was powerless to effect real change and estranged from many of the civil rights movements, he is said to have fought in his own way. However, the white man must accept the blame for his isolation from the more militant groups of young blacks. Many white liberals would ask, "Why do the young black students not want us to fight with them?" Others have even stated, "We are fighting the same man!" In many cases, the reply given is this: "You are fighting for different reasons, and depending on the reasons are the methods employed."

As the black movement became more militant, the alienation of the white liberal from the civil rights struggle was inevitable. He was outside the power base within the movement and felt trapped; he was not winning against "City Hall," nor was he a winner with black militants. The feeling of alienation may not be so intense today because of the change in the direction of the white liberal's behavior.

The experience of alienation is one from which the white liberal should have gained many lessons. This self-imposed alienation led to the forming of a new white man who would return to the fight for human liberation; a white man who could one day identify with the militant and radical attitudes of young blacks. The white liberal needed this alienating experience in America so that he could be on par with the black man who had inherited the status of slavery. Alienation has been a fact of existence for the black man, as an individual and as a group, down through history. He was wrenched from his homeland, loaded into ships, and brought to the New World to slave for his master without pay. He was separated from his friends and, more cruelly, separated from his family, removed from all connection with his culture and traditions and from the context of the meanings of his development. He was thrust into a totally new environment and required to work to exhaustion for men whose relationship to him was that of a property owner. Even after the black man was released from the chains he was forced to exist outside the mainstream of the society. The system kept him out and drew the white man in.

Jewish people have always felt that they are capable, more than any other ethnic group, of understanding and identifying with the black struggle in America. Their feeling is somewhat accurate for several reasons. Firstly, the Jewish people suffered persecution and religious repression. Second, they have experienced discrimination and segregation. Third, they have been placed in concentration camps and killed by the thousands. These experiences, as a total emotional force, justify the feeling of identity and understanding of Jewish-Americans relative to the struggle of Afro-Americans. Jewish-

Americans have also been oppressed to some degree, but for the most part they were permitted to maintain their Jewishness. Their traditions and many of their cultural traits persisted. Their history has never suffered distortion, and they have always enjoyed a very positive emotional identity with their homeland. They were never made to feel ashamed of their cultural past. As a result of these advantages the Jewishness of Jewish-Americans remained intact. Another advantage is that the color of black people, which easily identified them as subjects to be discriminated against, was not a problem of Jewish-Americans. Those ethnic characteristics which easily identified them were minimized and in some cases totally erased. Many Jews moved into powerful significant political, economic, and educational positions that placed them in control of those things for which blacks strived. What is often forgotten is the fact that Jews came to America to escape oppression, whereas Africans were brought to America to be oppressed.

In an attempt to expunge racism from the campus at New York University in 1968, black students ran into a wall of resistance from Jewish organizations. The employment of John F. Hatchett as the director of the Martin Luther King, Jr., Afro-American Student Center brought more resistance. John Hatchett was dismissed from the New York Public School system, where he had been serving as a substitute teacher. He had taken his students to a Malcolm X memorial program contrary to orders, which he claimed he had not received. One must bear in mind that the school system in New York, even New York University (NYU) is controlled by Jews. In their hands lie the economic and educational power. An article written by Hatchett which appeared in the November-December 1967 issue of the *African American Teachers Forum*, entitled "The Phenomenon of the Anti-Black Jews and the Black Anglo-Saxons," was the basis for the protest.[1] In this writer's opinion John Hatchett spoke the truth in his article. It should not be shocking and surpising for Jews to realize that some blacks don't like Jews. Hatred in this context may be the only positive and legitimate response, as it makes both parties aware of true feelings, which are brought into the open to be dealt with. The result will depend on what is done with such feelings and attitudes.

However, to the accusation of being anti-Semitic, Hatchett was very defensive. He declared that he was not, and had never been an anti-Semite. However, he was strongly against the systematic exploitation of black people in the city's schools, which were controlled and maintained by Jews. As a black man Hatchett's position was sound, but many of his critics, most of whom were in New York City, did not try to understand his position. After NYU decided to retain his services, Hatchett again attacked the system and three of its products. He termed the then presidential candidates, Richard Nixon and Hubert Humphrey, and the New York teachers' union leader Albert Shanker "racist bastards." He was not dismissed for free speech but for a poor choice of words. In the same speech, before more than seven hundred students, he asserted that "no white person in America was free of racism." After this speech the university officials quickly decided to dismiss him.

Black and white students talked about fruitless, disruptive protest actions. However, the objectives of the issues shifted from reinstatement of Hatchett to a demand for more student power and influence in formulating university policy. They wanted, it seems, to prevent the occurrence of a similar situation. Seemingly, whenever a group of people or even individuals with similar experiences of repression fight with black people to gain control of systems which determined their destiny, their objectives change after they become a part of the systems. Black people have experienced opposition even from their "liberal allies" because these allies lacked that emotional involvement in black causes and because they were not easily identifiable.

With the advent of the hippie and other movements with their identifiable cultural characteristics and objectives, it became possible for many whites to gain the emotional experience which lends itself to the forming of alliances with black people.

Many white liberals were also alienated from the black struggle because of a lack of understanding as to how oppressed people feel. The alienation of white liberals is the result of the reality of their progress over that of blacks. This holds true also for individual blacks who have experienced exceptional progress. Many times whites have admitted this lack in their lives. Two whites were daring enough to try living under the conditions that blacks faced every day. To have a total experience they had to change their pigmentation by medical means. The extent of their emotional experience depended on the degree and extent to which they could identify with blackness.

The Chicago convention, and the ensuing riot involving the police and whites, forced the demonstrators into a very healthy experience. Several persons were awakened to many of the situational realities blacks had been shouting about for years. Here was a group of people calling for a voice in the politics of their country and suggesting a change in the entire system. Repression was everywhere at that time in Chicago. Those in power got very concerned because the people wanted to change the system. Fear gave way to tactics which had no room for discrimination. The sick, lame, and lazy; the young, middle-aged, and old; the child, woman, and man; the visitor, bystander, and participant; the longhaired, shorthaired, and the bald, were all subjects of brutality and violence. Many whites began to admit that they did not fully believe in blacks and their cry of injustice and brutality until Chicago. Looking at policemen beat, kick, and drag women across the streets to wagons and throw them in does make one wonder how black people endured such torture for so many years. Black writers and the press brought the double standard of reporting to the attention of white writers and the press. One black woman said, "Now you know what it means to be subjects of violence, repression, harrassment, brutality, and oppression. We have been reporting it for years relative to black people in the black community. Where were you? You were nowhere around because you did not believe it nor did you care because it was levied against black people." Young white college graduates were talking about getting guns to protect themselves.

The incident at Kent State came as no surprise to the black community. Once a group of people begins to feel repressed and powerless it will take action to alter such conditions. Although color was not the significant identification in this case, the establishment and representatives of the establishment had other means of identifying the victims—an identification they felt justified the oppressive actions of the police. There is no doubt that the rhetoric of many of our top officials in America has resulted in a breakdown of social inhibitions against the use of guns to kill students in their home, the campus. This situation experienced by "sensible" whites, the one-time liberals, should have proved invaluable to them as a force for real change. This was the beginning and the end of a total experience that would have enhanced a deeper understanding of the black man's struggle.

The slowing-up of the pace of civil rights provided enough time to recognize in a significant way problems of pollution and other such issues. The white liberal, realizing that his efforts in the civil rights cause were futile, began to give his all to a relatively safe fight—a problem considered a threat to the lives of blacks and whites. The fight against pollution has brought Americans face to face with a problem basic to the racial problem—moral duplicity and moral pollution. America will fail to solve any of the problems facing its people until there is an attack on moral duplicity.

The minds of blacks and whites have been polluted with preconceived notions about each other. The more numerous their common experiences the greater the force of unity. There will be greater unity between oppressed people in America when those racial and cultural characteristics and experiences that set them apart are understood, respected, and cherished. There were those—blacks and whites—who were disturbed after 1966 when whites were asked to reevaluate their involvement in the black social movement. Black militants asked that they leave only after whites became uneasy with the apparent switch in strategies. "Any means necessary" was a call for aggressive action. There were those who argued that it was such language from the militants that caused whites to leave. However, several black organizations have always questioned the practice of having whites participate in their organization. When the NAACP was organized, the issues of white participation and the nature and extent of the white role dominated the various meetings. The Black Muslims refused whites membership and would not as much as cooperate with white groups. The rationale for this posture has changed with the change in leadership resulting from the death of Elijah Mohammad and the role accorded whites in the general world view of the new leader. In 1966, when SNCC expelled its white members and attempted to organize independent black political groups, it was following the lead set by Malcolm X, who in 1964 announced his separation from the Nation of Islam and established the black organization of Afro-American Unity.

Even though the integrationist groups continued to maintain white members, some blacks in the organizations believed that the white liberals among them were liabilities to the struggle for freedom and liberation. To define liberation in radical and racial terms made white liberals uncomfortable because those who participated in black organizations felt the need to take the initiative in demonstrating their seriousness in participation. The burden of proof rested with them. They had to prove their commitment to the struggle even though they were physical representations of the objects of the struggle. This burden was eased somewhat when the focus shifted to the system or the social order rather than those who owned, controlled, and benefit whites and blacks differently unless the arrangements are trans-assisted by white liberals was to be benefactors of the system. Liberals today sound like Marxists but act as liberals, not really willing to transform the system. Their analysis of the problem requires transformation of the arrangements of the social order, but they offer legislative reforms.

Coalition policies and politics where whites are involved will always benefit whites and blacks differently unless the arrangements are transformed.

Stokely Carmichael and Charles V. Hamilton have set forth the major arguments made against the traditional coalition policy. Kenneth M. and Patricia Dolbeare summed up their contention:

... there is a lack of identity of interest between the goals of blacks and most whites. Traditional coalitions, they argue, were based upon the assumption that what is good for white America is automatically good for black people. But this is an erroneous assumption because whites, in general, are opposed to the fundamental reorganization of the society which the black liberation movement has as its goal. Because it is in their interest, whites are consciously or unconsciously dedicated to the preservation of the prevailing norms and institutions. Further, it is difficult for whites to conceive of a society in which white Anglo-Saxon norms do not prevail. In contrast, the need of black people for self-definition challenges the preservation of these very norms and institutions and requires basic changes in the society.[2]

Coalition with whites has not been successful to the point of achieving substantial gains for blacks. There have been token accomplishments, but the "material condition of the black masses have either remained unchanged or actually declined in recent years. In addition, the coalition policy has been positively destructive to black pride and dignity because it reinforced the prevalent image of black inability to progress without white leadership."

If blacks are to make substantial gains along with others who are oppressed to the same degree and extent that blacks are oppressed, coalition politics is a must. In reality, there does not seem to be any viable alternative to coalition politics.

Oppressed groups are natural allies, and effective coalitions can be formed among and between such groups. Even in the case where there are genuine radical white groups, that is, white groups that understand and are committed to a total restructuring of the American social order, there should be caution in forming an alliance.

A new move of coalition politics has developed in Texas among Afro-Americans and Mexican-Americans, under the leadership of Congressman Mickey Leland. Other members of the Congressional Black Caucus along with Mexican congressmen are assisting. The primary goal is to organize the two groups around the various issues that concern them as oppressed groups and to develop strategies for dealing with such concerns.

It is important and significant that these groups recognize their common position in the political economy of America. What is also important to recognize, and to establish a mechanism to deal with, is the way the system perpetuates and maintains itself against the protest efforts of coalition groups. Initially, the groups focus their attention on the system and its set of oppressive arrangements. However, if there is an indication of progress, the focus shifts from the system and those who benefit from it to the groups themselves, especially in coalitions formed by black and white workers.

Coalitions are effective when and if they keep their focus on the system and its arrangements that oppress them. If they are forced, for economic or political reasons, to give attention to their individual group needs or to the relative advantage they enjoy over the other group or groups, for whatever reason, the collective effort is weakened to the point where the system will exercise control over the groups through distribution of funds, selection of certain of their leaders for token powerless positions, differential recognition of leader, and the like, causing conflict among group members and the ultimate destruction of the coalition. What really destroys the coalition and the collective efforts is the shift in perspective relative to the possibilities that result from the ability to endure. For the first couple of months the group's planning is intense and the outcome appears hopeful. Meetings are called, data are collected, and strategies are developed. By the third month or sometime later, the interest subsides and excuses are made not to continue.

Groups of oppressed coalitions must develop the ability to endure until they have accomplished something substantial. They should keep struggling until there is substantial evidence of change. The coalition efforts of Mexicans and blacks in Houston, Texas is an attempt at developing a history of coalition between and among oppressed peoples. Issues discussed at the town meetings and the ideologies expressed indicate the possibility for collective action. However, there is the possibility for conflict in ideology. There has developed a difference in the definition of the social order based on the perception of the groups' positions relative to the social order. The groups' perceptions are different because the social order defines Mexicans differently and at the same time treats them with the same oppressive realities. There is a degree of confusion among Mexicans and other such persons who are defined by the system as whites and are not receiving preferential treatment and deriving benefits based on the definition.

In the school system in Texas, for example, Mexicans are defined as whites. The school system has no obligation by definition to increase the number of Mexican teachers to approximate their student population in the schools. If the assessment of minorities for inclusion is based on the definition, then the Mexicans could be excluded if there are, by definition, sufficient whites. A significant number of Mexicans define their struggle in purely economic terms even though they might refer to themselves as being brown. The fact is, however, they were never slaves in America, and they do not pose the same threat as blacks to eliminate whites through interracial mixing. The driver's licenses of Mexicans identify them as whites. This identification has the effect of stabilizing the conflict between blacks and Mexicans and making ineffective any coalition efforts.

Blacks have had such experiences with Jewish Americans who were defined as whites but, at the same time, were not receiving the benefits through preferential treatment. Whatever coalition efforts were attempted never benefited blacks. However, Jews have achieved significant economic and political power in the American social order. On the other hand, blacks have not achieved any significant increase in political and economic power in America as a group of oppressed people.

Coalition efforts ought to be discussed in specific terms with an established agenda agreed upon by the groups forming the coalition. Contractual agreements should be signed by the groups relative to their goals and objectives and the strategies to be employed in achieving their goals and objectives.

The needs of most racially and economically oppressed groups are essentially the same. If these directions are followed the benefits derived from any coalition efforts would be shared equally according to the defined needs of each group identified and included in the agreed-upon agenda. Any other approach to coalition seems destined to fail, causing conflict of a nature that will not allow for any future attempt at coalition.

The power that is the potential of coalition among oppressed peoples of America is indeed a threat to those who have political and economic power. Consequently, any way those who now have such power can find to weaken the coalition will be employed to divert the attention away from the social order and those who benefit most from it to the groups that comprise the coalition. When there is a shift in focus the coalition weakens and those who benefit from the present set of arrangements are allowed to strengthen their position, making certain that the conflict intensifies between the groups. As the groups weaken, the social order is strengthened and those who control and exercise power in the social order make firm their position.

It has become rather difficult for a single oppressed group to challenge the power position of those who own, control, and benefit from the arrangements of the social order. Efforts to bring about change may mean that the group merely survives without any possibility of making progress. The greatest possibility for oppressed groups to bring about change in the social order that guarantees progress is for them to form a coalition that challenges the political and economic position of those who now exercise power over the affairs of the system. However, a number of possibilities for causing conflict and confusion among oppressed coalition groups are to be given special attention prior to and during the efforts for change by the coalition groups.

There are those who may argue that coalition policies among blacks and materially deprived whites have had some effect. This is true if the goal is inclusion into a racist-capitalist social order. There are token inclusions. There is evidence that the integrationist perspective has not been beneficial to the masses of oppressed people. It has allowed a few to experience a limited degree of vertical mobility, but mostly horizontal mobility. It is true that material deprivation is shared by whites and that they might be led to support certain changes in the system that blacks would support. However, there are both economic and racial policies and practices that oppress blacks, and while the change in economic policies and practices creates an identity of interest between blacks and whites, racial policies and practices achieve the very opposite.

Oppressed groups by themselves constitute a small minority of the American population. Therefore, if substantial transformation of the social order is to be achieved, allies are essential. Alliances with other oppressed groups create a majority. Its goal or objective, especially if the materially deprived whites join the alliance, should be a total restructuring of the American economic and political system. Any other form of objective and alliance is impractical and unacceptable for the purpose of liberation of racially and materially oppressed groups in the American social order.

Notes

1. John Hatchett, "The Phenomenon of the Anti-Black Jews and Black Anglo-Saxons," *African American Teachers Forum* (November-December, 1967).

2. Kenneth M. Dolbeare and Patricia Dolbeare, *American Ideologies: The Competing Beliefs of the 1970's* (Chicago: Markham Publishing Co., 1971), pp. 138, 139. See also Stokely Carmichael and Charles V. Hamilton, *Black Power: The Politics of Liberation in America* (New York: Random House, 1967), pp. 58-84.

4

Black Suicide and Individualism

The Question of Black Suicide

After doing research in the literature of sociology, criminology, and psychology, it is not difficult to realize that social scientists seem to suggest that if one is born black, somehow he inherits certain sociopathic criminal tendencies. Crime, mental illness, juvenile delinquency, and other forms of "deviant" behavior are almost always adversely associated with black or other "minority" groups.

Benjamin Quarles observes that "when we pick up a social science book, we look in the index under 'Negro'; it will read, see Slavery; see Crime; see Juvenile Delinquency; perhaps see Commission on Civil Disorders; perhaps see anything except the Negro. So when we try to get a perspective on the Negro, we get a distorted perspective."[1]

Aside from the fact that statistics are faulty and do not represent an accurate picture of what is defined and committed as "deviant," it is also significant to note that the group that has the power to define and operationalize the definition will do so to the disadvantage of others. Moreover, this position of power is enhanced by the fact that the group that owns the economic institutions and their attendant components and controls or influences the political machinery and its attending mechanisms will also be dominant.

It is argued that Dr. Charles Prudhomme (a medical doctor) was the first researcher to deal exclusively with the question of black suicide. He conducted a study published in *Psychoanalytic Review* (1938) entitled "The Problem of Suicide in the American Negro."[2] The study was an intragroup analysis of suicide among blacks in America. From all indications, this study was the only one for a long time that dealt exclusively with black suicide. Most studies, if not all, since 1938 focused their investigation primarily on white suicide, sometimes with a passing comparative mention of blacks.

In his discussion of suicide, Durkheim does ascribe importance to the state of poverty and its protective nature against suicide.[3] If the expectations and aspirations of individuals are low, disappointments of unfulfilled expectations will be so low as to guard against self-destruction. Durkheim also extended his analysis in his discussion of egotistic suicide, implying that when personal expectations are realized, individualism dethrones social ties—thus, the sacrifice that increases the possibility of suicide. This seems to be the basis for the suggestion that as more blacks embrace middle-class status, suicide among blacks will increase. This position is taken by Prudhomme in his study. In a study of African suicide, Bohannon also points out that because of strong social ties the suicide rates among Africans are very low.[4] From preliminary investigations on the issue of suicide in the Caribbean, the same thing is true.

Prudhomme suggests that:

The lower suicide rate in the American Negro is determined by a number of cultural factors each in its own way contributing to the reaction. These factors, on analysis, appear to be traceable to the peculiar and psychologically vicious environment which the majority group has imposed on the minority. As the environment approximates that of majority, the suicide rate becomes higher.[5]

Notwithstanding a few attempts to explain the phenomenon and the fact that black people in America are the most researched group, this question of black suicide has not been adequately dealt with. It could be that it did not justify or warrant intensive and extensive investigation. It is felt that if the rates were in fact very high among blacks, researchers would be suggesting, as they have done in other areas, sociological theories of self-hatred and pathology to explain the suicide phenomenon.

With respect to suicide rates, data have historically shown that the rates have always been much higher for whites than for blacks.

The data in Table 1 reveal that suicide rates among whites have been historically higher than the rates for "non-whites." For white males the rates have remained relatively constant yet higher than for black males and any other category. Nonwhite male rates have increased and nonwhite female rates have increased during 1962 and 1963. The white female rates have been higher between 1955 through 1962 than those for nonwhite females, but the rates for nonwhites increased over those for white females in 1963. However, these data do not reflect the rates for black females and males as separate categories. Included in the data for nonwhites are rates for other so-called minority groups. Consequently, the data in this table should not be used to indicate the rise in black suicide rates since 1963. Yet a careful look at the data reveal that even when we compare white rates with nonwhite rates that include other minorities the rates for whites on an average are higher.

Table 1
SUICIDE RATE PER 100,000 FOR NONWHITES AND WHITES IN THE
UNITED STATES, 1949 to 1963

| | NONWHITE | | WHITE | |
	Male	Female	Male	Female
1949-51	6.1	1.5	18.5	5.3
1955	6.1	1.5	17.2	4.9
1956	6.1	1.6	16.9	4.8
1957	6.8	1.4	16.5	4.6
1958	7.0	1.8	18.0	5.1
1959	7.4	1.9	17.8	5.0
1960	7.6	1.9	17.1	5.3
1961	7.2	1.9	17.6	5.3
1962	7.2	2.2	17.8	5.9
1963	7.9	7.9	17.8	6.3

SOURCE: From Table 1-20, Deaths and Death Rate for Each Cause by Color and Sex: United States, Vital Statistics of the United States, Vol. II. Mortality, Part A (Washington: U. S. Department of Health, Education and Welfare, for years listed). Data for 1949-51 from Jack Gibbs and Walter Martin, *Suicide and Status Integration* (Eugene, Ore.: University of Oregon Press, 1964), p. 62.

From the data shown in Table 2, we observe that black women, in spite of their problems, have the lower suicide rate (2.4) when compared to white women (6.3). The rate for black males (7.3) is much lower than the rate (16.9) for white males.

The indication is that blacks are less susceptible to suicide than whites, which in the light of the oppression of black people in America, speaks to a particular and peculiar strength among black people. These data indicate a very definite trend in a high rate of suicide for whites and a lower rate for blacks.

Table 2 reveals that for the black male the incidence of suicide remains relatively constant from ages 20 through 34 and drops by 4 percent from ages 35 through 79. From ages 85 and above, the incidence of suicide drops sharply, by as much as 10 percent. However, for white males the situation is quite different. Although the incidence of suicide remains rather constant from ages 20 through 35, it is slightly higher than that for black males (10 percent). The picture changes during the ages 45 through 79. The incidence of suicide among white males is not only higher (12 percent) than that for black males, but it increases by 17 percent. The incidence of suicide among white males over 85 years is even greater (56.8 percent).

The suicide rate among black females remains relatively constant throughout the life cycle. However, during the period between 20 through 49, the

Table 2

SUICIDE RATES PER 100,000 FOR SELECTED AGE GROUPS BY SEX
AND AGE, 1968

AGE	MALE		FEMALE	
	Black	*White*	*Black*	*White*
Total (All Ages)	7.3	16.9	2.4	6.3
5-9	—	0.0	—	—
15-19	4.7	8.3	2.2	2.2
20-24	13.1	15.0	4.4	4.8
25-29	16.0	16.3	4.5	7.0
30-34	16.1	18.3	4.8	8.1
35-39	12.0	22.0	4.7	10.6
45-49	12.1	27.0	3.8	13.1
55-59	13.3	35.8	3.1	12.3
65-69	12.8	35.6	3.5	8.3
75-79	15.0	42.5	4.7	7.2
85-up	5.5	56.8	2.8	4.9

SOURCE: Prepared by the National Urban League Research Department from unpublished data in U. S. Department of Health Education and Welfare, Mortality Statistics Branch.

incidence of suicide is about 1 percent higher than other years. For the white female, however, the suicide rate increases from age 20 to age 39 about 4 percent and increases through to age 59 by 8 percent. The highest incidence of suicide among white females is between ages 35 and 59. The rate gradually decreases by 8 percent between ages 65 and 85 years.

The data in this table indicate that suicide is lowest among black women, followed by white women, black men, and white men, especially older white men.

A few researchers (Hendin, 1969; Seiden, 1969, 1970; Peck, 1971) argue that the suicide rate for blacks is increasing and that suicide is no longer a white problem. There is little national evidence of this trend, even if this is the case for one or two cities.[6]

For example, Seiden argues that "at ages 15-19, the suicide rate for nonwhite females has for many years exceeded the toll for white females.[7] At ages 20-24, the suicide rate of nonwhite males has frequently surpassed that of white males. He suggests that the trend is not particularly new and sights Hendin, who notes that suicide rates for blacks of both sexes between ages 20-35 exceed the white suicide rates.[8] Furthermore, Seiden validates his generalization by grounding his position in records of New York City where he claims, the pattern of high youthful nonwhite suicide existed for over fifty years. Although Seiden does not specify the number and percentage of blacks in the study, he consistently uses the term nonwhite. In the same paragraph, Seiden says, "whereas white suicide increases in its direct relationship to advancing chronological age, black suicide reaches its peak at youthful years."[9] M.O. Ogden et al. in their study of suicide among Indians, assert also that for the Indians suicide reaches its peak at youthful years.[10] A footnote to Seiden's paper reads that the "terms black, nonwhite, and Negro were used interchangeably." For what was considered distorted information, Seiden received much criticism from the black community, particularly from those defined as "black militants."[11]

It is important that we return to Seiden's statement that the suicide rate for blacks has for years exceeded the toll for whites. What seems to emerge is an apparent confusion with regard to the composition of the rates, nature, and extent of black suicide, not to mention a lack of understanding as to the reason for black suicide. While Seiden, Hendin, and Peck suggest a dramatic increase in the suicide population among blacks, Hills and Henry and Short note that the population was smaller than the white population. Without this confusion and complication in statistics, the etiology of suicide is a difficult and complicated phenomenon to explain. Moreover, the etiology of suicides among blacks is even more complicated.

McLean predicted that the suicide rate among blacks would increase: "As more Negroes break out of the prison of Jim Crow and identify themselves with whites and lose their longtime explanation for the cause of their personal misery, their frustration will grow. Their fear and inner conflict will increase as their hatred of white men becomes less justifiable."[12] What seems implicit in McLean's discussion is that the cliches about equality in the North mystify blacks concerning the issues of equality. Their confrontation with denials in the North and their awareness of the operation of moral duplicity provides for them the understanding that the North is equal in cruelty to the blatant atrocities of the South. The point made rather explicitly is that as blacks lose their justification for hating white people by identifying with white cultural values, the suicide rates among blacks will nearly approximate those of whites. When blacks have a scapegoat for their conditions, she suggests, they need not kill themselves. "To kill themselves will be no revenge to the white population." A desire to belong and so the need by blacks for white approval seems critical to McLean's analysis and assertions. The blatant atrocities of whites clearly identified the enemy, which increased the need to kill whites (the enemy) rather than a desire to kill themselves. An interesting point in McLean's analysis seems to be the relationship she sees between the degree of open oppression and the rate of suicide by blacks. As discrimination becomes less evident and the conditions of blacks remain somewhat the same, the definition of whites as oppressors is weakened and forces blacks to turn on themselves. This explains for McLean the fact that the black suicide rate in the South is less than that of the North. Hating Southern whites was justified and blacks need not feel guilty for doing so, but in the North where blacks tended to feel as though inequality and discrimination by northern whites did not exist, scapegoating by northern blacks is more difficult.

Woodford notes eighteen years later an increase in the black suicide rate and attempts to explain the increase. He states that:

Since 1946, the suicide rate of Negro men has almost doubled. It is even more significant that of the thousand Negro suicides each year, almost two-thirds take place in the financially secure, even wealthy, group. For as the Negro wins his way into the material plenty of American middle and upper-middle class life, he inherits economic, social and psychological tensions possessed by his white counterparts. And suicide is part of this legacy.[13]

Woodford complements McLean's analysis by suggesting that suicide is a kind of luxury in that the rates are high among "those whose physical needs are satisfied enough to free them to will over personal, internal problems." He continues his point by asserting that: "The very trials of segregation have probably preserved the sanity of many Negroes. For when the mind is occupied by daily external problems, it cannot feed upon itself." Woodford cites the low rate of black suicide during World War II as compared to the "suicide boom" during the postwar economic boom to establish his point. He further gives credence to his argument by noting those blacks who commit suicide.

Most of them are Northern city-dwellers whose family roots were in the South. They have recently come into money and high social position is often less comfortable than they had expected.[14]

Woodford sharpens his perspective by arguing that the mere attainment of a certain economic level does not explain the high rate of suicide among middle-class blacks and whites, but that the high rate of suicide among this group is a function of the confusions and disillusions associated with such a status, with which middle-class blacks and whites are unable to cope. This interpretation suggests that race is not the determining factor, as is sometimes suggested. The argument that "suicide is monopolized by the sensitive, the rich, the intelligent—meaning the white" is dispelled by Woodford's position that suicide is a (black and white) middle-class phenomenon.

Woodford seems to rely on Durkheim's position that suicide rates are related to a group's relationship to its society's cultural style and the style of their civilization. Evidently, Durkheim did not believe that suicide is determined by religion, race, or nationality.

Woodford concludes his argument by stating that:

The very Negroes who take their lives are usually the ones who worked, studied and fought their way to an honored and rewarding position in American Society. Clearly, whatever these Negroes thought to be worth living for proved to be not enough, or what they wished to achieve was being withheld from them.[15]

We may discuss the question of rates, as many researchers have used official records to establish the issue of suicide rates. However, the official statistics and records of suicide alone are inadequate as a form of empirical evidence of suicide. Real-world cases of suicide can produce adequate evidence along with the official statistics and records to allow for an etiological explanation and description of the suicide phenomenon. There are certain drawbacks even in this case. The situated social meanings of suicide essential to any etiological analysis of the phenomenon are difficult to arrive at and study. Moreover, it is problematic to predict the suicide case in terms of abstract values against the event.

Although researchers realize the limitations placed on official statistics and official records of suicide for empirical evidence, they continue to use them to make sweeping generalizations concerning complex social problems. For example, government vital statistics[16] and Peck[17] indicate that the national rates and the rates of suicide for the youth in Los Angeles County have increased significantly, especially for black and Chicano youth. The Indians, they claim, have surpassed the rate for whites.

Suicide in Nashville

According to the records of the metropolitan police department, from 1963 through 1967 there were 237 deaths by suicide in Nashville and Davidson County, Tennessee. With regard to methods, over one-half of the victims used guns (56 percent); 13 percent used an overdose of medicine, and 11 percent died by hanging.

Of the 237 persons who committed suicide, 90 percent were white and 10 percent were black. Taking into consideration the fact that the population in the county is approximately 80 percent white and 20 percent black, it is safe to say that a significantly greater number of whites committed suicide than blacks during this five-year period. In terms of sex the distribution was 70 percent males and 30 percent females. Sixty-one percent of the deaths were of people in the 30-59 age group, evenly distributed among people in their thirties, forties, and fifties. The percentage was exactly the same for those in the 20-29 age group and the 60-69 age group; 13 percent. There was no significant pattern relative to monthly incidence; no month stood out as a time at which persons were more likely to take their lives.

Data concerning attempted suicide in Nashville and Davidson County are not available for the same period, 1963 through 1967. However, the data

Table 3

NUMBER OF SUICIDES FOR SELECTED AGE GROUPS BY SEX AND RACE
IN NASHVILLE, TENNESSEE, 1968

AGE	TOTAL	MALE		FEMALE	
		Black	*White*	*Black*	*White*
0-19	3	1	1	1	—
20-29	8	—	6	—	2
30-39	10	2	6	1	1
40-49	18	1	13	1	3
50-59	13	1	7	—	5
60-69	10	2	7	1	—
70-up	3	—	2	—	1
	65	7	42	4	12
	100%	11%	65%	6%	18%

Table 4

NUMBER OF SUICIDES FOR SELECTED AGE GROUPS BY SEX AND RACE
IN NASHVILLE, TENNESSEE, 1969

AGE	TOTAL	MALE		FEMALE	
		Black	*White*	*Black*	*White*
0-19	3	—	2	—	1
20-29	6	—	5	—	1
30-39	5	—	4	—	1
40-49	17	1	10	—	6
50-59	5	2	3	—	—
60-64	3	—	3	—	—
65-up	6	—	6	—	—
	45	3	33	—	9
	100%	7%	73%	0	20%

Table 5

NUMBER OF SUICIDES FOR SELECTED AGE GROUPS BY SEX AND RACE
IN NASHVILLE, TENNESSEE, 1970

AGE	TOTAL	MALE		FEMALE	
		Black	*White*	*Black*	*White*
0-20	6	1	5	0	0
20-30	14	1	9	2	2
30-40	10	1	6	0	3
40-50	10	0	8	0	2
50-65	19	1	11	0	7
65-up	7	0	0	5	2
	66	4	39	7	16
	100%	6%	59%	11%	24%

available for 1968 indicate that 295 persons attempted suicide and survived. Although the data for 1968 are methodologically inadequate to provide a comparative analysis, the data present certain trends that should be noted. Whereas most of the deaths during the 1963 through 1967 period occurred by the use of firearms, only a few of the attempts fall in this category. The greatest number (80 percent) recorded attempts were by overdose of drugs. Whereas 65 percent of the deaths during 1963 through 1967 were males, 65 percent of the attempts during 1968 were females. More attempts (62 percent) were made in the 10-30 age group than in all other categories combined.

From the date presented for 1963 through 1967 and the data for attempted suicides for 1968, several indications are made. More men commit suicide than do women. There are many more suicide attempts among women than men. Many more young people than older people attempt suicide. Suicide rates are higher for whites than for blacks.

Of the sixty-four persons reported to have committed suicide in the city of Nashville, Tennessee, in 1968 (Table 3) forty-two were white males, twelve were white females, seven were black males, and four were black females. The highest numbers for white males occurred between the ages of 40 and 69 with thirteen; most between ages 40 and 49. The lowest occurred among the elderly and youth. For black males the number was low in each age category with no suicides recorded among the elderly over 70 years old. For black women the number was one in most age categories with no number recorded in three scattered age categories. The number for white women was highest within the ages of 30 and 59, with most in the 50-59 age category.

In 1969 (see table 4) forty-five persons were reported to have committed suicide in Nashville, Of this number thirty-three or 73 percent were white males; nine or 20 percent were black males. Again the incidence of suicide among blacks is small compared to that of whites. In the case of black females, there were no suicides recorded during 1969. Again, the highest number (ten) of white male suicides occurred between the ages 40 and 49 (33 percent). In the other age categories, the numbers were equally distributed except in the age categories 20-29 with five, 17 percent, and 65 + with six or 18 percent. The other categories combined accounted for twelve or 36 percent of the suicides among white men. The highest number among white women occurred between the ages 40 and 49 (67 percent). The younger age categories accounted for one each; a total of three or 33 percent with no suicides occurring among white women above the age categories 50 through 65 + .

In 1970 (see table 5) sixty-six persons committed suicide in Nashville. Of that number thirty-nine or 59 percent were white men; sixteen or 24 percent were white women; seven or 11 percent were black females and four or 6 percent were black males.

The highest number of suicides among white males occurred between the ages of 40 and 65, and the highest number among white females occurred between 50 and 65. There were few suicides among black males in each category. The highest number (five) of black female suicides occurred at 65 + , and the other two occurred between the ages of 20 and 30.

Table 6
NUMBER OF SUICIDES FOR SELECTED AGE GROUPS BY SEX AND RACE
IN NASHVILLE, TENNESSEE, 1971

| | | MALE | | FEMALE | |
AGE	TOTAL	Black	White	Black	White
0-19	3	—	3	—	—
20-29	11	2	6	—	3
30-39	8	3	2	—	3
40-49	10	2	5	2	1
50-64	11	—	6	—	5
65-up	13	—	12	—	1
	56	7	34	2	13
	100%	12%	61%	4%	23%

Table 6 reveals that the highest number (thirty-four) of suicides occurred among white males (61 percent). White females followed with thirteen or 23 percent; black males accounted for seven or 12 percent, and black females accounted for two suicides or 4 percent. Suicides among white males were greatest among the age categories 40 through 65 + . Age category 20-29 accounts for the second highest suicide rate among white males. The highest number of suicides among white females occurred between the age category 50-64. The two black females who committed suicide were in the age category 40-49. All the suicides among males occurred among the age categories 20-29 (2); 30-39 (3); and 40-49 (3).

From the data presented in Tables 3-6, it does not appear that there is an increasing trend of higher rates of suicide among blacks. In Nashville, Tennessee, suicide among blacks does not appear to be a major health problem. Data currently being collected in Houston, Texas, support this position. The data in Nashville report suicide specifically on blacks and whites and indicate that a clearer picture can be obtained when the data on blacks are not included in the category of nonwhites. This category usually includes several other groups with the exclusion of whites. When data are specific with regard to racial categories for blacks and whites, it is apparent that the suicide rates for blacks, male and female, are very low. The data for 1972 do not make a distinction between black suicide and "other" suicide rates. Nonetheless, the suicide rates for blacks and non-whites are comparatively lower than that for whites, especially that of white males.

Attempted Etiological Explanations

Three categories of etiological explanations have been explored in the literature more than others at this point. They are status integration, urban stresses, and fatalistic suicide or victim-precipitated homicide.

Fatalistic Suicide or Victim-Precipitated Homicide

Hendin[18] argues that black suicide and homicide have a common factor that demonstrates itself in the way black youth cope with the violence and the rage James Baldwin[19] spoke of (rage which comes with being relatively aware), fostered and created by racial oppression, exploitation, and injustice. Hendin thinks that the years 20 to 40 are critical times that seem to provide a choice between coping with the difficulties associated with living and avoiding or escaping those difficulties. His thesis is that "black nationalistic activities may have constructive effects for individuals through allowing an external, socially acceptable method for channeling personal feelings of rage and anger."

W. Breed, after making a comparison of black and white males in New Orleans, found that over 50 percent of the black suicides had problems with the police while only 10 percent of the white suicides had such problems. Breed seems to imply that because of the excessive and oppressive regulation of blacks by the police and because blacks view force and the right arm of white domination and authority as counter to their interests, the stage is set for the appearance of fatalistic suicide. Breed's use of the concept (fatalistic suicide) is similar to Durkheim's use, that is, "suicide deriving from excessive regulation, that of persons with futures pitilessly blocked and passions choked by oppressive discipline."[20]

Durkheim had difficulty finding examples to fit this category, except the very young husband of the married woman who is childless. In fact, except to provide a category for every suicide, fatalistic suicide seems to have had no contemporary significance. Slaves who were said to have committed suicide because of certain oppressive regulatory and disciplinary conditions fitted into this category and provided for it historical significance.

The same argument is put forth by R.W. Marvis after his study in Chicago. He noted that black suicides had problems with the police to a greater extent than white suicides. The contrast established by Marvis between black and white suicides is that black suicides were the result of acute crises and long-established problems, that blacks acted from retroflexed anger and not as a result of feelings of hopelessness, and that they were apt to blame others for their frustration rather than accept the responsibility themselves.[21]

The central position put forth by Breed and Marvis seems to be weak, in that there are as many blacks as they had in their studies who have not committed suicide even though they have been confronted with the "certain conditions" that provide the strong arm for their etiological explanations of black suicide. However, they both seem to suggest a significant relationship between suicide and homicide to the extent that apparent homicide for blacks may very well be defined as suicide. This is true especially for the young black militants.

However, this notion is not new. In 1940, Hans Von Hentig expressed the notion that:

We can frequently observe a real mutuality in connection to perpetrator and victim, killer and killed. Although this reciprocal operation is one of the most curious phenomena of criminal life, it has escaped the attention of sociopathology. There is a new form of grouping, causal or permanent. When these elements meet, it is likely that a novel compound is set up in the world of human relations, explosive and big with ruinous conflicts.[22]

Out of a study of "Patterns in Criminal Homicides," Marvin Wolfgang employs the concept of physical force to suggest that in many criminal homicides the victim often precipitates his own death, thus becoming a direct participant in the crime. Wolfgang's definition of such a person is a "suicide-prone" individual desirous of destroying himself who engages another person to commit the act because he is not able or willing to perform the act himself.

Except for the fact that they fail to use the lethal weapon directly on themselves, they are in effect committing suicide. . . .A considerable portion of suicide is latent rather than manifest and is hidden among victim-precipitated homicide.[23]

Wolfgang extends this assertion to categorize and define certain behavioral patterns of young black militants who were said to have initiated the fatal confrontation by striking the first blow as victim-precipitated homicide. Such young blacks are viewed as having suicidal tendencies; rather than killing themselves, they put themselves in "certain situations" and take the initial action that evokes the fatal reaction of others, especially the police. Theoretically, this type of homicide is technically redefined as suicide, thus as an increase of black suicide.

However, historically, blacks have been killed by the police at a disproportionate rate far beyond any reasonable justification. In recent years (1964-1970) black male homicide by the police has been extremely high in age groups where "hardened criminals" are fewer, the very young (10-14) and the very old (65 +). Philip Buell and Paul Takagi argue that: "In proportion to population black youngsters and old men have been killed by police at a rate 15 to 30 times greater than that for whites at the same age."[24] The literature is replete with examples establishing the fact that "police have one trigger finger for whites and another for blacks." Moreover, whether actively seeking change or not, black people in America, because of a history of oppression, racism, and exploitation, are viewed as seeking change in those arrangements of the white power structure that hold them in bondage. The police are a law-and-order group whose job it is to keep things the way they are. Any change or attempt at change is threatening to the police, because it gives the impression that they are not performing their duties. For this reason, they employ threatening tactics to stifle their rising panic in confrontation and to deal with what they publicly and privately define as "black threat."[25]

Black people and their communities are, and under the present political and economic circumstances will remain, police targets. Moreover, in the face of their violations and injustices, the police are protected by their superiors, who assure them that even their killing of black people is excusable if not justifiable.[26] With this in mind, Hendin, Wolfgang, and Seiden are incorrect in that black militants do not strike the first blow; in an attempt to cope with the first blow thrown at them, they are caught face to face, not with those who threw the blows, necessarily, but with the protectors, the police who perform the final rites for the racists and capitalists.

The expressed notion that black militants "take it upon themselves to provoke and engage in Kamikaze-like activities such as sniping or police shootouts against overwhelming odds—a type of masked self-destructive behavior dynamically related to the phenomenon of victim-precipitated homicide"[27] is absurd, simply because history documents that blacks do not have to be militants for police to destroy them. The new type of militancy may have provided a more comfortable explanation for officials than that of excusable and justifiable homicide. To further suggest that such activities by black militants are uncontrolled, impulsive, and undisciplined behavior is to overlook the fact that individuals have private and public morals and call upon them at different times and in different circumstances depending on their definition and interpretation of the situation.

A statement by the Black Panthers on "revolutionary suicide" is used by Seiden to give strength to his argument: "That's suicide motivated by the desire to change the system, or else die trying to change the reactionary conditions."[28] Seiden argues that it remains unanswered "whether this is simply provocative rhetoric similar to the right-wing slogan 'Better dead than Red,' or whether indeed it is a valid suicidal threat."[29]

For committed black militants the liberation of black people takes priority over everything else, even, for them, life itself. This is black power and freedom in action. Of what profit is it to live and be devoid of liberty and freedom? For them it is indeed "better to die on one's feet than to live on one's knees." It is within this context that "Freedom Now" has pragmatic meaning. These black militants to whom Seiden refers hold freedom for blacks so dear that they are willing to risk their lives in the face of death so that the liberation of a people may be realized.

Many whites do not seem to understand this point but they should if they study the behavior of their forefathers who did everything to control this land. Now, according to some, they cannot make sense of this kind of black behavior. Henry Garnet argued the point being developed here when he said "rather die freed than live to be slaves."[30] The assertiveness of those blacks defined as militants is a demonstration of the courage that mystified many middle-class blacks and whites. There is within "militant" blacks the ability to affirm their existence. Their attempt is to strike out on behalf of all black people at those oppressive and dehumanizing forces that threaten black existence and development. Paul Tillich suggests that "the ethical act is one in which man affirms his being in spite of elements of his existence which conflict with his essential self-affirmation."[31]

Blacks (militant or nonmilitant) who understand the workings of an oppressive society realize that they live, despite the affirmation of their being, in the ever-present possibility of death at the hands of oppressors and their agents. Many black people prefer to die than submit to oppression and the denial of their being. Rollo May notes that the cry for death is the "most mature form of distinctly human behavior."[32] Seiden, Wolfgang, and others would dare classify the death of Martin L. King, Jr., and that of Jesus as victim-precipitated homicides, not understanding their basic philosophy of life. Jesus and King had consciously chosen a value they held more dear than physical life itself. In fact, King believed that the essence of being human is finding something one defines as worth dying for.

Frantz Fanon observes that "man is human only to the extent to which he tries to impose his existence on another in order to be recognized by him. . . .he who is reluctant to recognize me opposes me. In a savage struggle I am willing to accept convulsions of death, invincible dissolutions, but also the possibility of the impossible."[33]

Victim-precipitated-homicide theorists try to explain away the seriousness with which black people struggle for liberation. They take lightly the efforts of an oppressed people. To submit to an oppressive situation, not to resist it, is to them the only sensible way. In a struggle in which blacks consistently seek liberation in America, bloodshed, destruction of the being, and death of physical life at the hand of oppressors and oppressive forces are inevitably murder. Therefore, these statistics should not be used to indicate an increase in the rate of suicide among black youth.

Urban Stresses (Urbanization) and Suicide

It is believed that significant to the increasing rate of black suicide is the fact of the population shift of blacks from the South to the North, and from the rural areas of America to urban areas. What is being suggested is that any etiological explanation of black suicide must take into account this shift in population and the consequent problems.

D.O. Price and Mary Lou Baner provide substance and significance to the argument of population shift by presenting statistics showing that the increased suicide rates of blacks correlate significantly with urbanization. The contention is that since the 1870s the suicide rates for blacks have increased as they have moved from the rural South to the urban North.[34]

L.J. Banks presents data to suggest that compared with young whites, nonwhite youth suicide rates in Washington, D.C., Chicago, New York, Atlanta, and Los Angeles have steadily increased for many years along with urbanization. Banks attributes this raise to "unemployment, cramped quarters, raw filth, the hunger and cold of many tenents."[35] Before this, the Metropolitan Life Insurance Statistical Bulletin of March 1967 more specifically suggests that the "exposure to new and unfamiliar stresses" contributes to the increasing suicide rates.[36]

It is conceivable that unemployment in urban areas may present peculiar problems for urban youth. Such terms as devastating and catastrophic seem inaccurate in an attempt to explain the relationship employment has to suicide. No consideration is given to the ability of black youth to create alternatives (legal or illegal) to official employment. Moreover, if unemployment has suicidal effects of black youth then it should have the same effect on white youth. Simply because the Labor Department figures show a large percentage of unemployment among youth does not suggest that the effects of unemployment are more severe among youth in general or that they have a suicidal impact upon black youth in particular.

For the most part, black youth may not regard an 8-to-4 job as meaningful. Indeed, meaningful jobs for a great number of black youth may not be defined as legitimate for inclusion in their employment records. The history of black people (youth and adult) is replete with a consistent quest for what officials define as meaningful jobs. Because of this very fact blacks have had to create other means to survive. Therefore, to suggest, without any proof of the effect, that lower-class blacks are not able to support their families because they are unable to earn a living and consequently commit suicide is to discredit the creative survival strategies of blacks. Moreover, black lower-class people are a hopeful group with a great stake in tomorrow.

No doubt, there are other problems significantly associated with unemployment. However, these combined problems are faced by all oppressed groups in the American society, even exploited women who have problems of self-identity and self-worth and other psychological scars.

Several works (Leebow, Paffenbarger and Asnes, Stanley and Barter) associate fatherless households in urban areas and lower-class young blacks with suicide.[37] What is explicit is the argument that the absence of the father is related to the increase of suicide among black youth. No data are presented to show that the black youth that commit suicide come from father-absent households or the difference in rates for youth whose fathers are present. What is further suggested in the works just mentioned is that these blacks who move into urban areas are unable to cope with new and unfamiliar stresses associated with urban life. Again, no data are given to support this argument. What is suggested, however, is that there were several persons who killed themselves over problems which seemingly could be easily solved. If solutions to their problems were readily available and yet these young blacks insisted on suicide, then one may argue that those obvious problems are not really significant as causal factors.

Status Integration and Suicide

The theoretical notion of status integration was developed by Gibbs and Martin, who noted that the consequences of constructive social changes may be positive as well as negative. The realization of such changes can be both bitter and sweet for individuals.

Jack Gibbs and Walter Martin made a formal attempt to test Durkheim's generalization about suicide rates and social integration. However, they maintain that Durkheim's theory is difficult if not impossible to confirm or prove false because social integration is not operationally defined. To attempt a test of the proposition on status integration and suicide rate, they employ theory construction techniques and statistical methods.[38] The consequence of their efforts is the theorem that "suicide rate is inversely related to the stability and durability of social relationships." Although this theorem seems to be a translation of Durkheim's proposition of social integration, it also seems difficult to test. The theory predicts an inverse relationship between status integration and suicide rate. Their test of their operationalized theorem with varying status configurations confirms their prediction that there is a high correlation between suicide rate and status integration.[39] Status integration is defined as the "frequency with which a particular status configuration is occupied." The greater the frequency of "occupation," the higher the status integration and the lower the suicide rate.[40]

The works of other researchers on the subject do not support some of the notions of Gibbs and Martin. Chambliss and Steele argue that the studies of Breed and Maris show just the opposite of those of Gibbs and Martin. Although the effort of Gibbs and Martin to formally test the generalization of Durkheim concerning social integration and suicide rate is considered a significant contribution, many of the issues raised as a result of their efforts are still debated.

However, basic to the theory is a historical perspective of social change, which suggests that in the face of certain situations (breakdown in group identity and moral codes, a high rate of occupational and social mobility, and a great degree of ambiguity of customs) institutions responsible for the normalization of such situations prove incapable and demonstrate an inability to cope.[41] Thus, Seiden notes, "as individual freedom increases there is less need to conform to the demands and expectations of others, but this personal freedom brings with it the existential liability of increasing role conflicts, incompatible statuses, and consequently a low degree of status integration."[42]

With respect to status integration and black suicide, the theorists assert that the suicide rate is dependent on the degree of racial discrimination, racial solidarity, collective mentality, and the common definitions the community holds of its oppression and oppressors.

The theory states that "the suicide rate of a population varies inversely to the degree of status integration of that population; but the same factors which lead to social improvement often decrease the degree of status integration."[43]

According to the theory of status integration, the advocates of "integration" and "equality" may use as an indication of progress toward occupational and educational "equality" the supposedly increasing suicide rates among blacks. The theory does suggest that as the aspirations of blacks and other oppressed people are realized and they achieve higher status through their obtained goals (educational and occupational), suicide among these groups increase. This is the argument and, more accurately, the prediction of Prudhomme and McLean concerning the possible increased rate of suicide among black people. It must be remembered that this increase is predicted among those achieving educational and occupational mobility, not among the majority (the masses) of black people whose sense of historical peoplehood and kinship bonds are solidified. The sense of being in it all together and the feeling of we-ness along with a high sense of hope will not allow this group to destroy itself.

Conclusion

Most studies continue to show a smaller number of blacks committing suicide than whites. However, the problem of suicide should not go unnoticed if it is the case that suicide is the second highest cause of death among the youth in general and college students in particular and increasing among black women. It is true that a greater number of persons attempt suicide than those who actually successfully complete the act. As such, suicide may be said to be social communication. It also seems factual that persons who attempt or commit suicide experienced recent disruption in their sociopersonal relations with others or within certain significant socioeconomic situations. Usually this experience represents a build-up of alienation, frustration, and aggression that finds no release and thus causes the individual to communicate what he/she believes to be an intolerable situation to those around by attempting to commit suicide. Attempted suicide may thus be explained as an intense and vital need to communicate one's immediate problems rather than merely a wish to bury one's ego by self-destruction.

Suicide may be said to be a socially directed action, a social act, a cry for help rather than a completely inner-directed act of aggression against the self. Sometimes help comes from within or from others; sometimes, however, help does not come and the self destroys the self.

One speculation concerning the question of suicide is that people who take their lives are not satisfied with their perception of the acceptance by significant others of their projected self. The discrepancy between the view by others of the projected self and the view held by the individual of the "real" self leads the individual to develop a style to convey a positive view of the self acceptable to significant others. When the individual fails to confront the breakdown in this process and the crisis of the discrepancy in perceptions, suicide attempts and successful suicide are inevitable.

Researchers on the subject of suicide have evidently disagreed with one another concerning the causal factors that lead one to commit suicide. Causal factors mentioned are anger, frustration, the predicament of poverty, a realization of the stability of an unbearable situation, domestic crises, disappointments, hopelessness, isolation, low self-esteem, feelings of rejection, complex family problems, pathological relationships, economic pressures, racism, and political oppression.

Middle-class blacks who commit suicide failed to make the necessary distinctions between their historical identification with the majority of black people and black culture and their participation identification with middle-class whites who reject them even though they identify with whites in job participation and in club and neighborhood situations. The discrepancy is due to the fact that these blacks are a different ethnic group; but because they share the same social class and therefore the same behaviors with middle-class whites, they seek to share a sense of peoplehood with whites, with whom they share participational identification and whom they view as their significant others. In the process, these blacks seek to reduce their sense of peoplehood with those individuals of the ethnic group with whom they share historical identification. Because these blacks share certain behavioral similarities with middle-class whites, they believe that they should share the same privileges, opportunities, amenities, and resources of the white middle class. In the process, these blacks are alienated from the ethnic group that provided their historical connections and allowed for buffers against such discrepancies.

In this sense the black middle class is not a harmonious social group, integrated and regulated within the norms and values of the white middle class. Neither is the individual a central member of the white middle-class societal groups. Moreover, the black middle class isolates itself from its ethnic roots, which results in the absence of solidarity and cohesion within the group itself. The consequence is that which was predicted several years ago by Charles Prudhomme and Helen McLean: The suicide rate would increase among blacks as more blacks move into middle-class status.

It is not so much that these middle-class blacks have severe problems of social isolation and other forms of rejection from white middle-class groups that they define as their significant others. It is rather their separation from the normative order of their ethnic group with whom they share historical identification and peoplehood that reduces their ability to remain cohesive as an ethnic group. Individualism becomes important and is operationalized so as to cope with the contradictions and conflicts. This behavioral principle is also penetrating the communities of the masses. Consequently, what seems common to all the factors identified as causal relative to suicide is the inability of those individuals to cope with those causal factors in individual terms. Whether it is the middle-class black isolated from a sense of peoplehood and from his historical roots or the grass-root black who experiences isolation or alienation while still operating within the masses, they all suffer from individualism when they attempt or commit suicide because collective forces once used as buffers to the evils of a capitalist-colonial society are being destroyed.

74   Critical Issues

Notes

1. Benjamin Quarles, *Jet* 33 (12) (December 28, 1967): 32.

2. Charles Prudhomme, "The Problem of Suicide in the American Negro," *Psychoanalytic Review* 25 (2) (1938): 187-204 and 25 (3): 372-91.

3. E. Durkheim, *Suicide* (Glencoe, Ill.: Free Press, 1951).

4. P. Bohannon (ed.), *African Homicide and Suicide* (Princeton: Princeton University Press, 1960).

5. Ibid., p. 391.

6. Richard H. Seiden, "Suicide Among Youth," P.H.S. Publication No. 1 (Washington, D.C.: U.S. Government Printing Office, December 1969); "We're Driving Young Blacks to Suicide," *Psychology Today* (August 1970); Herbert Hendin, *Black Suicide* (New York: Basic Books, 1969); M. Peck, "Youth: Special Suicide Risk Group" (paper read at NIMH Suicidology Institute West, Los Angeles, January 1971).

7. Richard H. Seiden, "The Problem of Suicide on College Campuses," *Journal of School Health* 41 (5) (1971): 243-48.

8. Hendin, *Black Suicide*, p. 5.

9. Seiden, "Suicide on College Campuses," p. 245.

10. M.O. Ogden, M.I. Spector, and C.S. Hill, "Suicides and Homicides Among Indians," *Public Health Report* 85 (1) (1970): 75-80.

11. Seiden, "Suicide on College Campuses," p. 245.

12. Helen Vincent McLean, "Why Negroes Don't Commit Suicide," *Negro Digest* (February 1947), p. 6.

13. John N. Woodford, "Why Negro Suicides Are Increasing," *Ebony* (July 1965), pp. 89-100.

14. Ibid.

15. Ibid., p. 100.

16. Vital Statistics of the United States. Vol. II, Part A, 1965-1967. Mortality. Washington, D.C.: U.S. G.P.O.

17. M. Peck, "Youth," 1971.

18. Herbert Hendin, *Black Suicide, p. 5*

19. James Baldwin, quoted in Angela Y. Davis, *If They Come in the Morning* (New York: New American Library, Segret, 1971), p. 21

20. W. Breed, "The Negro and Fatalistic Suicide," *Pacific Sociological Review* 13, no. 3 (1970): 156-62.

21. R.W. Mavis, *Social Forces in Urban Suicide* (Homewood, Ill.: Dorsey Press, 1969).

22. Hans Von Hentig, "Remarks on the Interaction of Perpetrator and Victim," *Journal of Criminal Law, Criminology and Police Science* 31 (May 1940-April 1941): 303.

23. Marvin Wolfgang, "Suicide by Means of Victim-Precipitated Homicide," *Journal of Clinical and Experimental Psychopathology* 20 (1959) 335-49.

24. Philip Buell and Paul Takagi, "Code 984: Death by Police Intervention," *Journal of Afro-American Issues* 2, no. 2 (1974) 109-117.

25. L. Alex Swan, "The Politics of Identification: A Perspective of Police Accountability," *Crime and Delinquency* 20, no. 2 (1974) 119-28.

26. *Ibid.*
27. Richard Seiden, "Suicide on College Campuses," p. 244.
28. *Black Panther* (August 1970), 15, 1-3, 5.
29. Richard Seiden, "Suicide on College Campuses," p. 246.
30. Henry H. Garnet's address to the slaves in 1898. See *Cross Current* 27, no. 2 (Summer 1977): 152.
31. Paul Tillich, "Our Culture," *Anxiety*, ed. Paul H. Hoch and Joseph Zubin (New York: Hafner Publishing Co., 1964).
32. Rollo May, *The Meaning of Anxiety* (New York: Ronald Press, 1950).
33. Frantz Fanon, *Black Sin, White Masks* (New York: Ronald Press, 1967), p. 218.
34. Mary Lou Baner, "Differentials in Health Characteristics by Color," P.H.S. Publication No. 1000, Series 10, no. 56, Washington, D.C., National Center for Health Statistics (October 1969); D.O. Price, "Changing Characteristics of the Negro Population" (1960 Census Monograph), Washington, D.C.: U.S. G.P.O., p. 3.
35. L.J. Banks, "Black Suicide," *Ebony* 25, no. 7 (May 1970): 76-84.
36. Metropolitan Life Insurance Statistical Bulletin (March 1967).
37. E. Leebow, *Tally's Corner* (Boston: Little Brown, 1967); E.J. Stanley and J.T. Barter, "Adolescent Suicidal Behavior," *American Journal of Orthopsychiatry* 40, no. 1 (1970): 87-96; R.S. Paffenbarger and D.P. Asnes, "Chronic Disease in Former College Students, III. Precursors of Suicide in Early and Middle Life." *American Journal of Public Health* 56 (1966): 1026-36.
38. Jack Gibbs and Walter Martin, *Suicide and Status Integration* (Eugene: University of Oregon Press, 1964).
39. William J. Chambliss and Marion F. Steele, "Status Integration and Suicide: An Assessment," *American Sociological Review* 31 (1966): 524-32.
40. Mavis, *Social Forces.*
41. Ruth S. Cavan, *Suicide* (New York: Russell and Russell, 1965).
42. Richard Seiden, "Suicide on College Campuses," p. 246.
43. Ibid.

5

Branded for Life: The Case of Detained Black Youth

One of the basic problems facing the area of juvenile delinquency is the very concept, which not only covers a wide range of activities and a complex set of juvenile offenses but also is so vaguely defined that its meaning is often left to the discretion of law enforcement officers and the courts to define. Juvenile status offenses, for example, are a group of acts committed by juveniles that are regarded as illegal only for juveniles. For these acts adults would not be arrested. Within the context of broad notions such as "out of control," "beyond control," "habitually truant from school," "habitually refuses to obey the reasonable and proper orders or directions of parents, guardian, custodian, or school authorities," police and court officials exercise their discretion. The juvenile is faced with a vague notion of delinquency with a dual definition. The juvenile not only can be arrested for acts for which an adult may be charged and convicted but also may be arrested and convicted for "offenses" peculiar to the legal status of the juvenile.

However, the real problem that black youth face is the assessment of their acts or the social interpretation of their behavior in the community by outsiders who have the power to identify, treat, and label their behavior as delinquent or define them as needing supervision. It is not so much the act alone that constitutes a delinquent act, but the social interpretation or the assessment plus the act. Most police bring a different set of values, norms, and belief systems to assessing the acts of black youth. Usually police and school officials make an assessment of the black youth in terms of the acts, while parents make an assessment on the basis of the total character. This is the reason that police and school officials are often in conflict with parents regarding the social interpretation of juvenile acts and the disposition of actions to be taken. If parents and community members identifying the behavior do not assess the act as requiring the police, the behavior will not be judged delinquent.

When a juvenile is identified, treated, and labeled delinquent by the police and court officials there are serious consequences of further contact between the juvenile and criminal justice systems. We will return to this point later because it is the essence of our understanding of the typing process that brands black youth by institutional arrangements, stigmatizing black youth and their community.[1]

The Juvenile Justice System

The juvenile justice system is significant to the typing and branding of black youth. The system was once thought to represent a crucial improvement over the earlier handling of juveniles as adults. This view was later replaced by the belief that the penological philosophy on which the juvenile court and its related structure of delinquent control organizations were based was a progressive ideal that had never been translated into efficient action.

Platt argues that the establishments of a separate court and corrections system for juveniles grew out of sociopolitical interests and a penal philosphy that were not especially liberal nor radical in nature. As the main object of the child-saving movement was the discovery and control of juvenile delinquency, it "brought attention to and thus invented new categories of youthful misbehavior which had been hitherto unappreciated." The court system intervened in the youth's life to "save" him from a bad nature and environment, denying the youth freedom without due process even when no offense had been committed or when acts for which adults were not indictable were involved.[2]

The middle-class women who made up the majority of the child-savers were more concerned about the threats that urbanization, industrialization, and immigration posed to their values than with humanitarian concerns for the youth. Consequently, they promoted a system that incarcerated youth for long periods of time, indeterminately, allowing for the internalization of "middle-class values and lower-class skills."[3] Platt's original position, focused on middle-class interests, was a pluralist stance that argued that the success of the child-saving movement was due to the fact that it satisfied diverse interest groups.

Criticism forced Platt to reinterpret his earlier view. He argued later that his earlier work focused too much attention on middle-class reformers, reasoning that "impetus for delinquency legislation flowed from close and compromising links between members of the middle and upper classes" and that "the juvenile court system was part of a general movement directed toward developing a specialized labor market and industrial discipline under corporate capitalism by creating new programs of adjudication and control.''[4]

The juvenile court was considered to be a great advance in child welfare in that it was to remove youth from the stigma of the adult criminal process. The juvenile court was defined as civil rather than criminal, and the civil rights of juveniles were not protected. In order to "straighten them out" a more authoritarian approach was assumed as the child-savers engaged in procedures that denied children due process. Proceedings in the juvenile court were distinguished from those in the criminal court. The language was changed but the consequences remained the same. The changes were supposed to restructure the proceedings along the lines of the new clinical ideal and to further the goal of investigation, diagnosis, and prescription of treatment rather than to adjudicate guilt or fix blame.[5] However, critics say on the one hand that the system punishes when it says it doesn't and on the other hand that it fails to safeguard the liberty of individual juveniles when it is supposed to do so.

Decisions rendered by the U.S. Supreme Court in Kent v. United States,[6] even though this was a criminal case, in Gault[7] and in Winship,[8] resulting from charges that the courts subjected youth to arbitrary decisions and capricious procedures, established certain rights of juveniles. The implementation of these rights, however, is being resisted by juvenile court officials. Many juvenile courts have either ignored these decisions or by other subversive strategies have not enforced their principles. In many instances across America juveniles are not afforded the due process guaranteed by the Constitution to children accused of criminal conduct. The fact is that presently juveniles are subject to imprisonment whether they are tried for delinquent behavior or for status offenses. Status offenders are over-represented in state institutions, and the majority of these are poor and oppressed juveniles. Even those who are imprisoned for alleged delinquent acts are poor and oppressed. The juvenile justice system and especially the courts have come to be the process and mechanism for typing, labeling, and branding certain individuals as delinquents.

The Use of Official Statistics

When statistical information regarding the extent and nature of delinquency is published it creates a false image of delinquency in the American social order. It establishes the myth, through its typing and branding process, that delinquency it somehow associated with blackness and the urban community. The stigma of this myth has had a demoralizing effect on many black youth in the black community, and it also hampers the development of successful prevention plans to deal with delinquency and its root causes. This is the picture that is intended to be given and maintained of black youth. It is argued by others, Benjamin Quarles[9] and George Napper,[10] that this is the picture that is also presented of black people as a whole.

The disportionate numbers of black youth detained by the juvenile justice system is explained by the presence of racism at every level of the system. Those who have been critical of statistical records of police departments, courts, and prisons have established the fact that these records are inadequate and invalid. Yet there are those who continue to use these records and argue that regardless of race, youth of the lower "socioeconomic status" are more likely to engage in delinquent behavior, the logic being that as there are proportionately more poor and oppressed youth of this particular social class than other social classes it follows that there would be more poor and oppressed given to delinquent behavior. Studies that do not rely exclusively on official records argue that a large number of delinquent acts are unrecorded in these sources. One report suggests that the police never learn who commit most delinquent acts.[11] Moreover, wealtheir individuals who commit the same kinds of offenses are four to five times less likely to appear in some official record than poorer individuals.[12] Data collected by self-reporting methods demonstrate that official records exaggerate the extent of delinquent behavior of juveniles from lower-status homes and that police are more likely to record officially those offenses committed by lower-status youngsters, the children of semiskilled and unskilled parents. Middle- and upper-class youngsters, especially white youngsters, get away with delinquency, and poor kids get records.

The use of official records showing an overrepresentation of lower-class oppressed persons in criminal populations has been a controversial isuue that has led to the development of a theoretical position that focuses on factors of lower-class life as causal explanations of crime and delinquency even though only correlation and not causation is indicated. There is no doubt that law enforcement agencies exercise selective bias against lower-class and oppressed populations. The differential enforcement patterns such as detention of suspicious persons and harassment of certain community groups and saturated patrol of these communities are self-fulfilling practices that inflate arrest rates and criminal records. Official statistics are nothing more than indicators of official processing decisions. This argument is strengthened by evidence generated by self-reporting and victimization surveys. Crime levels exceed officially recorded rates by several times, and the statistical differences in criminal involvement are reflective of variations in the reporting of offenses and of the differential law enforcement practices among the various classes and races.

It is not just the disproportionate lower socioeconomic status among blacks and other oppressed people that explains the disproportionate number of them who comprise the criminal statistics and occupy the juvenile and detention homes. It is the definition of blackness that is operationalized by the police and court officials upon contact with blacks that translates into racist decisions that also explain the situation. The system of racism black men and women have been subjected to over a long period of time in the American social order is still operating and manifests itself in the administration of justice. Middle- and upper-class white youth who commit delinquent acts are defined by police and court officials in psychiatric and psychological terms, while the same acts committed by black youth are defined and handled in criminal and delinquent terms. [13]

Data collected in southern states indicate that even though black youth committed fewer officially delinquent acts over a period of five years (1970-1975) in the areas of burglary, larceny, auto theft, forgery and counterfeiting, vandalism, driving under the influence, drunkenness, vagrancy, and disorderly conduct, they make up the majority of individuals detained in state juveniles homes. [14]

The majority of these black youth come from communities that are politically and economically powerless. Their parents also lack contact with powerful persons or with institutions and organizations with some degree of power. Most parents are so busy making a living that they are afraid they would lose their jobs if they took time off to attend hearings about their children. Consequently, the youth usually lack legal representation and parental presence at hearings. Moreover, the practice of pastors appearing on behalf of the parents to assert some degree of moral persuasion and community concern has ceased in many communities.

The great majority of black youth processed through the juvenile system and detained are between the ages of 14 and 17. Aside from the fact that their parents do not have political and economic power to invoke upon the contact of their children with the juvenile justice system, their parents do not own their own homes, and many live in substandard housing. Their incomes are between $3,000 and $7,000 per year, and most of them have an education level between elementary and high school. However, the majority of the parents themselves have not had any contact with the criminal justice system or the juvenile justice system.

A significant number of detained black youth are detained for status offenses, that is, noncriminal acts. These status offenders are usually apprehended for subsequent delinquent behavior. It is argued that if they were not apprehended for those initial status offenses they would be less likely to be apprehended for index offenses and misdemeanors. Because police are more likely to stop and question black youth than white youth and because their dispositions are harsher toward black youth than white youth, black youth are more likely to be referred to juvenile court than white youth. Moreover, black youth are more likely to be sent to detention homes than to receive recommendations for psychiatric examination and treatment as do their white counterparts.

Nathan Goldman's study of police decisions and court dispositions of apprehended juveniles shows that 65 percent of black juveniles, in contrast to 34 percent of white juveniles, were referred to court and that they were more likely to be referred to the court for status offenses, malicious mischief, and property damages.[15]

Terence Thornbery also found significant racial differences between blacks and whites in processing through the courts.[16] Theodore Ferdinand and Elmer Luchterhand, using a random sample of 1,525 teenagers in six inner-city neighborhoods, found that black teenagers were disproportionately processed through courts more often than their white counterparts.[17]

In a study of five hundred juveniles in Huntsville, Alabama, and Nashville, Tennessee, the differential processing of black and white youth was very evident. Seventy-nine percent of the black youth were sent to juvenile institutions while only 23 percent of the white youth were sent to such institutions for the same offenses.[18]

There is little doubt that blackness is defined and operationalized at every level of the juvenile justice system in relation to whiteness. The consequence is that a significant number of black youth get typed as delinquents and a defined process is established and maintained which allows for a disproportionate number of black youth to experience the process and its typing. This is the case for the majority of black youth who come in contact with the juvenile justice system whether or not they committed an index crime, a misdemeanor, or a status offense.

The same selectivity that exists in the records of police also exists in the records of the courts and juvenile corrections, as a direct or indirect result of the function of arrest and the function of police discretion. The judicial system also allows a great degree of discretion to judges. Judges and police are products of their experience, class background, training, prejudices, racial notions and emotional conflicts. In fact, most of what the law is and has come to be is a matter of what judges think the rule of law should be. Judges and police have much leeway in the decisions that they make. Their failure to enforce and apply the same standards in all cases has resulted in racial and class injustices. It is implicit in the discretion of the police to arrest and the power given to judges that black youth get processed as delinquents and labeled in the juvenile justice system.

Labeling theorists argue that when we talk about delinquency reference is being made to someone who has been labeled by the juvenile justice system. The juvenile is forced to play the role he has been given once he is labeled, even if he prefers another course. It is important that attention be focused on the interactive aspects of delinquency, taking into account the delinquent activity and the performer as well as those who come to define the situation and the actor as delinquent. This is essential to an understanding of how only certain juveniles from certain communities get branded as delinquents even though all juveniles regardless of race and class commit acts that may be defined as delinquent. Reality is grounded in the symbols we use to talk about it. As W. I. Thomas puts it, "if men define situations as real, they are real in their consequences." Moreover, most juveniles who do not experience independence of identity come to see themselves as they are defined by others. A juvenile who has been labeled delinquent is more likely to commit acts consistent with this identity than is a youth who has not been so labeled.

A number of social, cultural, psychological, and economic factors may cause the original act, but what is more important is an adaptation to the official reaction to the original act in terms of social roles, social identity, and process in fixing a person in a delinquent category. The label is designed as a stigma and the process by which a person is discredited as stigmatization. The process separates the juveniles from others who are not stigmatized and brings those who are of like stigma into contact with one another.[19] The extent to which black youth get caught up in this process suggests the permanence of the brand. Most black parents whose children are identified by police to be processed do not have the social status, the economic resources, and the political clout to fight the attempt to fix stigma. It is because of this lack of economic and political power and not necessarily because of their greater delinquent activity that black youth are overrepresented in official statistics. Given the process, since blacks and the poor are more likely to be labeled and stigmatized as delinquents, they are more likely to be forced, by the process, into the role of delinquents and thereby actually to be involved in more delinquent acts.

Police and court officials have the power not only to define the situation and create the social reality of delinquency, but they have the power to make their definition stick. The juvenile is an active participant in the process, but it is in the direction of the definition and the power of the juvenile justice system. In the process of the identification, treatment, and labeling, the juveniles find it difficult to manipulate the process through impression management and performances. Most officials disregard the claims most black youth make for themselves. The identities of processed juveniles are made in these situations and follow them around as a constant.

Official agents are not mere responders to delinquent behavior; in a significant number of instances they initate certain actions in the lives of black youth whether or not delinquent behavior is displayed. The consequences of this situation are far-reaching. Most behavior is shaped in interaction with significant others in one's social world. Juveniles usually act in ways that are consistent with their reputation in their social world. In this regard the President's commission notes:

[w]hen the process of role definition moves from the informal labeling of peers and neighbors to the official stamp of the state, it is quite another matter and its ramifications are likely to be more serious. So long as the community's classification of young persons remain informal, the likelihood that it can be modified by changing circumstances remains possible. But the official labeling of a misbehaving youth as delinquent places him in a clear category which is difficult to escape. Once a youth is stamped delinquent, the resources of the police, the court services, the schools, and other official agencies respond to him on the basis of that label, in a manner different from those without the label. Further, this label becomes known to the public, whose view of the individual then becomes colored by it. Soon the individual who is seen by his community as delinquent and is treated by the official agents on the basis of this label, begins to perceive himself as delinquent and to act in accordance with it.[20]

What should receive our primary attention, therefore, is the initial contact of juvenile justice officials with black youth. For it is the police contact with black youth and their discretion to arrest that put the juvenile justice system into operation. Success in this regard ends in those arrested being sent to juvenile homes. The function is that it gives the appearance of police activity, satisfies the need of the juvenile justice officials, identifies apparent delinquency, creates a parasitical relationship between the subsystems of the juvenile justice system, and provides legitimation to the process. However, these functions are not fulfilled if certain juveniles are detained by juvenile officials. Furthermore, for these functions to be realized the initial contact must extend itself to the detention of those arrested. Those who are more likely to fulfill these needs and cause these functions to be realized are oppressed powerless people. It is at this point that efforts should be organized to change the juvenile justice system. It is the police function to arrest and the juvenile judge's discretionary function to define and detain that is the primary reason for the racial and class composition of the juvenile home population and the fixing of a stigmatizing brand on black youth.

A Question of Emphasis

It is not sufficient to simply divert the youth to community based programs. In 1977 the Law Enforcement Assistance Administration provided $10 million for public and private agencies with minorities programs that will divert juvenile offenders from the juvenile justice system. This action was taken for a variety of reasons, but the most important reason is that most delinquency prevention programs have failed. Reasons given for the failure vary from the argument of a strained relationship between theoreticians and practitioners to ineffective, inadequate, and imprecise techniques and strategies. One of the most important reasons, one that officials are reluctant to acknowledge, is the lack of adequate explanatory and descriptive data, especially about the lives of the youth into which the system attempts to intervene. Neither is there an appropriate political perspective that challenges the political and economic assumptions of delinquency and social control. Most of the theroretical notions, themselves competing and conflicting in their explanations, focus upon such factors as the kind of family life or personality of the juveniles. Very few tell in any detail what the youth thinks of himself, his community, and his behavior or what his daily life means to him. The focus must also offer an analysis of the social system itself and the character of its arrangements as it impacts the community of black youth. Then we would be in a position to understand the nature of human action and the process development of the executed act and the conditions created therefrom.

What can be said concerning black youth is that in the process of growing up in a hostile world where the definition of blackness is implicit in decisions and policies to dominate, regulate, brand, and subordinate individuals and their community, it becomes difficult for the majority of black youth to avoid the intent of the system to identify and label them deviants, especially if they make decisions that do not conform to the articulated norms of the wider society even when these norms are not practiced by those who articulate them.

The responsibility of the community to black youth is to provide protection from racism and oppression and to provide services that would enhance interpretations and judgments as our youth plan and proceed with action. This responsibility is crucial in light of the present political and economic condition that our youth face and the historical powerless position of black people and their community.

An Approach to Prevention

In 1974, an agency known as the Office of Juvenile Justice and Delinquency Prevention (OJJDP) was created by Congress to assist public and private services to those defined as delinquents. The rationale for the creation was that juvenile crime was so alarming, especially in urban communities, that a federal agency was necessary to assist in finding new approaches to control the problem. According to a congressional study, the federal assistance is not very significant in fighting juvenile crime. Juvenile courts are as busy as ever, and correctional facilities are overcrowded.

In 1976, the outline of an approach was discussed at the National Urban League Office among a group of criminal justice specialists and practitioners.[21] In the group was the founder of the House of Umoja in Philadelphia, who was anxious to respond to the outline, declaring, with a degree of excitement, that the content of the outline was an exact description of the operation of "The House."

In the *Washington Post* Jack Anderson reported on three neighborhood-based programs that have received no federal assistance but have record results.

Anderson's conclusion is that the "neighborhood groups are more effective than federal programs in combating juvenile crime."

In the Philadelphia ghetto, a black couple without social training established the House of Umoja on a shoestring budget. They persuaded members of youth groups to lay down their weapons and work on constructive projects. Police credit the couple with reducing gang deaths from an average of 42 a year to a single death in 1978.

In Hartford, half a dozen rival youth gangs agreed to support a unique dance. They policed the dance themselves, without incident. The proceeds paid for a Halloween party for younger children and food for the elderly.

In Baltimore, Pete Kambouris was a heroin addict at 16, a hardened criminal by 18. He was arrested 24 times for crimes ranging from shoplifting to burglary. After several years in prison, he was paroled and was recruited to help homeowners make their homes burglarproof. He abandoned his former life to help his community fight crime. Now he has a good job, is married, has a daughter and was pardoned by the governor.[22]

A report by Robert L. Woodson notes that "In Puerto Rico, the community service center of Ponce, organized by untrained nonprofessionals, has worked for the last seven years with young people to unite them in a common effort to rid their community of crime. The center tries to provide hope instead of despair to its young and poor with programs of job development and other activities geared to uplifting the spirit of the community."[23]

The OJJDP's efforts are focused on middle-income white youths, not on the low-income and minority youth who are faced with unemployment and underemployment. Woodson also found that the money awarded to states remains unspent. In 1975, although $181 million was given to the states, only $37 million was used. The remaining $144 million is sitting in banks.

Community Mechanism for Prevention

The basic principle for the operation of delivery service systems must be rooted in the broad lifestyles of the community and the philosophical context of the people.

There should be funding for the development of Juvenile Development Centers in each community where there is a significant number of children and families needing protection and services. These centers, adequately financed and properly organized and operated, can cut the number of referrals to the court, especially the truants, runaways, and the so-called unmanageables.

The processing of the juvenile must enhance the development of the juvenile's self-image and identity. When the juvenile's behavior is defined as delinquent or where there are emotional disturbances, the community should view this as a call for aid in the form of love, support, and concern.

Juvenile behavior must be allowed to be developed, nurtured, shaped, and influenced by increasing the juvenile's spiritual, critical and political consciousness rather than through drugs or psychosurgery or any other medical form of behavior modification.

The control and responsibility for processing juvenile referrals by parents who find it difficult to manage their children at home should lie solely with the center on behalf of the parents and the community. Whatever is decided as the process of development, the entire family should be involved in as far as possible. A community panel should assume the power and authority that the juvenile court judge and probation authorities presently exercise. The members of the panel should be compensated for their services.

The composition of the community panel should reflect the make-up of the community in terms of age, sex, and other important characteristics peculiar to the community. This is to assure the input from all possible perspectives in the process of development of the youth of the community. All referrals should be directed to the respective community panel. Referral agents coming in contact with the juvenile will describe the situation to the panel after a thorough investigation as opposed to labeling or categorizing the action(s). Decisions that are made by the panel in consultation with parents or guardians should take into account the various community resources and skills in the community to enhance the process of development.

The community panel should act as a supervisory commission consisting of various representatives exercising community (collective) control over the administrative activities and services of the Juvenile Development Center.

Juveniles who are released should be provided social assistance whether they are attending school or at work, with their parents or with guardians.

Voluntary community councils should be set up within the Juvenile Development Center to aid in the development process of the juvenile. For example, there might be a community education council, community work council, community political council, community economic council, community recreation council, and a community study council.

On no occasion should the juvenile be confined to a penal institution away from the community. For those juveniles requiring services that are not in the program for youth in the community, those services should be employed to enter the Juvenile Development Center.

The services of the Center should not be punitive or custodial in nature, and its management should take a humanistic approach. Commingling of sexes is a natural phenomenon and should be encouraged within the content of certain basic principles of trust, respect, and honesty to facilitate human development.

Each month the situation of each youth should be reviewed by the panel, and assistance and direction should be recommended after all parties are allowed to participate in the review. Whatever services are provided to the families should strengthen family ties to ensure that the youth continue to develop as viable members of the family and the community.

The creation of Juvenile Development Centers in the communities will provide an opportunity for community members to collectively use their philosophy and values in the process of developing their children.

As it is agreed among most experts in the area that most of the episodes that juveniles engage in disappear as they grow older, it is most important that these centers are established to assist families and youth in the development of judgment, appropriate interpretations, discretion, and decisions.

The present services rendered to juveniles are fragmented, and many are duplicated from one agency to another. They are inadequate, ineffective, and insufficient in quality. Consequently, many jurisdictions perpetuate a cycle of abuse, neglect, and delinquency in the lives of thousands of juveniles each year.

Given these examples of success, there is a great opportunity for funding agencies to assist in the development of juveniles. The resulting assistance to needy families in the communities would make a difference in terms of serious acts of violence and the deterrence from a career in criminality among young adults and adults. Moreover, the present practice where the neglected, dependent, and abused children who end up with delinquent records become a part of the recycling phenomenon may be corrected. The vast number of petitions presently filed each year in juvenile courts, unnecessarily removing a large number of children from their homes and communities, will also be corrected.

Notes

1. Howard S. Becker, *Outsiders: Studies in the Sociology of Deviance* (New York: Free Press, 1963).

2. A.M. Platt, *The Child Savers: The Invention of Delinquency* (Chicago: University of Chicago Press, 1969), p. 137.

3. Ibid., p. 137-138.

4. A.M. Platt, "The Triumph of Benevolence: The Origins of the Juvenile

88   Critical Issues

Justice System in the United States," in *Criminal Justice in America: A Critical Understanding*, ed. Richard Quinney (Boston: Little Brown, 1974), 356-89.

5. President's Commission on Law Enforcement and the Administration of Justice (Washington, D.C., 1967), p. 3.

6. Kent v. United States, 383 US 541, 1966.

7. In re Gault, 387 U.S.I, 1967.

8. In re Winship, 397 U.S. 358, 1970.

9. Benjamin Quarles, *Jet* 33, no. 12 (December 28, 1967), p. 32.

10. George Napper, "Perception of Crime: Problems and Implications," in *Black Perspectives on Crime and Criminal Justice System*, ed. Robert Woodson (Boston: G.K. Hall & Co., 1977), pp. 5-22.

11. Fred J. Murphy, Mary M. Shirley, and Helen L. Witner, "The Incidence of Hidden Delinquency," *American Journal of Orthopsychiatry*, 16, (1946): 686-96.

12. Martin Gold, *Status Forces in Delinquents* (Ann Arbor: University of Michigan Institute for Social Research, 1963).

13. Bruce McM. Wright, "Bangs and Whimpers," unpublished manuscript, 1977.

14. L. Alex Swan, "Juvenile Delinquency, Juvenile Justice and Black Youth," in *Black Perspectives on Crime and Criminal Justice System*, ed. Robert Woodson (Boston: G.K. Hall & Co., 1977), pp. 55-77.

15. Nathan Goldman, *The Differential Selection of Juvenile Offender for Court Appearances* (New York: National Council on Crime and Delinquency, 1963).

16. T. Thornberry, "Race, Socioeconomic Status and Sentencing in the Juvenile Justice System." *Journal of Criminal Law and Criminology* 64 (March 1973): 90-98.

17. T.N. Ferdinand, and E.G. Luchterhand, "Inner-City Youth, the Police, the Juvenile Court, and Justice." *Social Problems* 17 (Spring 1970): 510-27.

18. L. Alex Swan, *Black Youth, Delinquent Behavior and the Juvenile Justice System* (Department of Sociology, Fisk University, Nashville, Tennessee, 1978).

19. Erving Goffman, *Stigma* (Englewood Cliffs, N.J.: Prentice-Hall, 1963).

20. President's Commission, 1967, pp. 86-87.

21. Swan, "Juvenile Delinquency," 1977.

22. Jack Anderson, *The Washington Post* (January 7, 1979).

23. Robert L. Woodson, *The New York Times* (February 10, 1979).

6

Criminal Behavior and the Reentry of Formerly Incarcerated Black Men into Society

Introduction

Before an adequate analysis can be made of black men in America's prisons and their reentry into society, a proper context for such an analysis must be established. The nature and character of the political economy of the United States provides such a context.[1]

The first systematic and organized attempt to confine blacks in prisons came soon after 1863 when blacks were assured, resulting from the Lincoln gesture, that they were free to leave the plantation under a forced labor system. Capitalism had created the need for free labor to which black people were subjected. The enactment of vagrancy laws continued the system of enslavement and forced cheap labor.

Vagrancy laws were first enacted in 1349 in England. "There is little question that these statutes were designed for one express purpose: to force laborers to accept employment at a low wage in order to insure the landowner an adequate supply of labor at a price he could afford to pay."[2] "These laws were a legislative innovation which reflected the socially perceived necessity of providing an abundance of cheap labor to landowners during a period when serfdom was breaking down and when the pool of available labor was depleted."[3]

Vagrancy statutes adopted in America to control the labor of recently freed slaves provided for the arrest of people with no visible means of support.[4] The landowners were assured of cheap labor after the former slaves were arrested and hired out to plantation owners.

The Crime Picture of Black Men

Black men are imprisoned for crimes such as burglary, robbery, drug dealing, mugging, and hustling of various sorts. These crimes against property are pursued because of the need to survive. They are not profitable crimes[5] for the purpose of making profit and economic progress.

Personal crimes are usually directed against members of the same class. These are the crimes of rape, murder, and assault, which seem to be more antagonistic to the capitalist social order. Consequently, the criminal justice system, especially the police, are actively engaged in processing individuals who commit personal and property crimes.

Data indicating crime rates of which black men participate tend to reveal that these crimes are committed more in urban areas than in rural areas and more in larger cities than in smaller cities. The crimes are committed closer to the center of cities than farther from the center.

Quinney argues that:

Ecological patterns of crime reflect the larger class struggle in the society's overall political economy. In a class-divided, capitalist society, all aspects of life are affected by the ownership and control of the means of production by the capitalist class. The working class, the poor, and the oppressed minorities are constantly in conflict and struggle with the capitalist class. Included in this basic antagonism is the struggle for living space and for living conditions. Those who own and control the means of production have different access—because of their economic and political power—to property and housing. The conflict and struggle that locate people geographically also produce the geographic distribution of crime rates.[6]

That urban crime rates are higher than rural crime rates is a consistent pattern. Crime rates in urban areas increase with the size of the city. For all "major" offenses, except murder, the urban rates are higher than the rural. The difference can be explained in terms of the difference in cultures and structures of the urban and rural areas. The structural characteristics and the cultural and behavioral norms in the urban areas provide more opportunities for the execution of such crimes as burglary, larceny, robbery, and auto theft. The structural environment of the urban community also accounts for a greater degree of class conflict. Domination and control of oppressed and exploited urban dwellers intensifies class conflict and struggle, which tends to influence urban crime. Crime is more pronounced and prevalent in larger cities with a great extent of capitalist development. These are the cities in which the oppressed gather and live, seeking to better their conditions. However, in these areas they are more likely to become victims of criminal behavior.

Many urban dwellers are worried that they will be physically assaulted by strangers. Surveys tend to indicate that personal violence is more likely to come from family members and other persons previously known to the victims.[7] It is estimated that 75 percent of willful killings, two-thirds of aggravated assaults, and 70 percent of forcible rapes are less likely to come from strangers. In larger cities such as New York and Chicago, this trend is changing and the victim is increasingly less likely to know or have any acquaintance with the assailants.[8]

Given the urban context and intensity of capitalist development and

Table 7

CHARACTERISTICS OF OFFENDER AND VICTIM BY RACE IN CRIMINAL
HOMICIDE IN SEVENTEEN CITIES, 1967

RACE OF OFFENDER	RACE OF VICTIM White	Black	Total	(victim)[a]
White	24.0%	3.8%	27.8%	(159)[b]
Black	6.5	65.7	72.2	(412)
Total	30.5 (174)	69.5 (397)	100.0	(571)

[a]Total row and column percentages may not exactly equal 100.00 percent because of the weighing procedure and rounding.

[b]Number of victims are given in parentheses.

SOURCE: Crime of Violence, Vol. II, Staff Report submitted to the National Commission on the Causes and Prevention of Violence, Donald J. Mulvihill and Melva M. Tumin, Co-Directors (Washington, D. C.: U. S. Government Printing Office, 1969), p. 210.

activities, crimes of violence are carried out against persons of one's own racial group. Whites victimize whites and blacks tend to victimize blacks in such crimes as homicides, aggravated assaults, forcible rapes, robbery, and the like.

Table 7 reveals that 24 percent of the homicides in seventeen large cities were between whites and 65.7 percent were between blacks. Only 6.5 percent of the homicides involved blacks killing whites and 4 percent whites killing blacks.

Alex Pokorny found in his study that in Houston, 97 percent of the black victims were killed by blacks, 91 percent of the white victims were killed by whites, and 86 percent of the Latin Americans were killed by Latin Americans.[9] Other studies have indicated that aggravated assaults, forcible rapes and the like are primarily intraracial crimes.[10]

Crimes of violence are suffered by the oppressed poor and working class in disproportionate numbers in a racist, exploitative, and capitalist society. The cultural and structural environments of the urban area created by the conditions and forces of a capitalist-racist society create among its members interpersonal relationships that foster violence intraracially (against one's own people) as displacement, as convenience, and as a personal solution to the oppressive and exploitative problems generated by the wider society.

Blacks and other oppressed of the capitalist-racist society are disproportionately victims of violent crimes. Victimization is highest among blacks in all categories of violent crimes except larceny. In fact, blacks and the poor working class of America are the major victims of violent crimes.

When criminal conduct is expanded to include profitable crimes of a corporate, governmental, and organized nature, the majority of the population become victims.

Criminal sanctions exist for every citizen in America. However, these sanctions are applied more often against those whose economic and political positions in society render them powerless. Consequently, it would be expected to find the majority of those in custody in prisons poor and oppressed minorities from urban communities.

In 1978, the number of prisoners in custody in state and federal prisons was 293,882. Juveniles held in juvenile and correctional institutions and persons confined to local jails are not included (see tables at the end of this chapter).

Prisons are institutions of control for the poor and exploited working class, those who have committed the survival crimes of burglary, robbery, larceny, assault, and so on. Criminals of the middle and upper classes who participate in profitable crimes, causing more economic and social loss to the society, are not counted in the criminal statistics or in the prison population.

Prisoners are the surplus population that is not really needed in the larger society for capitalist production but become a part of the capitalist production of the prison in satisfying certain production needs of the state.

Erik Wright notes that:

Forty-one percent of the general labor force falls into white-collar employment categories (clerical and sales, managers and owners, and professional and technical workers), compared to only 14 percent of the prison population. At the other extreme, 43 percent of the prisoners are manual or service workers, compared to only 17 percent of the total labor force. The same pattern is found for education: 55 percent of the prisoners have an elementary school education or less, compared to only 34 percent of the general population; 45 percent of the general population are high school graduates compared to only 18 percent of the prison population.[11]

Wright also indicates that a very large number of prisoners in America's prisons are black. The estimate is that one in every twenty black men between the ages of twenty-five and thirty-four is either in jail or prison on any day compared to one of every 163 white men in the same age group.[12] Ninety percent of the black men are in prison for committing survival crimes.

A Theory of Survival Crimes

Criminologists and criminal justice practioners tend to pay more attention to and spend more time and money trying to explain and solve survival crimes committed by the oppressed and exploited populations of America than on profitable crimes committed primarily by white middle-class individuals and those who occupy certain political and economic positions of power in the social order.

The national attention has always been brought to focus upon survival crimes almost to the exclusion of profitable crimes. The Uniform Crime

Report has identified certain crimes as index crimes, which some have labeled street crimes. Swan[13] and Napper[14] have argued that to continue the primary focus on index crimes as a measure of crime in the social order is to continue the distortion of the nature and extent of crime and the false image of who are the criminals in the American society, who benefit most from crime, and who are the primary victims.

Muggings, robbery, burglary, aggravated assault, and auto theft are survival crimes committed to enhance the economic and political power position of the perpetrators and to facilitate the survival of those in a society who perceive the social order as having few acceptable and available alternatives to address their powerlessness. The perception of their powerless position—without marketable skills or adequate and appropriate education, exploited and oppressed by the political and economic arrangements—allows for the employment of the definition of individualism and the operation of the notion, "What is thine is mine and I will take it." This is the reason that in survival crimes the object is more important than the subject and often the subject is subjected to physical violence, especially when the subject intervenes to protect the object or to prevent the completion of the common design.

Homicide committed by the majority of those involved in survival crimes is committed after-the-fact to the common design of survival crimes. The conversation in the process of the commission of survival crimes indicates that the intent is not to commit a homicide. For example, the instructions of a person attempting to commit a robbery might be, "If you don't do thus and so, I will have to hurt you"; or, "I don't want to hurt you so just do thus and so." The weapons are to make such threats stick—to make serious the intent and importance of the completion of the transaction. The weapons used are also designed to protect the victims and the perpetrators and to assure that the common design is complete. In the other, fewer, homicides that are committed in the context of the family, social interactions with friends or associates, where there is a quarrel and the like, the perpetrator is attempting to assert and/or protect his/her self-esteem and his/her sense of self-worth. For the subject (victim) to disallow this means that the victim is perceived by the perpetrator as blocking the completion of the common design, the intent of which is to display the importance of self and for the victim and those around to pay attention or give recognition to the self-worth and importance of the perpetrator.

The completion of the common design in a robbery or in any other survival crime is just as important to the perpetrator as the assertion of self, the display of self-worth and the solicitation for recognition or the enhancement of self-esteem in family conflicts, or conflicts with friends, or in the politics (exercise of power over the perceived status of the subject) of rape.

Survival crimes are not profitable crimes as are organized, governmental, and white-collar crimes. The mugger has no vacation; the perpetrator does not retire after many years of mugging activity in a very expensive neighborhood with financial investments and a fat bank account. Those who participate in profitable crimes can choose to retire because their criminal achievements mean monetary success. The perpetrators of survival crimes do not become well off from such activities. Their efforts are more intense, more dangerous, and much more difficult than the efforts of the perpetrators of profitable crimes. However, in a society that promotes individualism, where the definition of the object is more important than the subject, in the presence of a sense of plenty, survival and profitable crimes tend to flourish and even increase.

Survival crimes are treated more seriously by citizens and the criminal justice system because of the definition of violence and because such activities are more apparent. However, profitable crimes are more dangerous and violent than survival crimes: for example, the case of Hooker Chemicals and Plastics Corporation and its dumping of poisonous chemicals that has brought harm, financial tragedy, and a future of agony and worry to thousands of Americans. Burglars, muggers, robbers, and even embezzlers could not have accomplished so much financial damage and physical harm to the people of the Love Canal area near Niagara Falls, N.Y., as did Hooker. For generations, Hooker has dumped some of the most poisonous chemicals known to mankind in areas where families with pregnant women live and where little children play. Experts who have examined the complaints of residents concerning headaches, birth defects, mental illness, and a variety of other health problems testify that the damage to human beings and the environment is irreversible.

Dumping of toxic waste is the most serious health problem in America, and the Hooker case is only one of many. If crime is primarily intraracial, then it is irrelevant to put emphasis exclusively on black or black crime, or "minority" crime. In doing so the tendency is to continue the myths about the nature, extent, and character of crime and criminals without capturing what is common to criminals and criminality. What is common to all crimes is that there is a common design and the object of the common design is more important than the subjects in the common design. Action in criminal behavior (whether that of the perpetrator or the victim) is the result of the definition of the subjects involved, including the victim(s) and the perpetrator(s) and the meaning of the object to the lives of both the perpetrator and the victim.

In a social order where greed and materialism are complemented by individualism, it is very easy for the oppressed and exploited, as well as the oppressor and would-be materialists, to perpetuate crimes in society. The difference is the positions they occupy in the social order and the avenues available and the mechanisms employed to accomplish the object of the common design. For the oppressed, however, the behavior is more apparent. For others it is not that apparent, but just as real and in many cases more violent and destructive of human life.

Institutional Treatment and Reentry

In another work, I examined the reentry process of the parolee, and logically determined the way the parole conditions enhanced or improved the successful reentry of the parolee. An analysis was also made of the relationship between the important elements in the parole process—the parolee, the community, and the parole system—to determine the extent to which they contributed to the failure or success of the parolees in transition.[15] In another work, the use of inmates, especially black inmates, for the purpose of research and experimentation and its impact on reentry success is analyzed and discussed.[16] Here the concern will be with institutional treatment, its impact on the reentry possibility for success, and the importance of community-based efforts to allow successful reentry of the formerly incarcerated black male.

Modern trends toward corrections continue the objective of punishment as a strategy of treatment for the purpose of rehabilitation, especially for those who threaten public and prison order. Prisons are thought of as theraupeutic units for the management and change of offenders for successful reintegration into society. Extension of the model allows for the definition of society as a therapeutic environment within which many offenders can be treated and changed. However, neither the prisons as therapeutic units nor society as a therapeutic environment have been responsible for successful reentry of the offender.

Prisons are good at confining and punishing inmates. They have never really had a true rehabilitative function. Inmates have always been subjected to punishment in custody and punishment in institutional treatment. Punishment has also been extended to inmates' families and their friends.[17] Moreover, it is not possible for professional workers and prison authorities, under the present condition of prison life, to determine when an offender is successfully rehabilitated. The employment of the indeterminate sentence allowed for such persons to make process judgments regarding the inmates, but many inmates have testified that professional workers and prison authorities have tried to coerce them into changing and conforming to the needs and interests of the prison community.

Jessica Mitford has observed that confinement is the dominant mode of business in prisons.

In prison parlance, "treatment" is an umbrella term meaning diagnosis, classification, various forms of therapy, punishment as deemed necessary, and prognosis, or the prediction of the malfeasant's future behavior: Will/won't he err again? While the correction crowd everywhere talk a good line of "treatment"—phrases like "inadequate personalities," "borderline sociopaths," "weak superegos" come trippingly off the tongue of the latter-day prison warden, having long since replaced the sin-stained soul and fallen men or women with whom his predecessors had to cope —very few prison systems have actually done much about implementing it in practice. Nationwide, only 5 percent of the prison budget goes for services labeled "rehabilitation," and in many states there is not even the pretence of making "therapy" available to the adult offender.[18]

The members of the outside society assume and expect inmates to be reformed during their prison experience. Indeed, the professionals and prison authorities also expect them to change during confinement. However, these two groups have conflicting objectives and establish different priorities in dealing with inmates.

Custodial workers are concerned with maintaining control and this concern is reflected in their priorities of action in a given situation as well as in the considerations they express in planning and supervising inmates' activities. On the other hand, treatment personnel tend to be concerned with mitigating the psychological or interpersonal problems of inmates. Conflict engendered by these different priorities is exacerbated because custodial and treatment workers, by virtue of their different responsibilities, are also frequently confronted in a different manner by inmates. These workers thus develop different conceptions of the inmates and each staff group becomes convinced of the correctness of its view and decides that of the other.[19]

Inmates recognize the conflict and also perceive the treatment programs to be nothing more than a cover-up for control, inmate domination, and repression in prison.

On ex-inmate disclosed:

I'd go into a room and be treated like a human being and the possibilities seemed unlimited. Then I'd leave the room and my reality was the prison. Then some hack would holler "line up, bend over and spread your cheeks. Stand up, move out. . . ." and I would be angry and resentful—as much against the people with the programs as I was against the hack. I began to resent the outsiders because they teased me. They let me think I was a human being with dignity. I stopped going to the meetings.[20]

As a means of rehabilitation institutional treatment (imprisonment) has had little success. It has not been effective primarily because treatment programs within the prison tend to be dehumanizing. In such an environment there is little preparation for reentry. There is the argument that rehabilitation will work, and the consequences would be the reduction in recidivism if treatment programs are individualized. However, most of the treatment programs in prisons, whether designed to meet individual needs or not, operate on the basic assumption that the individual is a criminal. In spite of the institutional treatment, many inmates do not return to prison. What seems to account for this trend is the particular circumstances the inmate faces upon release and the legitimate opportunities acceptable and available to him/her during the first four to six weeks after release. The facilitating circumstances must be created by the inmate or others. He/she must be able to avoid the power of others to define him/her in criminal terms and must be convinced that it is no longer necessary to participate in criminally defined activity.

During the mid-1960s an increase in coercive behavior-modification techniques for managing and controlling those inmates who threaten the social order of prisons became rampant. Such techniques as electronic surveillance, electrical and chemical stimulation, and psychosurgery were the techniques employed. There are suggestions and recommendations today that the brainwashing techniques used on American prisoners of war by North Koreans could be employed to rehabilitate and change inmates' behavior.[21] Several tactics are identified in the brainwashing techniques, which prisoner groups have referred to as the Manifesto of Dehumanization.[22]

Given the increasing awareness of black prisoners, cooperation with the various treatment programs will decrease. In fact, "they will actively resist these attempts to strip them of their humanity and their consciousness that it is society's ills rather than their own individual psychological problems which perpetrate their plight."[23]

Release from Prison

Parole is the major form of release from prison. Over 75 percent of those released from prison each year are on parole or are under some form of mandatory supervision.[24] Parole supervision is conducted by a parole officer whose responsibility it is to determine, over a period of time, whether the parolee's behavior conforms to the rules of the parole. The parolee is forbidden to associate with those who have a criminal record and other questionable persons. There are restrictions on employment, mobility, change of residence, travel, and purchasing. If the parolee wants to get married or change his or her intimate friend, permission of the parole officer must be gained.

There are many discrepancies between the expectations imposed on the parolees and the realities of their situation as convicted offenders. John Irwin describes such a condition relative to the status of being parolees.

This status has for its underpinnings several premises which are often not shared by many deviants and ex-deviants. Two of these premises are self-evident axioms: (1) society, i.e., the existing political organization and government agencies, the laws and the government institutions, are both necessary and "good" per se; and (2) this society, especially the existing political organization and government agencies, has the right to imprison some of its members for acts which it has outlawed, to deny the ex-prisoner full citizen rights, and to impose special restriction upon him. Furthermore, the conditions are underpinned by the belief that to be a worthy member of the society and, therefore, to be allowed to remain a free person, the ex-felon must live according to a puritanical code of conduct—he must work steadily ("steady employment is an essential for anyone's satisfactory adjustment in life"), not drink to excess ("it is conceded that total abstinence from the use of alcohol would benefit most parolees"), not use narcotics or dangerous drugs, not associate with persons of "bad" reputation, and conduct himself as a good citizen.[25]

Irwin further suggests that the perception of the parolees is likely to be different from their official status.

Parolees often do not share the belief in the "goodness" of society or the existing social organizations, agencies, and persons filling positions in these organizations. Some deviants believe that conventional people, legitimate businessmen, and public organizations are corrupt. Often they believe that the laws and the workings of the public agencies are part of a power struggle where the big and powerful are protecting what they have from the small and weak. . . .They, the deviants or ex-deviants, do not feel that the conventional society, the dominant society, the government agencies, are "right." Parolees (that is, the criminal parolees) have other definitions of good and proper conduct. Even those who have resolved to live a conventional life—resolved to "straighten up their hand" and to "make it" in terms of a conventional life—are in disagreement with the conditions of parole and tend to believe that it is all right to break many of the rules. From their viewpoint, the only restrictions the agency should impose are on extreme criminal behavior.[26]

A modification of the custodial setting of institutional treatment are work-release programs outside the prison, halfway houses where offenders receive residential treatment while they attend school or work. These techniques and measures are employed because professionals and prison reformers have come to believe that prisons do not rehabilitate and that inmates are not successfully treated in the prison environment.

Saleem A. Shah presents the argument in this way:

During the past many years there has been considerable evidence justifying the increasing disillusionment with the rehabilitative and treatment effectiveness of traditional correctional institutions. It has become glaringly evident that such institutions have been designed primarily to meet the societal objectives of restraint and containment, rather than the stated concerns with treatment and rehabilitation. Indeed not only are correctional institutions generally ineffective in regard to attaining their rehabilitative objectives (which objectives they cannot be expected to meet without considerable efforts in and by the larger community), but the deleterious and destructive effects of such incarceration appear further to add to the problems of correctional clients.[27]

The U.S. Bureau of Prisons has in recent years given strong support for community-based treatment and correctional programs for adult offenders. One director said during a congressional hearing:

We in corrections know that offenders can change—can be reintegrated into the community—if provided the proper assistance, support and supervision. The focus of this effort is, of course, the community-based programs. We must continue and expand these programs and develop new ones of promise. All of us at every level of government, in public and private agencies, must share in this work.

Two of the major goals of the Federal Bureau of Prisons are: to increase the program alternatives for offenders who do not require traditional institution confinement, and expand community involvement in correctional programs and goals.

In achieving the first goal, we will attempt to minimize the corrosive effects of imprisonment, lessen the offenders' alienation from society and reduce the economic cost to the taxpayer. We must achieve the second goal because only with the successful reintegration of the ex-offender into the community will we have fulfilled our mission—the correction of the offender.[28]

There is express admission that the process of imprisonment is corrosive and that this effect must be dealt with to achieve success in reentry. The alienation from society is achieved by employing certain exclusionary rules and regulations. The solution to the problem of prisoner alienation is within the grasp of prison authorities. However, there are those who are successfully criminalized and those who are not. Those that are as a result of the prison experience come to see themselves as criminals with no alternative but to pursue a criminal career. This is an extension of the perception of the professionals and prison authorities who have developed measures designed to find a solution to the problems of crime in the offender's makeup, behavior, and personality. While the offender has a significant degree of responsibility for his/her decision and resulting behavior, social, political, and economic factors combine to create a set of circumstances that are interpreted in such a way as to allow for criminal behavior. Until solutions are found for these factors (social, political, economic) that maintain an oppressive and racist social environment, it will continue to be relatively easy for the oppressed and poor to interpret their situation in terms that allow a significant number of them to participate in survival crimes. We must remember that only 15 percent of the blacks in prison are career criminals; that is, they commit crimes as a way of life.

Given the failure of the prison process to assist the offender in avoiding the criminal justice system, and the failure of community-based programs, for a variety of reasons,[29] to effectively assist ex-inmates to stay in the larger society, the black man finds it extremely difficult after the prison experience to successfully reenter society. Because of what blackness has come to mean in a capitalist-racist social order, the economic arrangements of the society have rendered these black men poor and powerless with no real possibility for successful competition and vertical mobility. The racist arrangements of the social order have defined them as would-be criminals, and those who are reentering society from prisons have simply lived up to or conformed to such a definition. These sets of circumstances are difficult to challenge and overcome. Those who overcome them and achieve smashing victories are those who reject the definition of criminality imposed upon them by prison authorities, professionals, and the society, seeing themselves as convicts rather than as criminals. There are those who seek a set of circumstances created by relatives, friends, and those who care to assist that would enhance their successful reentry. For some a job establishes the basis for the set of circumstances. For others interested in pursuing an education, the college establishes the basis. There are, however, a significant number of offenders who have embraced a religious experience, which accounts for a high rate of success among those who reenter society from prisons. When these factors are brought to bear on the person reentering, a network of support systems interact to assure success.

Environment for Success

The network of support systems that provides the basis for successful reentry constitutes an environment into which the ex-inmate enters. The environment consist of four subsystems (the family, work, school, church) that interact with each other to produce an environmental condition conducive to reentry. Consequently, the subsystems must be prepared for the reentry of the ex-offender. If they are not prepared, there is rejection and alienation, conditions sufficient to produce high rates of recidivism.

In those cases where the men have been in prison for long periods of time, the family makes adjustments necessary to continue its scheme of life. The adjustments often exclude the physical presence as well as economic and emotional input of the men. Consequently, reentry requires readjustments for the inclusion of the men if they are to enter the families and receive assistance for a successful reentry.

It is not very easy to change people or to help them adjust constructively. The problem is often in controlling the direction of the change or adjustment so that the individual's life becomes more successful and more self-enriching, rather than less so.

If the family decides to admit the person and attempts readjustment, the role of the person must be clearly defined. In the process of establishing effective family relationships, the members must focus upon and reemphasize what was and is positive in their relationship. Complaining and focusing on the negative aspects of their relationships can be seriously disruptive to successful reentry of the person. When family members switch their own emotional focus, the family problem becomes a family strength. Most people reentering society from prisons build up ego defenses; by shifting their emotional focus, family members allow these people to let down their built-up ego defenses and begin to appreciate themselves more positively. This is usually a gradual process, but adjustments and changes are achieved and experienced by all members. It becomes easier for the family members to establish joint action in the fitting together of their lines of action to the actions of others in the family.

Further, family members must seek to reinforce what they like about their relatives' behavior and not reinforce what they do not like. Dislikes and likes must be carefully ascertained, and members must take note of those situations that produce or stimulate positive reactions. There are times when certain actions of the persons will have to be ignored, especially when they remind family members of behavior prior to imprisonment. A step-by-step upward rebuilding of relationships can provide the strength necessary and sufficient to make the relationships even better than before the separation.

Most people who reenter are inclined to be silent about their feelings and experiences. The family context is a very safe place to assist them to improve their communications. Communication is the only way to understand what they are feeling. Understanding is a first step to acceptance and assistance in making the adjustments crucial to successful reentry.

The prison experience is perceived by ex-inmates and the general public as a handicap. Consequently, ex-inmates feel severely restricted in terms of social, political, and economic activities. Even though the definition and the effect depend largely on the individual ex-inmate, the self-concept of the individual labeled as handicapped by his prison experience determines in a large number of cases his relationship with others. It is the perception of others, or adjusting to others, especially in the job environment, that most ex-inmates have problems dealing with. In the majority of cases, the family is prepared or assisted by family members, relatives, friends, and sometimes social agencies in preparation for the reentry of the ex-inmate. However, very rarely is the job environment prepared for the inclusion of the ex-inmate as a legitimate partner and worker. Often the disposition is that he will always be a "criminal" and that the assistance given by the company, in the rehabilitation effort, is a waste of time. In all cases investigated, the ex-inmates discerned the negative attitudes and quickly removed themselves from the environment. Whispering about their status as ex-convicts and the care with which the workers interact with them, removing valuable items from their immediate presence, suggest that they are not really welcomed and not to be trusted.

For this reason, probation and parole officers are persuaded that it is not always the best gesture to find employment for ex-inmates until and unless the total environment is thoroughly prepared for their inclusion. It is not enough to inform the foreman or the supervisor of the convict status of the individual. The attitudes of the appropriate associates should be determined. If there are negative attitudes they should be expressed and dealt with in the open prior to the inclusion of the ex-inmate into the work environment. It must be very clear to the workers that the company is not just engaging in public service.

Often when certain skills and abilities are demonstrated and promoted by supervisors (posing no threat to the workers) there tends to be greater acceptance of the person entering the work environment. However, 95 percent of those entering the work environment do not have special skills demanded by their jobs and the companies employing them. Consequently, they are not defined as being significant to the job situation or very important to the outcome of the product (goods and/or services). In such cases the ex-convict occupies a peripheral role in the work environment and is not taken seriously as a significant or dependable worker or one who need be depended upon. This situation is easily and quickly perceived by the ex-con. What is especially frustrating for ex-convicts is the perception of them, by those who found them jobs, that they are unable to hold a job. The emphasis placed on the ability to hold a job is oppressive. Emphasis should be placed upon the hostile work environment and its preparation to include an ex-convict and the preparation of the ex-con's coping skills to adjust to the work environment as it presents itself. It is the breakdown in this preparation for joint action that allows the interpretation of ex-cons to exclude themselves from the job environment.

The majority of the jobs secured by ex-convicts are dead-end jobs with wages inadequate to restore them as primary breadwinners. In many cases they are unable to take care of the basic necessities of food, shelter, and clothing. If they are married, the survival strategy employed by spouses and family members to continue their "scheme of life," coupled with the satisfactory participation of the people in the work environment, helps them to be able to achieve and maintain a successful reentry experience.

In other cases, where the responsibilities are not great, requiring significant financial attention, single and married persons, especially if they have started an interest in academic (educational) matters in prison, should pursue their interest in college either in the technical, professional or academic fields. The school environment is not usually so hostile as the work environment. Many students, especially those representing oppressed countries or those participating in acts that are private but are clear violations of the law, realize that the ex-con could have been any one of them; he was merely the one adjudicated.

College students tend to perceive the ex-con as one who has certain kinds of information regarding the nature and character of the criminal justice system. In the classroom, especially in courses in criminology, deviance, and various courses in criminal justice, he is treated as an expert with inside information as a participant. Most ex-cons who enter the college environment tend to disclose their status as ex-cons to fellow students either inside or outside the classroom. Seemingly, the college environment is more tolerant and accepting of the ex-con, and little or no prior preparation for his inclusion is necessary. The perception of the ex-con as an expert on matters pertaining to crime and the criminal justice system enhances his acceptance in the college environment and is therapeutic in the sense that the ex-con accepts the expert status, which means that he does not need to repeat the experience. Even though students may tend to be cautious in establishing intimate relationships with ex-cons on the college campus, they do not alienate them from social gatherings. If they attend they are never denied participation.

The classroom and the college environments provide a network of support systems for the ex-con that are not yet clearly defined nor adequately identified. It is within the context of this environment that ex-cons feel free to discuss their experiences frankly, openly and freely. Ex-cons take pride in disclosing how tough the prison system is and how rough they have had it on the inside. Their disclosure is usually a warning to students to suggest that they not participate in criminal acts and that they not get caught. Such disclosure might not scare many to conform, but it causes many to become cautious about their deviant activities. The emphasis placed on the difficult experiences encountered in the criminal justice system by the ex-cons allows fellow students and teachers to perceive them as survivors and persons who can endure hardship and even oppression. In this sense, ex-cons come to see themselves as superior to their fellow students and even their teachers who might have not have had such experiences.

Some assume that the church would be filled with born-again ex-convicts, and there are those who worship in churches who have been changed by conversion experiences. The fact of the matter, however, is that very few ex-cons participate in the environment of the church as members in good and regular standing. This is not to suggest that churches are not engaged in prison ministry or that a good number of inmates have not been influenced by the efforts of the church.

Data tend to indicate also that the membership of the black church does not contain many persons who have had very extensive public deviant careers. This fact suggests that the church has not been very interested in

Table 8

STATE AND FEDERAL BLACK MALE PRISONERS, 1978 (by region)

REGION AND STATE	MALE PRISONERS	BLACK MALE PRISONERS	
Northeast			
Connecticut	3,360	1,351	40.2%
Maine	695	8	1.2
Massachusetts	2,738	1,008	36.8
New Hampshire	277	6	2.2
New Jersey	5,693	3,502	61.5
New York	19,635	10,485	54.4
Pennsylvania	7,685	4,194	55.0
Rhode Island	648	152	23.5
Vermont	453	1	.22
TOTAL	41,184	20,707	50.3
North Central			
Illinois	10,918	6,304	57.7
Indiana	4,754	1,376	28.9
Iowa	1,985	355	17.9
Kansas	2,193	737	33.6
Michigan	14,323	8,101	56.6
Minnesota	1,871	301	16.1
Missouri	5,455	2,728	50.0
Nebraska	1,264	422	33.4
North Dakota	196	4	2.0
Ohio	12,569	6,536	52.0
South Dakota	514	10	1.0
Wisconsin	3,286	1,266	38.5
TOTAL	59,328	28,140	47.4
South			
Alabama	5,213	3,116	59.8
Arkansas	2,511	1,304	51.9
Delaware	1,261	706	55.9
District of Columbia	2,784	2,672	95.9
Florida	19,936	10,156	51.0
Georgia	10,852	6,498	59.9
Kentucky	3,279	947	28.9
Louisiana	7,083	5,099	71.9
Maryland	7,722	5,843	75.7
Mississippi	2,785	1,860	66.9

REGION AND STATE	MALE PRISONERS	BLACK MALE PRISONERS	
North Carolina	12,718	6,856	53.9
Oklahoma	4,010	1,139	28.4
South Carolina	7,086	4,028	56.8
Texas	23,570	10,015	42.5
Tennessee	5,574	2,647	47.5
Virginia	7,985	4,735	59.3
West Virginia	1,156	180	15.6
TOTAL	125,525	67,801	54.0
West			
Alaska	678	176	25.9
Arizona	3,275	641	19.6
California	20,178	6,743	33.4
Colorado	2,419	533	22.0
Hawaii	688	14	2.0
Idaho	775	17	2.2
Montana	675	10	1.5
Nevada	1,274	373	29.3
New Mexico	1,526	172	11.3
Oregon	2,769	228	8.3
Utah	875	71	8.1
Washington	4,327	843	19.5
Wyoming	414	0	—
TOTAL	39,870	9,821	24.6

SOURCE: Unpublished data, National Prisoner Statistics, Demographic Service Division
—U. S. Bureau of the Census, Washington, D. C., 1979.

attracting such persons to membership, even though they are not actively discouraged from church participation. It could also suggest that the church shares the common definition of the general public that "once a criminal always a criminal." Consequently, their interaction with ex-convicts is not attractive or inviting. Many church members feel safe working with inmates who are safely behind bars, but once they are released, even when there is testimony of conversion experience, the members are usually afraid to associate freely with ex-cons. In the case of male ex-convicts, the experience has been that mothers with daughters in the church discourage any form of association that would suggest an interest.

Several churches in the black community are being encouraged to establish prison ministry programs to increase their influence in the lives of prisoners and ex-convicts. Despite some reluctance to develop such programs, the discussion continues. Some individual members of churches work with prisoners as a commitment to their religious faith.

In several cases in Nashville and Huntsville, the membership of black churches had to be worked with to allow the inclusion of a professed converted ex-con. Some who professed conversion but were still serving time did not receive an open-armed welcome from the church. In fact, one pastor wanted the matter to be kept a secret for fear the members would be scared away. This condition suggests that the definition of criminality and the deviant label attached to ex-convicts and behavior are significant in the minds of individuals and come to bear on their dispositions, attitudes, and beliefs as they interact with those representing such definitions and subjected to such labels. It is ironic that church members have such attitudes and dispositions when it is their declared mission to introduce salvation to sinners.

With the exception of the Nation of Islam, there is no organized group of religious persons systematically focusing upon the prison population with the intent to reduce recidivism. The Nation has an impressive record in resocializing prisoners. It is possible, given the nature of human behavior and the ability of individuals to develop in the process of interaction, for church organizations to create environments and establish a set of circumstances for the successful reentry of the black ex-convict.

Conclusion

The family, the college, and the church have the potential to create environments that act together or separately to produce a conducive set of circumstances for the successful reentry of black ex-convicts. Given the racist-capitalist nature of the social order, reentry success requires a restructuring of the economic, political, legal, and educational arrangements of the society. However, the black family, the black college, and the black church have developed coping strategies for survival and progress that can be transferred to the inmate who is attempting to develop coping skills for successful reentry.

Handling the problem of crime and criminal behavior might come only as the nature and character of the social, economic, legal and political character of the social order is changed. In the absence of a restructuring of the arrangements of the social order, the therapeutic environments made possible by the efforts of the family, the college, and the church create imperative circumstances for the successful reentry of black ex-convicts. The history of struggle and survival of these support systems speaks to their ability to transfer or bestow survival qualities to those ex-convicts needing assistance and protection from deviant labels and criminal definitions.

Institutional treatment has varying effects of inmates. Some inmates do not return to prison in spite of the treatment; some because of circumstances encountered upon release. Some do not return because of a decision that it is no longer necessary or wise to engage in criminal activity. Other ex-convicts do not return to prison because they are able to avoid the criminal definitions and labels of those in positions of power to make such definitions and labels stick.

Institutional treatment has made some inmates angry, frustrated, passive, and radical. It has caused some inmates to internalize definitions of themselves that are negative and destructive to their growth and development. This fact is unfortunate and oppressive. Seventy-five percent of the black males in prison convicted for survival crimes are not career criminals but tend to become career criminals if they are not significantly impacted by the environments of the network of support systems mentioned earlier. Consequently, to identify, label, and treat black men as criminals through the process of adjudication has consequences for their further participation in criminal activity. The support to black ex-convicts found in the community within the context of the family, the church, the work experience, and the college can allow for success circumstances that can challenge the negative circumstances created by the prison experience, the need of the state for prison labor, and the need of the police and the other subsystems of the criminal justice system to be legitimate.

Notes

1. See chapter 1, "Nacirema Society."

2. William J. Chambliss, "A Sociological Analysis of the Law of Vagrancy," *Social Problems* 12 (Summer, 1964): 67-77. Also see George Rusche and Otto Kirchheimer, *Punishment and Social Structure* (New York: Columbia University Press, 1939), pp. 32-41.

3. Ibid., p. 76.

4. *The New York Times*, July 8, 1967, pp. 1 and 9.

5. L. Alex Swan, *Crime Policing, Corrections and the Social Order* (forthcoming), chapter 2.

6. See John Rex and Robert Moore, *Race, Community and Conflict: A Study in Sparkbook* (London: Oxford University Press, 1976). Richard Quinney, *Criminology* (Boston: Little Brown and Co., 1979), pp. 222-23.

7. President's Commission on Law Enforcement and Administration of Justice, *The Challenge of Crime in a Free Society* (Washington, D.C.: U.S. Government Printing Office, 1967), p. 18.

8. Selwyn Raab, "33% in New York Don't Know Killer," *The New York Times*, June 13, 1976, p. 1. See also Robert A. Silverman, "Victim-Offender Relationships in Face-to-Face Delinquent Acts," *Social Problems* 22 (February, 1975): 383-93.

9. Alex Pokorny, "A Comparison of Homicide in Two Cities," *Journal of Criminal Law, Criminology and Police Science* 56 (December, 1965): 479-87.

10. *Crimes of Violence*, Vol. II, a staff report submitted to the National Commission of the Causes and Prevention of Violence, co-directors Donald J. Mulvihill and Melvin M. Tumin (Washington, D.C.: U.S. Government Printing Office, 1969), p. 209.

11. Erik-Olin Wright, *The Politics of Punishment: A Critical Analysis of Prisons in America* (New York: Harper and Row, 1973), p. 26.

12. Ibid., pp. 31-34.

13. L. Alex Swan, *Crime Policing, Corrections and the Social Order* (forthcoming).

14. George Napper, "Perception of Crime: Problems and Implications," in Robert Woodson, *Black Perspectives on Crime and Criminal Justice System* (Boston: G.K. Hall & Co., 1977), pp. 5-22.

15. L. Alex Swan, "Reentry and the Black Parolee," *Journal of Social and Behavioral Sciences* 21, nos. 2 and 3 (Spring-Summer 1975): 104-116.

16. L. Alex Swan, "Research and Experimentation in Prison," *Journal of Black Psychology* 6, no. 1 (August, 1979): 47-51.

17. L. Alex Swan, *Families of Black Prisoners* (Boston: G.K. Hall and Co., 1981).

18. Jessica Mitford, *Kind and Usual Punishment* (New York: Alfred A. Knopf, 1973), p. 97.

19. Irving Piliavin, "The Reduction of Custodian-Professional Conflict in Correctional Institutions," *Crime and Delinquency* 12 (April, 1966): 125-34.

20. Quoted in David Rothenberg, "Failure of Rehabilitation: A Smokescreen," *National Catholic Reporter* 12 (April 16, 1976): 10.

21. Edgar H. Schein, "Man Against Man: Brainwashing," *Correctional Psychiatry and Journal of Social Therapy* 8, no. 2 (1962): 91-92.

22. Quoted from Federal Prisoner's Coalition, "The Mind Police," *Penal Digest International* 2 (August, 1972): 8-10.

23. Chicago People's Law Office, "Check Out Your Mind: Behavior Modification, Experimentation and Control in Prison," *Chicago Connections Newsletter*, supplement No. 1, n.d., p. 4.

24. National Criminal Justice Information and Statistics Service, "Prisoners in State and Federal Institutions," *National Prisoner Statistics Bulletin*, no. SD-NPS-PSF-2 (June, 1976), pp. 28.

25. John Irwin, *The Felon* (Englewood Cliffs, N.J.: Prentice-Hall, 1970), pp. 155-56.

26. Ibid., pp. 156-57.

27. Saleem A. Shah, foreword to Marguerite O. Warren, *Correctional Treatment in Community Settings: A Report of Current Research* (Rockville, Md.: National Institute of Mental Health, 1972), p. iii.

28. "Future Role of the U.S. Bureau of Prisons," Hearings before the Subcommittee on National Penitentiaries of the Committee of the Judiciary, United States Senate, 92nd Congress (Washington, D.C.: U.S. Government Printing Office, 1971). See also Elmer K. Nelson, Jr., "Community-Based Correctional Treatment: Rationale and Problem," *Annals of the American Academy of Political and Social Science* 374 (November, 1967): 82-91.

29. L. Alex Swan, "Diversion and Community-Based Corrections Programs," pp. 1-25.

7

Family Relations, Family Therapy, and the Black Family

As a social unit, the family is one of the community's basic social institutions. However, today, as in the past, the black family is faced with various problems, some of which are so complex there seems to be neither understanding of nor solution for them.

This chapter will delineate some of the many problems in black family relations and the various possible techniques and approaches for handling problems and crises in the family. The primary aim of black families is to stay together as families and experience growth and development, but they need assistance to understand their particular situation and organize their efforts to handle divisive forces that affect them. Although most families are aware of those forces, they do not always fully understand their nature and character nor have appropriate and effective ways of dealing with them. Once this understanding is achieved, the employment of adequate, appropriate, and effective means of handling these forces becomes the major concern of the families.

Many black families suffer emotionally, economically, socially, and otherwise, either because they have not developed family coping mechanisms or strategies for dealing effectively with such matters; because they are unwilling and incapable of doing so; or because, once coping schemes are established, certain family members are not committed to the schemes. The resultant breakdown is usually blamed on economic, social, psychological, or emotional problems, not on the absence of coping mechanisms nor the unwillingness and inability of certain members to follow such coping mechanisms. Black families will always have problems of one kind or another arising out of various situations they did not create and over which they might not have any control. The important matter for the family is the presence of appropriate and effective coping mechanisms, essential if families are to survive, grow, and even make progress as families. If the family is to accomplish certain tasks, the family scheme of life is also essential This should be clear to all members, especially crucial members of the family.

There are times when one individual will have to assume several roles to fulfill the family scheme of life. Many of the problems faced by families today could be dealt with if roles were clearly defined and understood by all members. The willingness to assume anticipated and expected roles is very crucial to effective family functioning, allowing emphasis to be placed on the collective unit and not merely on the individual within the unit. Such an attitude creates the appropriate atmosphere for family functioning and the survival of operative family schemes.

At least four basic family schemes should be operating in each family. (1) A social and interpersonal scheme is needed for handling social matters such as conflicts, crises, stress, frustration, recreation, and play. (2) An economic scheme should be in place to deal with economic issues and matters of finance. (3) A religious scheme for dealing with religious and spiritual matters is often important. (4) An educational scheme for dealing with matters pertaining to the education of parents and children should be in place. Absence of such family schemes means that the family lacks an adequate mechanism for dealing effectively with matters of grave importance to the survival, progress, and successful functioning of the family as a unit. Families with no effective means for dealing with their many and often complex problems find their units struggling to survive and unable to make any progress. They might be poor, working-class, middle-class, or upper-class families. Poor and working-class families are less likely to take it for granted that their families will survive and make progress without constant attention to developed and established family schemes for getting certain tasks accomplished.[1] Middle- and upper-class families tend to assume that economic and social positions are sufficient unto themselves and abrogate the necessity for establishing clearly defined and stated mechanisms for handling various family matters, which may be potentially destructive to the family unit.

Scholars in the field of family relations and family therapy have identified several fundamental issues that tend to be sources of problems for the family.[2] Communication and the discrepancies in communication among family members surface as the number one source, with finances, sexual difficulties, openness and honesty, identity, self-worth, and feedback following closely behind.[3] Family therapists, for the most part, have agreed that if the discrepancies in communication among families are worked out and members share their feelings clearly and honestly, the various other problems could be solved with a minimum amount of difficulty. In fact, many therapists work with families on their problems in communication as the mechanism families need to cope independently without therapeutic assistance.

Families generally suffer from problems that should be distinguished. To do so is important for the therapists who are sought out for solutions. Problems may be structural, generational, or supportive in nature. Structural problems are related to the breaking up of the family. Whether the husband and wife separate or the parents and the children, the structure of the family changes, often leading to adjustment difficulties. Generational conflicts stem from discrepancies among the values held by parents, grandparents, and children. Often, as a result of generational conflicts, family members experience much rejection and hostility. Supportive difficulties have to do with the emotional support or lack of it experienced by family members. These distinctions are essential for sociological diagnosis, and the proper therapeutic treatment is dependent on a clear indication of the nature and character of the problem.[4]

Family Relations

Most family members tend to believe that a successful partnership is free of conflict. In most developing relationships, however, this is not necessarily the case. In fact, conflict is often an intrinsic part of the growing relationship.[5] As a grandmother once remarked, "Son, you can't expect to see eye-to-eye with your wife all the time."

In ongoing relationships the tendency is to assume in a conflict that someone is "right" and should be vindicated when the "wrongdoer" is determined. In the final analysis the wrong is condemned, and so is the wrongdoer. This is not always the best approach in dealing with conflict situations.

Undoubtedly it is more difficult to avoid conflicts in ongoing relationships than in casual and occasional relationships. The old West Indian adage, "Come see me and come live with me are two different things," confirms this fact. Certainly all situational conflicts should be appropriately managed, but a growing relationship must not be dominated by conflicts. Problems and ensuing conflicts are in many instances unavoidable but are usually the basis for growth and development when appropriately, adequately, and creatively managed.[6]

Trouble Spots and Sources of Conflict in Family Relations

Family members should be most aware of the many trouble spots in intimate relationships. Although they will vary from family to family, families seem to have difficulty coping with certain ones in type, nature, and degree.

The most potentially troublesome spot is sexual relations, because it is the most intimate aspect of the partnership. In a partnership where the partners are sexually incompatible, a great deal of patience, cooperation, understanding, and love is required if a mutually satisfying sexual relationship is to be achieved. The term compatible does not denote sameness or similarity; it simply suggests that the behavior, likes, approaches, styles, positions, and the like of one partner complement the behavior, likes, approaches of the other. Sex is a communication process within intimate partnerships and may be used, for the most part, as a way to communicate the tender, loving, and gentle aspects of the relationship as well as its passion. Partners may express through sex their desires to be dominant, submissive, seductive, and so on. Sexual adjustment helps to keep the relationship from becoming static. The need to openly and honestly discuss feelings, desires, attitudes, and dispositions toward sex is an important part of achieving a better understanding of partner and self. This practice is rewarding, satisfying, and enriching to the growth of the relationship.

A majority of sexual difficulties in family relations result from personal and interpersonal problems, though a small percentage stem from physiological difficulties. Even when the physiological and psychological problems are solved, the resulting interpersonal difficulties may continue. A variety of fears—such as the fear of failure or displeasing one's partner—may lead to intrusive thoughts during sexual relations and be highly destructive of sexual satisfaction. Partners have admitted to substituting for their own partners, in fantasy, some more desirable but unattainable one during the sexual experience. This is possible when the image of the psychological substitute is fresh and vivid; but when it is not, the process breaks down and sexual performance becomes less than satisfactory and even unpleasant.[7] A marital relationship characterized by conscious commitment and love can have latent hostilities, anxieties, and ambivalence that impact on sexual functioning. An atmosphere of pressure and tension, subtle power struggles, a repulsive attitude, and frustrated desires of partners may create difficulties in a relationship and ultimately lead to sexual problems.[8]

As the political economy becomes more oppressive, families find it more difficult to manage their income to cover their needs and desires. Consequently, money and income management become an increasing form of conflict in most partnerships, especially among "middle-class" black families. Every family must make decisions about how money is going to be spent, and these discussions must be influenced by established priorities within the context of a plan or what I have previously referred to as an economic scheme. The most effective spending plan or economic scheme is a budget, a tool to help families spend money wisely and at the same time achieve family goals. Adherence to a budget also allows the reduction and elimination of inefficient spending. If the family takes the time to plan a budget and is determined to follow it, with the cooperation of every family member, many interpersonal conflicts can be solved. The family budget must be workable and adapted to the needs of the family and the family's actual income.

The essential problems in having a budget in place are related to choices that must be made, sharp lines that must be drawn, and negotiation of priorities with consideration for the habits and attitudes of all family members. If habits are unfamiliar, partners tend to note carefully how money is being spent by their mates. Financial difficulties can be effectively avoided and even solved with mutual awareness of each other's spending habits. Moreover, respect for each other's judgment regarding the family's financial situation creates an atmosphere of sensible resolution of any conflict over money matters.

Partners come into marital situations with different expectations of each other and of the relationship. Often these different expectations become trouble spots when partners' behavior does not conform to expectation. This conflict in expectation can occur over the way a partner behaves in sexual relations, how he or she relates to in-laws and friends, how a partner spends money, or how the partner dresses. Some expectations might seem trivial, but they should be aired if they are not to become sources of conflict that may ruin a happy and satisfying relationship. Each individual brings a cluster of values, expectations, beliefs, and assumptions to every partnership. The task is to establish joint action, resulting from or based upon the different frames of reference. Having an understanding of the frame of reference that establishes the difference in perspectives and interpretations allows for the management of potential conflict and the resolution of situational conflicts.

Varying degrees of esteem for in-laws account for the different expectations partners have for dealing with in-laws. Many partners are nervous around in-laws, especially if uncertain how to interact with them or what to say in their presence. Some partners experience social distance from their in-laws because they do not know how to establish close relationships with them. If they are not living in the same household, establishing close relationships takes a little longer and carries a greater degree of uncertainty. Each partner expects the other to feel close to his/her in-laws, especially parents-in-law. If the partners are having difficulty expressing such closeness, they should discuss it first with each other, then with the particular in-law(s).

When partners come together in a marital relation they by definition shift loyalties from their parents as primary family to their partners as primary family. This shift often is so traumatic that it is never really made. At times one partner expects the shift to be immediate while the other tries to shift gradually. On the other hand, some partners make the shift long before the partnership. Whatever the situation, conflicts sometimes develop. These conflicts could become more acute if the in-laws become jealous or if questions of commitment are raised between the partners. In-laws can become rivals for the loyalties of their daughters and sons who have established partnerships. Partners can sense this rivalry and often allow it to become a troublesome spot. A partner who is slow to shift loyalties might frequently visit his/her parents' house, causing the other to complain. Frequently the telephone, used as a means of maintaining loyalties, becomes the basis for situational conflicts with accusations that one partner is always on the phone with his/her parents. Partners (more often the females) tend to seek parental advice even after marriage, and it is not unusual to find that a daughter will continue for some time to do her shopping with her mother and even allow her to make choices for her. If there are complaints regarding these matters, it could mean that a partner is jealous of the other's relationship with his or her family. This jealousy could erupt into open and constant conflict if not properly managed.

Partners should pay keen attention to several other sources of conflict. Partners should always attempt to understand the issues they face and try to sort out workable solutions to their problems. Recognizing that the issues are real allows for an atmosphere that contributes to the resolution of the situation that produced the defensive behavior. Defensive behavior tends to intensify conflicts and is often an inadequate means of coping with conflict in intimate relationships.[9] Failure to meet a need or an attempt to alleviate tension and self-depreciation causes some individuals to develop defensive behavior. Defensive behavior allows the individual to achieve a substitute end to reduce the tension yet fails to attain the basic goal of eliminating the tension.

Defensive behavior can take the form of fantasizing, withdrawal, rationalization, excessive sleeping, substitution, and psychosomatic illness. Defensive behavior originates when issues threaten the self-image or when situations are especially unpleasant.

Accommodating one another is essential to full development of a relationship, but this becomes somewhat difficult when individuals have significantly different backgrounds and perspectives. Differences in views and background can have a profound effect on the potential for growth and joint action.[10] Where there are major differences, partners should realistically anticipate problems and willingly confront them together in open discussion. Couples will come to enjoy the experience of learning from each other different ways of looking at and doing things together. More options are learned and alternative responses to situations are made available as they engage in the process of fitting their lives together.

Because the process of change can be uncomfortable and painful, some individuals stubbornly resist giving up prior comfortable ways which they have come to view as best. Yet, for a variety of reasons, including geographical mobility and range of potential mates, there is the increasing likelihood that more partners who differ greatly in background and perspectives will establish families. In any event, partners should not expect their partners to treat them as their parents treated them. If a partnership is to be productive, it is crucial that the partners seek to fit their actions to the actions of each other, using their backgrounds and outlooks as a basis.

Different backgrounds and outlooks might include different approaches to child-rearing and discipline. Conflicts over this matter are bound to be destructive to the relationship if a child-rearing scheme acceptable to the partners is not worked out. If the children are old enough or are capable of participating in the establishment of such a family scheme, they should be participants.

Children learn how to put parents and their divergent outlooks in opposition. This practice must be managed effectively or children will destroy family relationships and make unity difficult to achieve. The focus must be upon the issue, the behavior, the situation, and not on the individual parent or children. A distinction must be made between the individual and the behavior.

Another potential source of conflict stems from multiple feedback. This means that partners in their relationships with each other often give and receive multiple messages that create confusion. In response to behavior, partners give feedback to each other. It is expected that these messages will be interpreted into behavior modifications or action adjustments. Adequate feedback is essential to the growth of interpersonal relationships. If the feedback is confusing because of its multiple messages, it prevents appropriate assessment and interpretation of the situation and as a result inhibits proper adjustment and modification of actions. Adequate feedback allows partners to perfect joint action appropriate to their objectives. Because feedback is usually ambigous, partners must encourage each other to interpret clearly and correctly the message received. They should encourage and give support to each other to reduce ambiguity in the feedback relayed to each other. Families can maintain a very healthy and productive relationship among and between members when feedback is clear and precise, allowing for appropriate and adequate interpretation. Partners must be willing to establish such a process so that one or the other does not feel pressured to modify his or her behavior while the other remains unaffected. Failure to do so could cause a feeling of being shaped according to the dictates of the dominant partner. Eventually the relationship, marked by frustration and anger, breaks down with partners always on the defensive and lashing out at each other.

When affairs, inside or outside the family, do not go as expected, frustration and even aggression may set it. Frustration turned inward leads to depression, but a more common response in such instances is to project onto an innocent person or object the responsibility for the frustration experienced. The ability to recognize the real source of the experience helps both the partners, and the entire family to deal with the situation in an appropriately effective manner. A misunderstanding of the situation not only does not help the relationship but leads to defensive behavior instead of an offensive attempt to get at the real souce of the problem.

Within some family structures, conflict is allowed to get out of control. When this happens family relations deteriorate, and in the end such families are torn apart. They did not make distinctions between the real worth of situational conflicts—which are worth struggling over and which are not. It is also important for the family to be clear as to what is being struggled over. Some families get into struggles not really knowing what the real struggle is about.[11]

If couples and families are to make progress and grow in their relationship they must learn how to handle conflict creatively. Controlling conflict and using it as a constructive part of the relationship helps the relationship lead to eventual growth.

In this regard, there are several points couples and family members should bear in mind. (1) Partners should be regarded as equals, and each member of the family should be recognized as important to the family process. (2) The personhood of the partners should be recognized, and partners should avoid reducing each other to the status of a nonperson through abusive language, accusations, and other negative behavior. (3) Even when ideas expressed are in direct conflict, there should be appreciation and respect for the ideas and thoughts of each other. Opinions, views, dreams, and ideas are real and valid and must be taken into account in intimate relationships in families. (4) Partners and family members should respect, appreciate, and learn to accept the feelings of each other, even if they find such feelings unacceptable. Feelings expressed with honesty can be most revealing in family relations and can provide the basis for collective struggle. (5) Partners and family members should avoid competitive situations. Most competitive situations in intimate relations create a win-lose situation in which someone is usually hurt. This win-lose situation is often unfair because one person might be at a disadvantage, for a variety of reasons, at different times. (6) Partners should learn to accept anger and hostility as real and legitimate; at times their legitimacy may be questioned, but their reality should be faced. (7) Partners should learn the art of patience and develop the skill of allowing the other to save face especially at the peak of a conflict. (8) Finally, partners must learn how to take risks and use tact in dealing with each other when risk is taken. There are times that are more appropriate for risk taking. It is best that partners know those times and use them when dealing with certain matters.

If partners and family members are willing to develop and have a growing relationship, no trouble spot or conflict should be able to destroy their family or partnership. Making commitments to each other is a good approach to take when attempting to establish willingness to grow and develop.

However, if complex trouble spots do develop, they should be so managed that they do not dominate family relations. Because family relations are extremely intricate webs of emotions, partners should be careful that, in the process of finding a way to manage their conflicts or potential conflicts, relationships are not damaged to the point where they cannot recover, survive, or make progress.

The problem is that in many cases, partners wait until too late to discuss conflicts or potential conflicts with each other. Usually, the best approach is to discuss these trouble spots with each other before doing so with friends, other family members, or a professional counselor. Partners do well to pay heed to the proverb that "an ounce of prevention is better than a pound of cure." However, if problems become complex and difficult to manage and if partners, seriously concerned about their relationship, cannot provide the sociological diagnosis themselves, professional help should be sought at once.

Seeking Therapeutic Assistance

As the traditional role of the black preacher as a counselor and therapist of sorts has changed somewhat, more black people are visiting professional therapists as well as entering psychotherapy. This move is an indication of the growing nature of individualism among oppressed blacks. The collectiveness that once served as a buffer against the evils and difficulties of racism and economic oppression is disappearing. This situation is of great importance for a variety of reasons, one of which is that there are not many definitive answers to many questions addressed by psychotherapy. Consequently, blacks must give serious consideration to the complex problems and risky nature of choosing to become involved in therapy. Even if blacks continue to enter therapy as individuals and families, the process must be clarified to allow for more control by blacks over their lives as participants.[12]

Families get into therapy either voluntarily or involuntarily. Because therpists have come to realize that involuntary participation is usually not very helpful and that people who are coerced or forced into therapy resist whatever help is possible, they usually attempt to get the involuntary participant and even the voluntary participant to understand what therapy is abut and why most people participate. It is desirable, however, that the participants have some understanding of what they want out of therapy and why they want to get into therapy. Initial involuntary participation and even voluntary participation is usually useful only after the participant(s) has come to such understanding.[13]

There are times when participants come to the realization that they can be helped by therapy only after they have entered. In those cases the participants might be anxious and even desperate to get help and enter therapy in faith, blindly hoping that satisfying outcomes will result.

Entering therapy without really knowing why one wants to get into therapy and what one really wants out of the experience can be dangerous and may cause additional psychological pain and social conflict. The need for immediate relief from suffering can also interfere with a careful consideration and selection of the therapist and the therapy most appropriate to one's needs. Not every therapist is competent, kind, considerate, patient, trustworthy, responsible, and reliable; nor is every therapy appropriate or suited to every individual or family need. It is simply not enough for the individual and families needing relief to believe in the professional status of the therapist and the power of therapy. They should also have some idea as to why they need therapy and what the resultant outcome of the therapy is likely to be.

Not every family or individual enters therapy for the same reasons. There are broad categories under which the various reasons might be listed. One category is that of personal crisis with extreme emotional distress and a feeling that one's whole world is falling apart and that one's life is out of control. Usually the difficulties center around personality and identity problems. Often these problems impact family functioning.

These difficulties might result from the fact that a significant person in close social contact might have defined the individual as "insensitive or unresponsive" to certain needs in the relationship. This characterization is interpreted as negative to the growth of the person and the relationship. How to change and how to become responsive and sensitive becomes very important, especially if the individual wants to continue with that relationship. In addition, what kind of person the individual wants to be and what he/she wants out of family relations provide the motivation for entering therapy.[14]

Another motivational issue within this category is severe depression resulting from emotional distress usually precipitated by the loss of a lover or rejection by a loved one. The need for attention, love, and affection from significant others, especially within the family structure, may also be a precipitative cause. Coming to grips with one's identity and reevaluating one's sense of self-worth are good starting points in situations where personality and identity problems develop within the family.

In some relationships where one person is insensitive or unresponsive, the situation may not lead to emotional collapse. Instead the following scenes may be acted out: attempts are made to point out limitations; resistance develops to such revelations; the other partner is taken for granted;

a false sense of security ensues; complacency sets in; demands are made but little is given in return.

In conflicts where there is physical violence, real damage to the relationship is checked by the reasonableness of the other person.

Although entry into therapy can have negative effects if certain preentry cautions are not considered and dealt with satisfactorily either before entry or soon after, there are very positive effects that might be derived from participation as an individual or as a family. First, the individual or the family could bring to an end a stressful pattern of behavior caused by personal or family crisis that plagued social relations and family life for months or even years. Second, the crisis can provide learning opportunities for dealing or coping with future conflicts. Third, the crisis can also be a helpful source of learning for understanding and revealing one's self. Fourth, entering therapy can help individuals alleviate distress and restore themselves and their families to a satisfactorily functioning level. When individuals and families think they have reached this level, they should terminate their participation in therapy.

Some individuals feel that their lives have not been meaningful and suffer from chronic depression. To them their lives have been empty. These are usually the bored individuals, successful in many ways and without severe emotional personality problems. These individuals do not portray problems associated with therapy. There is a degree of aimlessness in their lives, and they avoid the sense of loneliness with distractions like movies, television, compulsive work, and parties. Such individuals who enter therapy stay participants until they have learned as much as they can about themselves and their social world. Success or satisfaction for such individuals is the acceptance of who they are and the possibilities of extending the dimensions of themselves into social activities and into the lives of other people. On the other hand there are those who feel that they need someone to whom they can talk on an intimate basis because they do not feel free to do so within the context of the family. Participation in therapy is the means to achieve this need. Many people, not good at risk taking, enter therapy in order to learn ways of taking risk.[15]

Therapy has become somewhat idealized and has evolved into a process of search for a large number of people. Traditionally, therapy was used mainly as a treatment for mental illness. Today, in addition, it is used for personal and family growth, personal freedom and liberation; for understanding the dynamics of family relations as well as the means of exploring the mystery of being human.

As racism becomes more subtle and covert in its expression and black people become more individualistic in their relationships with one another inside and outside the context of the family, and with the wider society, blacks and the black family will be faced with more emotional and social crises at the individual, community, group, and family levels. Individualism is being substituted for collectivism, an approach to life that provided the basis for survival, personal and interpersonal growth. Consequently, more and more black families will be requiring professional help and assistance in their interpersonal and intrapersonal experiences.[16]

Family Therapy

Early psychoanalytic formulations accepted the notion that early family conflicts and alliances are important factors in the individual's character formation. Most psychotherapy developed on the basis of early psychoanalysis, focusing on the individual to resolve personal and intrapsychic conflicts.[17] This focus has been influenced or enhanced and in some circles replaced with the focus on the group that is the context for interpersonal experiences and transactions.[18] Consequently, family therapy and several forms of group therapy have come to represent real life more closely. As personal and social conflicts are believed to stem from and are reinforced by interpersonal relationships with family members, friends, neighbors, and schoolmates, therapeutic experiences with groups can help individuals work through these conflicts. Such group experiences can aid self-awareness, increasing sensitivity to the feelings of others and to feedback from significant and generalized others. Therefore, in our discussion of the basic forms of family therapy we will comment on group therapy and the advantages not possible in individual therapy.[19]

Entry into the family at birth is the first experience of the individual in group life. Consequently, for a significant period of the individual's life the properties of the image and the content of those properties are shaped by group experience in the family. Later the content of those properties are shaped and influenced by friends, neighbors, school, church, and work. There is a time in the experience of the individual, however, when the individual exercises control over the nature, degree and content of his or her socialization by others. This means that individuals do exercise power over perception of themselves by others and can regulate the internalization of that perception. Individuals, through the process of interaction, can manage the way others see them by the manner in which they display properties of partially or fully developed image-content.

In the process, the individuals are seen as they want others to perceive them. This independence is essential, especially if the individuals are in the process of rejecting negative labels forced on them. It becomes crucial that others see them as they see themselves and interact with them on the basis of their perceptions of themselves rather than on the basis of others' perceptions of them.[20] For a significant number of people this independence is never experienced. Continual participation in groups regulates and sets the pattern for individual behavior. Clinicians, especially clinical psychologists and psychiatrists, are beginning to understand this position more.[21] Family therapy and certain forms of group therapy are believed to simulate real life more closely. Until recently, clinicians worked primarily with the individual to resolve his/her personal and intrapsychic conflicts. However, there has been a shift in perspective to the family itself as a functioning social unit. The individual who is experiencing the difficulty is considered the *identified patient*. In family therapy, the family situation becomes the context for diagnosis and treatment. The identified patient, including the child in the family, might simply be the expression of the problem and conflict in the family. Therefore, treating the identified patient would be a mistake unless the problem has gained independence in the individual. In such a case, the other members should assume responsibility for the situation and assist in arriving at or managing the solution.[22]

Children are most vulnerable in a family situation and are often the identified patients because they are not always able to interpret correctly and adequately the contradictory messages emanating from parents whom they love. Sometimes they are rejected, avoided and pushed aside and other times they are loved, sought after, and hugged affectionately. Children, usually the most passive among family members, are safe objects for displacement and dumping, especially if one parent cannot displace or dump feelings of hostility and anger on the other parent or another adult family member.

Clinical sociologists and increasingly other clinicians are accepting the notion that the identified patient might simply be the expression of symptoms signaling the fact that something is the matter with the family as a unit. Therefore a careful study of the family and the relationship among family members will provide the context for therapeutic intervention and family therapy for the entire family.[23]

The practice of family therapy varies from therapist to therapist. All therapists tend to have as their primary objective, however, the improvement of the family in terms of its function as an interdependent, working group. To this end therapists work with families as a group to help remove obstacles to their relationships so that growth and developement might be experienced. Most family therapists encourage open communications and honest expressions for the exposing of truth among family members.

As a treatment technique, family therapy is not very old.[24] The development of theories that suggested the role of the family in mental illness provided the basis for the technique. The belief is that if change is to occur in the individual and in the family relations, the family as a group must be involved in the process. In other words, the family as a group is the context for change because it is the reciprocal relationships of the family members which determine individual behavior. However, the primary focus for change in the family is the disordered process.

Major Therapeutic Frameworks

Conjoint family therapy has become the most popular form of family therapy. In this approach, one therapist simultaneously works with parents, children, and other significant relatives and nonrelatives of the household. An example of this approach might be found in the works of Virginia Satir. Her approach is simple and straightforward; she functions as a resource person who helps the family members understand the discrepancies in their communications. The task then is to show them how to correct such discrepancies to achieve a more satisfying family relationship.[25]

N.W. Ackerman's approach is to focus on the immediate problems facing the family. Past events and relationships are not considered very important. He is also direct, forthright but confronting. In so doing, he attempts to get family members to become more open to him and in turn more open to each other. The underlying view is that in the family process, individuals tend to develop defenses against exposure for a variety of reasons. These defenses must be broken down if the family and the family members are to achieve more mutually satisfying outcomes.[26]

Concurrent family therapy is used by therapists who simultaneously treat various family members in separate sessions. This approach is not widely used, but the therapists who employ it argue that focusing on the same social event and transactions in the family with different family members at separate sessions allows for a broader perspective from which to understand the events and transactions. Once this understanding is achieved, a more precise and appropriate solution might be followed.

A rather complete picture is made from the various views of family members relative to the functioning of the family. Some conjoint family therapists work primarily with the identified patient and periodically with other family members, explaining the patient's condition and pointing out to them those social situations or transactions in the family that are detrimental to the progress of the patient as well as those that are helpful and inviting their assistance in times of crises.

Another approach which is identified as collaborative family therapy allows for the treatment of various family members separately by different therapists. The therapists then collaborate with each other, comparing the views of their clients relative to the events and transactions of the family. This approach is less common than the previous approaches, and some argue that it tends to produce less favorable results. The primary advantage of this approach, however, is that the therapists collaborate in their work relative to the problem of the family after securing different perspectives from their clients. This approach can also be very expensive to the family when the identified patient is the child, and a therapist sees the child and separate therapists see the mother, father, and any other significant member of the household. Where therapists work together as co-therapists with a family the collaboration is enhanced by the interpretation of each other's perceptions or understanding of the views of the family members.

The collaborative approach can be a drawback or an advantage if the therapists embrace different theoretical orientations from which they interpret what is going on in the family. The therapists have to describe and diagnose the problem and address it with theoretical insights. It is essential in diagnosing clinical situations in collaborative family therapy that the theoretical perspectives of each therapist is known by each other. Once an appropriate theoretical perspective is ascertained, the therapist can confront the specific problems. There are instances in collaborative therapy when therapists maintain their different theoretical perspectives until one or the other is achieving success in dealing with the problem. In the majority of instances all practicing clinicians note the kinds of problems being diagnosed and search for and/or select a theoretical perspective that contains assumptions closely related to the nature of the problem, the social life of the individual or family, and the possibility of change. What most clinicians tend to avoid is assessing the relative weight and methodological support for the various theoretical perspectives they use. The primary concern, however, is usually, how best to intervene therapeutically in family problems.[27]

A basic objective of family therapy is to improve the functions and relationships of family members as an interdependent social group. Family members are helped in communicating better and in removing obstacles that impede effective functioning of the family as a social unit. Growth and development of individuals within the family is possible. Even though individuals benefit from family therapy, this type of therapy does not simply mean treating individual members of a family in a family context. The family situation provides the context for changing the disordered family process, or for correcting discrepancies in communication, restructuring and refocusing interpersonal relationships, and establishing equilibrium in family life.

Conclusion

As the society becomes more complex and the arrangements of the social order more oppressive, black families, especially those in urban areas, must be helped to achieve a stronger sense of collectiveness and unity, an enhanced ability to communicate, and the willingness to work together to achieve satisfying and productive relationships. Even though there is little empirical evidence to indicate that family therapy has been successful, many family therapists know subjectively that they have helped families to change a process of disorder and disorganization to relative order and organization. Family therapy has helped to change feelings, attitudes, dispositions, and approaches in interpersonal relations and enhanced the chance for honesty and openness in communication between family members.

Black families experience major economic and political disruptions and social disturbances in their patterns of interaction. The traditional orientation of collectiveness and family and kinship ties suggest that the family as a collective unit is the context for achieving the goals in family therapy. Family therapists working with black families must seek to open up the family members to a recognition of their potential for growth and development as individuals and as a family unit. New ways of caring and interacting, especially with the person affected by disordered relationships within the family, must be sought so as to maintain the sense of collective culpability. The recognition that all family members are part of the problem faced by an individual within the family structure provides the basis for reciprocal relationships in the solution of interpersonal and family problems. In other words, the therapist must seek to put into operation the African philosophical/behavioral principle of the oneness of our being and the survival and progress of the family.[28] This principle provides the basis for the survival and progress of black people and their families.

An approach that seems to be effective in working with black families in therapy is to use the church as the place for therapeutic intervention. Most black people do not like visiting for counseling in the traditional office of the professional therapist.[29] The facilities of the church provide a very comfortable place for the therapist, the individual, and the family. Moreover, the church provides an appropriate context for dealing with individual and family problems. Most blacks are connected with the church, and the church is viewed as a legitimate intervention mechanism. Black clients tend to be more open in the church and seem more willing to be honest and capable of taking risks in that setting. Commitments made within the facilities of the church are more likely to be kept. At least there is a sincere attempt to do so. Blacks also feel more hopeful of dealing with their problems in the church setting. The pastor's role is that of a middleman. Although he might not know the details of the problem, the pastor stays in touch with the individuals and families and informs the therapist of their needs. In many cases, it is the pastor with whom the individual or family makes contact in their search for hope and counsel regarding family problems.

A most effective way to work with the church in offering services to individuals and families is to conduct a series of family life seminars and workshops at the various churches during the week. I have found Monday,

Tuesday, and Thursday nights most appropriate. Wednesday night in most black churches is scheduled for regular prayer meeting. Friday is a busy day, and attendance would most surely drop. Sessions should be conducted between 7 and 9 P.M. and may include a variety of issues. Experience has shown that it is during these sessions that individuals begin to get a glimpse of their individual and/or family difficulties. A question box provided for personal and general questions has proven useful; however, if the questions require detailed responses, it is best to suggest personal contact.

There are several advantages to the use of the church as the context for therapeutic intervention in the family. (1) The therapist is known to the church body and especially the pastor, who approves of the seminars and workshops. (2) The church setting is familiar to the members and the religious climate makes more believable the diagnosis and prognosis, or the clients are more susceptible to believing the diagnosis and prescription suggested by the therapist. (3) It frees the pastor to do spiritual work. (4) It reinforces the importance of the relationship between the college from which the professional received his/her training, the family, and the church as vital community institutions for the growth and development of an oppressed people.

To start the service, the professional should visit all of the churches in the city and then follow up with letters to the individual pastors. If they respond, a conference for discussing and outlining the details of the services may be suggested. The more successful approach is that of working through one pastor with whom the family counselor has developed a bond of friendship. Other pastors could then seek the opinion or testimony of their colleague when approached by the family counselor.

A significant number of church members cannot afford to pay the fee for counseling. However, most of them contribute to the tithe and offerings of the church, and very often, the services rendered to such persons are paid for by the church. Some churches establish an account for the poor or they have an account entitled "mission fund" from which such payments are made. The therapist would submit to the pastor a statement signed by him/her and the client showing the number of counseling hours each week. At the end of the month, the church board, pastor, or executive committee governing the church would authorize payments. As the fees are usually half the regular fees of an outside professional, most churches regard this program as a service to their membership rather than a burden. As families are helped, the church grows stronger and the pastor is held in high esteem for introducing such a service as part of the total mission of the church.

Occasionally, the therapist may speak to the entire church on topics such as "Child Development in the Home" or "The Father's Role in the Family." At times a sensitivity session for the entire church might be conducted to bring the church members closer together, especially if there are large numbers of church members who do not know each other and have no mechanism, except an occasional picnic, to get to know each other. These sessions have a purifying and cleansing effect in the church, if conducted correctly.

Increasingly, black families will need more professional assistance to help them struggle against the systems of racism and oppression. These systems create alienation among and between families and black men and women. Racism and oppression produce complex trouble spots that must be managed so that they do not dominate interaction and family relations.

However, because the systems of racism and oppression have created constant problems for black families, interpersonal interaction, harmonious development, and plain getting along have been difficult to achieve. Consequently, an understanding of the systems and how they impact the lives of black people in general, and black families in particular, is necessary, along with therapeutic intervention if black families are to wage a successful struggle to survive and make progress.

Notes

1. Herbert G. Gutman, *The Black Family in Slavery and Freedom, 1750-1925* (New York: Pantheon Books, 1976); Andrew Billingsley, *Black Families and the Struggle for Suvival: Teaching Our Children to Walk Tall* (New York: Friendship Press, 1974); *The Evolution of the Black Family* (New York: National Urban League, 1976); L. Alex Swan, *Families of Black Prisoners* (Boston: G. K. Hall and Co., 1981).

2. Nathan Ackerman, *Treating the Troubled Family* (New York: Basic Books, 1966); Peter J. Stein et al. (eds.), *The Family: Functions, Conflicts and Symbols* (Reading, Mass.: Addison-Wesley Publishing Co., 1977).

3. Herbert Goldenberg, *Contemporary Clinical Psychology* (Monterey, Calif.: Book/Cole Pub. Co., 1973), pp. 371-408; Rebecca M. Smith, *Klemer's Marriage and Family Relationships* (New York: Harper and Row, 1975).

4. Andrew Ferber et al., *The Book of Family Therapy* (Boston: Houghton Mifflin, 1973).

5. Carl E. Williams and John F. Crosby, *Choice and Challenge* (Dubuque, Iowa: W. C. Brown, 1979); A. Lynn Scoresby, *The Marriage Dialogue* (Reading, Mass: Addison-Wesley Pub. Co., 1977); George R. Bach and Peter Wyden, *The Intimate Enemy: How to Fight Fair in Love and Marriage* (New York: William Morrow & Co., Inc., 1969).

6. George Roleder, *Marriage Means Encounter* (Dubuque, Iowa: WM. C. Brown, 1979); Gail Fullerton, *Survival in Marriage: Introduction to Family Interaction, Conflicts, and Alternatives* (New York: Holt, Rinehart and Winston, Inc., 1972).

7. W.D. Winters and J. Ferriera, *Research in Family Interaction* (Palo Alto, Calif.: Science and Behavior Books, 1969).

8. Ibid.; Nancy Van Pelt, *The Compleat Marriage* (Nashville: Southern Publishing Association, 1979).

9. John H. Scanzoni, *The Black Family in Modern Society* (Boston: Allyn and

Bacon, Inc., 1971); Jeffrey K. Hadden and Marie L. Borgatta, *Marriage and the Family: A Comprehensive Reader,* (Itasca, Ill.: F.E. Peacock Publishers, Inc., 1969).

10. Herbert Blumer, *Symbolic Interactionism.* (Englewood Cliffs, New Jersey: Prentice-Hall & Co., 1969).

11. Scoresby, *Marriage Dialogue.*

12. Clifford J. Sager, Thomas L. Brayboy, and Barbara R. Waxenberg, *Black Ghetto Family in Therapy: A Laboratory Experience* (New York: Grove Press, 1970).

13. Nathan Ackerman, *The Psychodynamics of Family Life* (New York: Basic Books, 1958); Ted Clark, *Going Into Therapy* (New York: Harper and Row, 1975).

14. Ibid.

15. Don D. Jackson (ed.), *Communication, Family and Marriage* (Palo Alto, Calif.: Science and Behavior, 1968), pp. 63-86. See also *Therapy, Communication, and Change* (Palo Alto, Calif.: Science and Behavior, 1968).

16. L. Alex Swan, "Clinicial Sociologists: Coming Out of the Closet," *Mid-American Review of Sociology* vol. 5, no. 1 (Spring 1980): 87-98.

17. Ackerman, *Psychodynamics.*

18. Marshall Edelson, *The Practice of Sociotherapy* (New Haven, Conn.: Yale University Press, 1970); Swan, "Clinical Sociologists."

19. Vincent D. Foley, *An Introduction to Family Therapy* (New York: Grune and Stratton, 1974).

20. L. Alex Swan, "The Context of the Image and the Development of Properties of the Self." unpublished manuscript, 1978.

21. M. Edelson, *Sociotherapy and Psychotherapy* (Chicago: University of Chicago Press, 1970).

22. Goldenberg, *Contemporary Clinical Psychology.*

23. John E. Bell (ed.), *Family Therapy* (New York: Jason Aronson, 1975).

24. Donald A. Bloch, *Techniques of Family Psychotherapy* (New York: Grune and Stratton, 1973).

25. Virginia Satir, *Conjoint Family Therapy* (Palo Alto, Calif.: Science and Behavior Books, 1967).

26. Ackerman, *Psychodynamics.*

27. Ira D. Glick and David R. Kessler, *Marital and Family Therapy.* New York: Grune and Stratton, 1974.

28. Wade W. Nobles, "Africanity: Its Role in Black Families," *The Black Scholar* 5, no. 9 (June 1974): 10-17.

29. Swan, "Context of the Image."

8

Suffering Is Redemptive: The Religious Experience of Afro-Americans

Recent years have seen a sustained debate among blacks relative to the role of the church and the preacher in the struggle of black people. One view is that the church and the preacher must assume a primary role in the revolutionary struggle of blacks for freedom and liberation. Another view is that the church must advocate a social gospel that finds it in the social arena doing good for mankind. The view that the church has a spiritual role in society that transcends all other roles seems to be the dominant belief. However, there is agreement that all of these roles are to be assumed by the church with varying degrees of emphasis if black people are to survive and make progress.

Historically, the church has served as an anchor institution in the affairs of black people. The content of its message of love, hope, unity, and its physical facilities, which are usually owned by the members, have served the emotional, physical, and organizational needs of the community. The black preacher, more than any other leader or professional, has had the most influence in the affairs of the black community. Consequently, it is safe to suggest that the black church and the black preacher have been the primary forces around which black people have attempted to survive and make progress. The difficulty of the church and the preacher, as perceived by a significant number of black people, has been the contradictory nature of its character, which promotes restraint on the one hand and aggressive action on the other. Another difficulty is the perception of blacks that the content of the preaching, if not a central doctrine, is that suffering is redemptive. In fact, one of the most influential preachers of the last several years, the late Dr. Martin Luther King, Jr., articulated this position, capturing the religious culture that provided the context for the religious experience of black people.

Carrie Hunter argues that:

the early Black Church existed as the arena out of which all issues relating to Black life and existence could be addressed. It served as a social hall where Black people could fellowship and share talent. . . .In addition to serving as the social hall in the Black community, the Black church was and is the chief property-owner, business activity supporter, and Black education promoter. Out of meager resources, during crucial periods in Black history, the Black church struggled to build educational institutions at all levels.[1]

African people have always been deeply religious. Africans believed in God as the supreme being and their "religious codes were integrated into the daily life of its adherents."[2] Africans did not separate their religious beliefs from their daily business and social practices. African art, sculpture, masks, carvings, ivory, and horns expressed the religious concepts and represented the mode of worship and the entire life experiences of Africans. Geoffrey Parrinder argues that:

Most if not all, African people have had a belief in a Supreme Being as an integral part of their world views of practiced religion. . . .Missionaries have found, often to their surprise, that they did not need to argue for the existence of God, or faith in a life after death, for both these fundamentals of world religion are deeply rooted in Africa. . . .The nature of God in African belief can be gathered from the qualities attributed to Him. These correspond generally to many of the divine attributes postulated in other religions. That God is almighty is one of the most obvious assertions, since supremacy implies it. All-powerful is a common name for Him and He receives many similar titles: creator, all other, giver of rain and sunshine, the one who began the forest, the one who gives and rots, maker of souls, father of the placenta, the one who exists by Himself. The omnipresence of God, less commonly expressed, is found in sayings as "the one who is met everywhere," and "the great ocean whose head-dress is the horizon." More clearly God is omniscient: the wise one, the all-seeing, the "one who brings round the seasons." These attributes imply the transcendence of God, and to some extent his immanence. God is always creator and ruler, the one beyond all thanks, the ancient of days who is from the first, the everlasting who has no limits, and he who alone is full of abundance.[3]

Parrinder goes on to note that:

African psychology sees in man a living power, the greatest of all created beings. Though he is not the strongest man he is able by his intelligence, like the hare in popular African fables, to outwit those who are physically more powerful. His power is both physical and mental, and the coordination of the two makes him a full man. But man is dependent on God, and on powers greater than himself and so religion is essential to his well-being.[4]

Africa and Africans in the Bible

The Bible records the account of Moses, who wrote the first five books of the Old Testament, who was born and educated in Africa. He grew up in the palace of King Pharoah after being adopted by Pharoah's daughter. He was royally tutored in the affairs and wisdom of the Egyptians. Moses was the one who led God's people from bondage to the borders of the Promised Land. This story has always been of interest and a source of inspiration to black people because, like those in bondage in Egypt, controlled by an oppressive system, blacks defined their situation in America in similar terms and looked forward to a Moses for leadership out of suffering and bondage to freedom and liberation.

Herod's attempt to kill Jesus was averted when Joseph received a message from God to take the young child to Egypt for safety and security.

Simon of Cyrene, a place in Libya, Northern Africa, bore the cross of Christ and carried it to Calvary. The Ethiopian treasurer who was baptized by the evangelist Philip joined the Ethiopian church that for centuries has observed the seventh day as the holy Sabbath of God according to the Bible. The story of the Ethiopian's conversion is very interesting.

Long before Europe became a Christian continent, churches in North Africa and Ethiopia grew into prosperous institutions. It is recognized that Christianity took roots on the mainland of Africa during the first century. In fact the first missionaries were based in Africa and Asia Minor, from which Christianity was carried to the barbaric tribes in Europe.

When the white man began to expand the Christian doctrines in Africa, preaching freedom from sin through the Blood of Christ, Africans found it contradictory and surprising that they brought with them slavery and bondage, which they have been struggling against ever since. It is within the context of this contradiction and the beginning of this process of Christian socialization that the doctrine of suffering and redemption began to take root in the African experience. It has become a strange and complex issue that plagues the church today.

Another contradiction that enhanced the process is suggested by Vernon E. Jordan's observation that "the founding fathers included a dispro-portionate number of slaveholders, including Thomas Jefferson, the man who wrote the immortal words of the Declaration of Independence, 'all men are created equal, that they are endowed by their Creator with certain inalienable rights, that among these are life, liberty, and the pursuit of happiness.'" These contradictions and hypocrisies continued for over a hundred years. Nonetheless, the basic religious belief of Africans in a supreme being as omnipresent, omniscient, and omnipotent continued. All through the oppressive experience of slavery, Afro-Americans demonstrated an unfaltering faith in God, believing that He would one day deliver them out of their misery and distress.

The black church in America was born out of these experiences and within the context of suffering and became the institution in which blacks could find solace from the bitter realities of dehumanization, powerlessness, and racial and economic oppression. W.E.B. Du Bois notes that the power and validity of the church is so far-reaching that its functions are almost political.[5] The activities of such ministers as Gabriel Prosser, Nat Turner, Denmark Vesey, Richard Allen, and many others have displayed the black church as a religiopolitical movement.

The black church was the home of the birth of many national organizations and of the civil rights movement. It has become a most powerful institution because it is a definer of social norms and collective ideas and serves as a bulwark in the shared spiritual experiences of black people. The church has also been a force advocating economic, political, and social mobility for blacks. Gabriel Prosser, Denmark Vesey, and Nat Turner, all of whom were ministers, acknowledged a call by God in a vision to lead black people, as did Moses, from racial and economic bondage to freedom and liberation. The strategy and methods of resistance were clearly defined. They were to resist to the point of death, even the death of their oppressors. Suffering at the hands of the oppressor was not redemptive as far as they were concerned. Freedom was redemptive, and they fought to be free. The failures experienced by these religious leaders forced to consideration the concern to engage the church in political matters, thus demonstrating a commitment to change, within religious doctrines and ideologies and the realities of the racial and economic conditions of black people. This has been the nature of the debate since 1800: What is the most sound and spiritually safe strategy for the church in its role as definer of socioreligious norms and an advocate of freedom and liberation for the oppressed in a capitalist-racist social order?

There were those who believed that God was on the side of Moses and those who left Egypt seeking freedom and liberation from the oppression of Pharaoh. It was God, they argued, who destroyed Pharaoh's army on behalf of the oppressed. On the other hand, there were those who argued that justice would triumph over injustice and that because of the righteousness of their position against oppression, their course would eventually succeed. This position is rooted in the Christian message that one should absorb hatred and transform it through love and endurance rather than inflict violence. Dr. Martin Luther King, Jr., preached that suffering is redemptive and that blacks were to avoid physical and spiritual violence. That is, blacks should refuse to inflict physical violence on whites and should also refuse to hate their oppressors. Moreover, King preached that blacks should be willing to accept violence to themselves without retaliation; to accept blows from their opponents without striking back. The focus of the efforts and struggle of black people should be upon the evil itself, not on the person victimized by evil. The basis for this disposition is love and that history is on the side of justice.

This cultural tradition that established the mood for the church's involvement in liberation struggles was brought into serious question during the late 1960s. No doubt this cultural tradition, with deep religious concepts and emphasis, evoked a reconsideration of the role of the church and the traditional strategies employed that are appropriate and successful in the struggle for freedom and liberation. Whatever strategies were to be developed were to make comfortable the participation of all deeply religious persons. The church experienced a change or underwent a degree of transformation during the changing mood of black people. The ideological unification that resulted confirmed the religiopolitical role in the affairs of black people. It is not so much that the church assumed a new political role in struggle as much as it became very evident that the black church was involved in socioeconomic protestation and was concerned with worldly conditions and issues that affected the presence and religious position of black people. The church continued to find itself in the social center of the affairs of blacks and the spiritual life of the community. Increasingly, preachers were interpreting the Bible in terms of the material conditions of blacks and their spiritual needs.

This role had been a tradition with the church, although it had come in a different form. Preachers would confine their remarks to the Bible, quoting it to provide the context and focus for their concern. They would preach about Jesus and God's activity to deliver the oppressed. They would point out how God punished the wicked and rescued the down-trodden and dominated. They would say: Didn't God deliver Daniel? Didn't He destroy the Pharaoh's army? Didn't he deliver the three Hebrew boys from bondage? Indicating their position on racial equality, black preachers would again quote the Bible, saying: Didn't God create of one blood all nations of men to dwell on all the face of the earth? Didn't He send His son into the world to save all mankind—white and black, yellow and brown and red? Sermons were also preached around the notion of the importance of each person in the sight of God. Preachers would say: Didn't He say that the life of every person is sacred unto God; so much so that every strand of hair on the head is numbered? Didn't He say that not one sparrow falls to the ground without God taking notice and caring? These beliefs sustained the slaves on the plantation, and their songs in the fields spoke of their immediate, planned, and ultimate deliverance. Consequently, the partial victory of emancipation was viewed as an act of God, not of Lincoln, and the result of the Civil War.

To most blacks, suffering not only was redemptive but was thought to be the process of purification for the saints. The various problems and difficulties were thought to be the means by which characters were made strong. In many cases the concern was not for the problems to be removed but rather that strength be provided to endure. The problems appeared necessary to test the endurance of blacks and to establish strong and determined personalities. This is the attitude and disposition powerless and oppressed people tend to assume. The notion is not that the degree to which one suffers is the degree to which one is redeemed. Suffering is redemptive in that it provides the process and mechanism for powerless and oppressed people to survive. The oppressed and powerless could not survive if they did not develop an ability to understand, manage, and endure suffering. It is not an acceptance of suffering but a way of perceiving one's position in relation to the social order, and what is necessary to develop character and personality of endurance.

The church has assisted blacks in the process of character and personality development. Instead of establishing a balance between its role in assisting blacks to survive suffering in the form of racial and economic oppression and its role as an interpreter of the scriptures for spiritual growth for now and eternity, the church focused its attention on character and personality development for endurance in the present. This is the result of the pressure placed on the church and on the college during the 1960s to be relevant. Today the church hardly deals with essential doctrines that are important to liberation for eternity. Even the books written between 1965 and 1975, especially by black theologians, addressed themselves essentially to the necessity of developing character endurance for the present. This pressure is understandable not only because of the traditional role of the church in assisting blacks in struggle but also because the church provided the place for the meetings, discussions, and strategizing for social change. The leadership and the members of the leading churches in the community either became converted to the new theology during such sessions or were converted prior to such times. The church should continue to concern itself with worldly conditions, but it must also teach its members basic doctrinal teachings that are essential to the very purpose and mission of the church. Many preachers have been heard to remark, "We have to learn how to live here on Earth before we learn how to live in Heaven." The confusion is with the notion that suggests that people cannot love a God that they have not seen if they have not or do not love their visible fellowman.

Vincent Harding argues that:

There was a time when we blacks' (well dressed) and whites' voices blended together in accent, recalling the good old days of fighting together for the same cause. Days when Dr. King was a prophet and when we were certain that the civil rights movement was God's message to the church. But now there is a veil between then and now.[6]

The black nationalistic theology with a black God began to dominate the church. Demonstrating its will to live as a meaningful institution in the lives and affairs of black people, the church modified and even became silent on certain doctrines, especially the hell and destruction doctrine, and shifted its focus in an attempt to fulfill the needs of the people.

Black religious leaders were faced with a difficult question. Turn the other cheek and love your enemy were not very popular. How to be a

Christian in a racist social order was a popular but difficult question for religious leaders to address. The answer did not come in terms that advocated suffering as redemptive; rather, Christ had to be seen as being a part of the revolution, in a theology of the oppressed whose aim was to destroy racism in society. Christian obedience was viewed within the context of revolution and liberation. Within the gospel of Christ and otherworldly concerns, intellectuals in the field of theology argued that the church could not alienate its interpretations from the struggle of the oppressed for freedom and liberation and the gospel.

James Cone states: "Christianity begins and ends with Jesus, and his work is essentially one of liberation. Through an encounter with him, man knows the full meaning of God's action in a historical context with man in it."[7] Cone argues that the church has developed an eschatological perspective that adheres to the belief that one's God is totally uninvolved in the suffering of black people. In such a case then, God is preparing black people for another world. Such a perspective is heavenly and other-worldly oriented, and Cone argues that this is a divergence from the realities of life where black people are concerned. The black church is not encouraged to adopt a philosophy that promotes the belief that otherworldly conditions should be the black churches' primary concern of life. Cone suggests that the black church and black theology must present themselves to black people on an earthly basis. Further, they should speak of self-determination here and now on earth, as opposed to concerning itself solely with the earth's inevitable destruction and future state.[8] The gospel cannot be secondary to the experience of black oppression and black liberation. The gospel and the efforts of the black church are inseparable, as both seek to free and liberate black people from racial and economic oppression. We cannot completely divorce liberation from the concepts of Christian theology. There are those religious leaders who firmly believe that the black struggle and suffering is a religious experience.

Black people agree with the authors of the Declaration of Independence who argued that God created human beings with certain inalienable rights, that among these are life, liberty, and the pursuit of happiness. However, blacks question even those who wrote the document and most Americans who act contrary to the concept that God created all persons equal. Thomas Jefferson, one of the writers of the Declaration of Independence, commented on slavery and said, "I tremble for my country when I remember that God is just." Yet, Jefferson did not tremble enough to free the slaves he owned, not wanting to live without the convenience of having them. Because of the contradictory nature of this stance, which is typical of the many contradictions of America relative to the material and racist position of black people, blacks have not come to believe in the intent of America to liberate blacks. Within this context and understanding, the black preacher and the black church have struggled to protect the life, liberty, and the right to pursue happiness that are God-given.

To some people, the black church has not seriously and actively worked for the equality of black people. However, a historical analysis does not support this accusation. What has been the case is that the efforts of the black church and that of the religious leaders in the political and economic arena of the American social order have failed to achieve the desired goals of justice, freedom, and liberation. Those who blame the church and its leaders do not seem to understand the impact of the social order on the efforts of blacks to achieve liberation. The absence of liberation and freedom for black people is not the function of the inability of the church to obtain liberation for blacks. The nature and character of the social, economic, and legal arrangements of the American society provide the context for understanding the failure. What the church has failed to do, however, which might not have been controlled by the social order, is to teach blacks the truth about such crucial doctrines as the "State of the Dead," "The Seal of God," "The Judgment," "The Sanctuary," "Probation," "The Sabbath," "The Law of God," "The Holy Spirit," "Baptism," "Health," and other such teachings in the Bible that are important to the ultimate salvation of black people as Christians. Thousands of blacks who go to church every week believe that the dead do not really die, a deception that motivated the rebellion of Adam and Eve. There are others who eat anything and drink anything as if their bodies were not the temples of God. The church must occupy itself with providing the community with an understanding that it is not possible in a capitalist-racist social order for oppressed people to experience political, economic, and social liberation and freedom. The church's role therefore is to assist individuals in the process of character transformation and the understanding and practice of essential teachings of the gospel so that the nature and character of the social order of America and the world might be fully understood, along with their relationship to it and a sense of their destiny. This responsibility is not being fully demonstrated today by the black church.

The AME church was born out of struggle. But there was a Black Baptist Church in South Carolina in 1793. In 1841, blacks in Richmond, Virginia, established their first Black Baptist Church. The AME Zion Church was also born out of struggle. However, the physical separation did not force blacks to rely on their own interpretations and analysis of the teachings of the scriptures. The very fact that the white alleged Christians refused to accept blacks as their equals before God and refused to accept the black individual as a brother or sister on earth should have raised the suspicions of blacks regarding the religious teachings they shared and accepted from white theologians. That God created all persons equal is a basic teaching of the scriptures. That Christ came to save all persons is also a basic teaching of the gospel. Consequently, a basic doctrine of the scriptures is that all persons who accept the sacrifice of Christ and apply the provisions of grace—pardon and power—are brothers and sisters in Christ. This belief and meaning of the death of Christ provide the basis for Christian interaction, fellowship, and worship.

If black people are to be ultimately liberated and experience some degree of individual freedom here on earth, truths regarding the essential teachings of the scriptures must be made clear. The false teachings that they now embrace must be corrected, or their experience now will be oppression and then it will be destruction. It is the church's responsibility as the instrument and agency of God to provide a correct understanding of the teachings of the scriptures, at the same time providing the psychological, social, and even the economic resources for the survival process and the endurance of suffering, which is a process of character purification. The challenge to the social order of America and the world is performed within the context of these responsibilities and the understanding of the destiny of mankind. "It is appointed unto man once to die, and after this the judgment."

The black church has been accused of not involving itself in the black community. It has also been criticized for worshiping as it has been taught by the white church. The criticism and debate regarding the role of the black church provide an opportunity for the church to synthesize its worldly and otherworldly functions and responsibilities. The black church cannot be either, or; it has to perform both. The role of the black preacher simply expands within the expansion of the role of the church. It means, however, that the black preacher not only must learn how to develop and deliver a sermon but also must be a scholar of the scriptures.

The church cannot succeed preaching false doctrines and focusing primarily upon the here and now. To continue in this practice means greater oppression and exploitation. The black church cannot continue to fail to comprehend the physical as well as the spiritual nature and character of human beings. The church must not negate the physical and material needs of black people while addressing their spititual needs. Ultimate salvation and liberation is inseparable from historical liberation and freedom. Any gospel that speaks the Truth of God in the black community must deal with the issues of life here and now as well as with the transcendent dimension of the proclamation.[9]

The black church has historically involved itself in the struggle for freedom from injustice, racism, and oppression. This has always been an essential part of its defined task. M. Shawn Copeland in "The Atlanta Statement" said:

The Black church, then, must reject a ministry concerned with institutional trivia if it is to be authenticator of the community and if it is to be authenticated by the community. In other words, the Black church must continue to be a servant church engaged in the concrete tasks of black life and liberation. The Black church must continue to provide an institutional framework for the political/social/economic/educational struggles of its people lest that same church be guilty of the sin of failing to fight against injustice, of absenting itself from the liberation task.[10]

The white church has condemned, for the most part, the efforts of the black church in its struggle for freedom and liberation, arguing that such a focus is un-American and un-Christian. Such efforts are, however, not a contradiction of Christian love. They are the sociopolitical expression of the truth of the gospel of Christ. There is no question then of the theological legitimacy of the role of the black church in the historical struggle of black people for freedom.

James H. Cone, in his attempt to explain why many black theologians and preachers had difficulty accepting the concept of black power, argues that:

Many of us had been trained in white seminaries and had internalized much of white people's definition of Christianity. While the rise and growth of independent black churches suggested that black people had a different perception of the gospel than whites; yet there was no formal theological tradition to which we could turn in order to justify our definition of Black Power as an expression of the Christian gospel. Our intellectual ideas of God, Jesus, and the church were derived from white European theologians and their textbooks. When we speak of Christianity in the theological categories, using such terms as revelation, incarnation and reconciliation, we naturally turn to people like Barth, Tillich and Bultmann for guidance and direction. But these Europeans did not shape their ideas in the social context of white racism and thus could not help us out of our dilemma. But if we intended to fight on a theological and intellectual level as a way of empowering our historical and political struggle for justice, we had to create a new theological movement, one that was derived from and thus accountable to our people's fight for justice. To accept Black Power as Christian required that we thrust ourselves into our history in order to search for new ways to think and to be black in this world. We felt the need to explain ourselves and to be understood from our own vantage point and not from the perspective and experiences of whites. When white liberals questioned this approach to theology, our response was very similar to the bluesman in Mississippi when told he was not singing his song correctly: "Look-a-heah, man, dis yere mah song, en I'll sing it howsoevah I pleases."[11]

The black church must be the model of the creative integration of the struggle for justice and the theology of truth. This integration expresses the necessary praxis of the experiences of black people and the socioreligious reality of the gospel. Only as truth is presented to black people can they make sense out of their struggle for freedom in this present world and ultimate liberation in the world to come.

Every week black people gather together in churches of all sizes and shapes in various locations in the community to understand their destiny and the significance of the teachings of the scriptures to their present condition. The dream of freedom on earth and gaining entrance to the promised land constitute their deepest concerns. The church has attempted to expand its role in order to achieve these goals and has demonstrated its commitment to the struggle for liberation of the oppressed. However, the failure of the black church to secure freedom and liberation for black people in spite of its history of struggle, and the apparent incompatibility of black theology and the Western theological tradition have caused most blacks, especially young blacks, to raise questions such as—Will we reach the Promised Land? How will we get there? The black church and black people will not reach the Promised Land promulgating half-truths to their people. In so doing the church will deny its faith and guarantee its destruction as a source of spiritual and religious power and direction to black people, committed to the liberation of the oppressed. The black church will be a hindrance to black liberation not only because of its weakened position relative to its interest in raising money for new buildings and its reduced involvement in the struggle for liberation and freedom on earth but also because of its failure to correct many of the false teachings it has accepted from white churches.

From David Walker to Martin L. King, Jr., the black church has had a rich tradition in struggle, reacting to racism, protesting the economic, political, legal, and social injustices that dominate the lives of black people. But little attention has been given to what black people know to be true concerning many of the essential teachings of the scripture.

State of the Dead

A few examples will demonstrate this point. The story is told of a pastor who received a telephone call at about 1:10 one morning from a woman whose husband he had buried weeks before. "Can you and your wife come to my house immediately? Something awful has just happened!" The pastor and his wife quickly dressed and made it over as fast as they could to the home of the woman. They were ushered into her bedroom. "Pastor, he, or maybe I should say it, was standing right at the door where you just entered, and then he sat down in the chair where you are now sitting. He looked and talked just like John when he came home from work, with his hat in his hand and his coat over his arm. His voice was just like John's! He wanted to know if I got the full payment check from the insurance company to pay all the funeral expenses, and if I paid off the house mortgage. He also wanted to know if I had been feeding Birdie, the dog, regularly, and if I got all the matters cleared up at the bank about our savings and checking account." Then the woman confessed that, "I looked John straight in the face and said, 'What a dirty trick for you to try and play on me, a widow, Satan. In the name of Jesus, get out of here for you know the living knows that they shall die, but the dead know not anything!' '' The widow knew that dead men don't talk. However, a large number of black people who attend church every week do not really know that fact. They believe that their grandmothers, grandfathers, mothers, and fathers who have died are in heaven. In many instances, the belief extends itself to a position where it is thought that the kind of life and beliefs experienced by these relatives are sufficient for them.

The Bible is the standard of conduct for black Christians and should be used for information, direction, and testing of every belief. The scripture states, for example, in Ecclesiastes 12:7, "Then shall the dust return to the earth as it was: and the Spirit shall return unto God who gave it." This does not suggest that the spirit of the body given to man at his creation roams around the earth paying visits to relatives and friends. The dead are dead and do not come back (Revelation 16:14; Job 7:9, 10). The Bible states that when one dies he/she decays and returns to dust. His/her respiration stops, and his/her spirit or breath returns to the control of God. Nowhere in the 379 instances that spirit is used in the Bible does it denote an intelligent entity or personality capable of existence apart from a physical body so far as man is concerned. Teachings that suggest that a conscious portion of man keeps thinking, communicating, or reasoning after death are unscriptural and unbiblical. Further, in Psalm 146:4, the point is made plain that when a person dies "His breath goeth forth, he returneth to his earth; in that very day his thoughts perish." Consequently, if the breath leaves him/her the person cannot think, nor can he/she talk. All mental functions discontinue at death.

Those who preach and believe that persons go to heaven or some place else upon death are also suggesting the immortality of the individual at the time of death. The Bible teaches that immortality will be given only to those who have practiced a living and loving obedience to the gospel, and even then, it will not be conferred upon these obedient persons until the resurrection of the righteous dead, which takes place at the second coming of Christ (1 Thessalonians 4:16, 17). Nowhere in the scriptures is there any teaching that the soul is immortal. In all the passages that mention the term it is not spoken of as being "neverdying," or conscious apart from the body.

The Bible teaches that "the Lord God formed man of the dust of the ground and breath in him the breath of life and man became a living soul" (Genesis 2:7). The soul of man, therefore, consists of two basic elements: the dust of the ground, which is the body of muscles, organs, glands, tissues, and bones, and the basic living electrical current found in the breath of life, which only God can give and which permits an immobile collection of orderly placed muscles, organs, tissues, glands, and bones known as a body, to come alive and respirate, circulate, and intellectually inspire air, blood, chemicals, and thoughts. A living soul, therefore, is a body consisting of the essential parts of the body plus the breath of life. Similarly, it is the properly organized parts of the automobile plus the electrical and chemical power of a battery and fuel that constitute a running (living) automobile. When these elements are not combined we have a dead automobile. When the breath of life is removed man becomes a dead soul. It is not until the resurrection of the righteous from their graves at the second coming of Jesus in the clouds of heaven that the righteous are given eternal life and are taken physically, bodily, literally to heaven as living never-dying souls (II Thessalonians 4:16-17).

Jesus made it clear in John 11:25, by declaring, "I am the resurrection and the life: He that believeth in Me, though he were dead, yet shall be live." It is a clear contradiction to believe that the dead are not in their graves. What need would there be for Christ to return and have a resurrection? In John 14:2, 3 Christ said, "I go to prepare a place for you, I will come again, and receive you unto Myself; that where I am, there ye may be also." There would be no need for this trip if we will be there upon death. Satan and his angels are upon the earth imitating the form and sound of the dead, perpetuating the false belief that the dead are not dead. But the scriptures are clear that dead people do not come back to talk with their friends and loved ones. Black people should know the truth about the state of the dead.

Laws of Health

According to some recent data, there are approximately 13,000 people in the United States who are 100 years of age or older. About two-thirds are women; 75 percent are white, the other 25 percent of various other racial categories. About 80 percent of this population are farmers for a significant portion of their lives. They give a number of reasons for their long lives, including "following the Ten Commandments," "looking on the bright side of life," "trusting in the Lord to give health and strength," and "working hard, being active in community affairs, and eating sensibly."

The Bible records the fact that persons lived almost 1000 years, like Methuselah who lived to be 969 years old.

Given the statistics on the longevity of blacks, the church must teach black people the ordained laws of health. If blacks want to live healthily and have long lives, they must obey the laws of health for their bodies. By living out of harmony with these laws, the inevitable result is ill health, sickness, disease, and finally premature death. The reason that there is so much sickness, disease, and suffering is largely that people are disobedient to the laws of health, either ignorantly or knowingly. Many suffer because of errors in regard to diet.

Even though what Christians eat or drink has much to do with their religion, very little is heard by the church regarding health and the importance of obeying the laws of health. The Bible argues that Christians have no right to eat or drink as they please. "Whether therefore ye eat, or drink, or whatsoever you do, do all to the glory of God" (I Corinthians 10:31). What one puts into the body through food and drink has much to do with the soul.

In the first book of the Bible (Gen. 1:29) the statement is recorded: "And God said, Behold, I have given you every herb-bearing seed (grains and rice, wheat, oats, beans) which is upon the face of the earth, and every tree (fruit trees) in which is the fruit of a tree yielding seeds (nuts); to you it shall be for meat." This is the diet God pronounced as good for mankind. This was the original diet consisting of *fruits*, *grains*, and *nuts*. In Gen. 9:3-5, diary products were added to the diet. God did not permit man to eat the flesh of animals until after the Flood. It became necessary to clarify to mankind what animals, fish, and fowl are fit for food. In this regard, two chapters of the Bible (Lev. 11; Deut. 14) are devoted to making clear this matter. Again, very little attention is given to the directions given in these chapters by black churches.

An animal that is commonly eaten by many black people, and especially black Christians, today that is condemned as unfit for food is the swine. "And the swine (pig, hog), because it devideth the hoof, yet cheweth not the cud, it is unclean unto you: Ye shall not eat of this flesh, nor touch their dead carcass" (Deuteronomy 14:8). God has permitted man to eat the flesh of sheep, cows, deer, and any other animals which "parteth the hoof and cheweth the cud." Such animals as the rabbit, possum, and squirrel are condemned along with the hog (Deuteronomy 13:3-8). All fish that have fins and scales are pronounced good for food, but such creatures as catfish, eels, lobsters, oysters, clams, and shrimp are directly condemned as not good food for mankind.

Many black Christians do not really know why the pig is unclean and unfit for food. As Christians, they should accept it as fact because God said it is unclean, but pork is also frequently infected with microscopic worms or parasites, known as trichinae, which produce a disease known as trichinosis in those who eat pork products. Normal cooking and government inspection do not eliminate the danger of getting trichinosis from pork.

Public health officials in Washington, D.C., suggest that: "Sicknesses that are called typhoid fever, intestinal flu, malaria, rheumatism, heart disease, intercostal neuritis, and many other diseases are nothing but thousands of these little worms encased throughout the muscles of the bodies." Christians, of all persons, should know and follow the health instructions of God who said that the swine (hog, bacon, fatback, pork chops, ham, etc.) is not good for human beings to eat. The pig has its function. God placed the animal on earth as a four-footed garbage can to clean up the earth; instead, human beings are cleaning him up, especially black Christians. There are many individuals who have come to the understanding of this fact on the basis of medical information and data. Black Christians had this information long before medical and public health experts came to this understanding. Yet, thousands of such Christians continue to buy, cook, eat, and share such unclean food with others, including their children. Jesus' death was to clean up mankind, not the swine. The swine will remain ''unclean until Jesus comes back with chariots (or angels) like a whirlwind.'' The scriptures teach that those who are found eating the pig's flesh would ''be consumed together, said the Lord'' (Isaiah 66:15-17; Revelation 18:2).

Some persons argue that Peter's vision of the great sheet with all types of animals and creeping things teaches that no animal should be called common or unclean. The vision recorded in Acts 10:1-35; 11:1-8, was not to tell Peter to eat swine and other unclean food. The vision was to teach Peter that racism had no place in the plan of salvation and that racial inequalities should not exist in the Christian church because God was utterly displeased with racial bigotry. Peter learned when he met Cornelius that God was telling him to stop calling Gentiles (Blacks, Indians and non-Jews, etc.) common and unclean (Acts 10:28).

Black Christians are confused regarding the use of intoxicating beverages and tobacco. The Bible condemns the use of beer, wine, hard cider, whiskey, gin, moonshine, and other such liquors. Paul suggests that ''Wine is a mocker, strong drink is raging: and whosoever is deceived thereby is not wise (Proverbs 20:1; 23:29-35). In Cor. 6:10 Solomon advises the Christian not to touch, handle, or taste such drinks. Drinks such as cola, tea, and coffee are also dangerous because they contain a poisonous alkaloid known as caffeine. The Bible is also clear in its condemnation of Christians who use tobacco for smoking, chewing, and dipping. The Bible states that the Lord will not spare the individual that useth ''a root'' (rosh, or poisonous weed). In Deut. 29:18-20 it is stated: ''. . . and all the curses that are written in this book shall lie upon him, and the Lord shall blot out his name from under Heaven.'' Five of the worst curses found anywhere in the Bible are pronounced upon these who knowingly defile their bodies with this ''weed'' tobacco, for tobacco is neither a fruit or a vegetable. It is what God called it—a poisonous weed. Snuff is called ''wickedness'' in the mouth (Job 20:12-15). The Bible condemns opium, morphine, marijuana, LSD, glue, banana peelings, and all drugs used as dopes. Tobacco gives heart trouble, cancer, jumpy nerves, short wind, high blood pressure, Bright's disease, ulcers of the stomach, tumors, and a guarantee of a slow suicide. Black people should be encouraged to practice drinking plenty of fresh water, exercise moderately each day, get as much fresh air as possible, eat sparingly, avoid agitation, eat regular well-balanced meals, including fresh fruits, nuts, vegetables, and some dairy products, and get to six to eight hours or more of sleep nightly.

The health of black people is essential to their struggle for freedom and liberation. Jesus paid attention to the health of those who were physically sick, but He paid attention also to those who were spiritually sick. The black church and the black preacher must also assume the role of attending to the health needs of black people. Most of the information just discussed is not discussed in the churches, and the members have not been taught that these are the health laws they must follow for socioreligious reasons if they are to experience freedom and liberation.

The Moral Law

Thousands of black Christians believe that the law of God was "done away with" at the cross, and their preachers continue to perpetuate the lie, not understanding the differences among the three laws described in the Bible.

There are the Ten Commandments, usually referred to as the moral law and the decalogue; the ceremonial laws, often thought of as the law of Moses, describing ritualistic ordinances; and the civil code, which embodies ordinances of health and sanitation. Most black preachers experience difficulty distinguishing among these laws and usually confuse the moral law with the ceremonial laws.

It is important to note that the moral law or Ten Commandments are the eternal code for conduct that God himself wrote (Exodus 20:1-17; 24:12; 32:15,16). As the process of character development is the primary process of socialization for Christians, the law serves as a guide designed to govern the conduct of created beings for all times. Furthermore, the code is a reflection of the character of God (Psalm 103:17-20; John 14:10). In the scripture the moral law is described as being perfect (Psalm 19:7), spiritual (Romans 7:14), holy and just and good (Romans 7:12), righteous (Psalm 119:172), and truth (Psalm 119:142, 151).

The Ten Commandments stress, in the first four commandments, man's relationship and duty to God, and in the last six, man's relationship and duty to human beings (Matthew 22:37-40). The moral law is, therefore, the embodiment of love to God and love to mankind.

Even though the moral law has no power to save an individual, its function is to reveal sin to mankind and point the transgressor to the Saviour, Jesus. Sin is the transgression of the Ten Commandments and it separates the sinner from God. A recognition of this fact in a specific way, relative to the moral law, causes the transgressor to seek forgiveness. The moral law is a guide that transgressors may employ to come to Christ and salvation (Matthew 19:16, 19; Romans 7:7-10). In the final analysis, the Ten Commandments are the standard of judgment. The character of human beings will have to measure up to the character of God. This is the reason that Jesus came, to vindicate the character of God as revealed in the Ten Commandments and to provide pardon and power (Grace) so that human beings could accomplish ultimate liberation and freedom. The citizen is free when not a violator of the law of the land. However, the citizen will soon be found under the jurisdiction of the law when it is violated. Sin separates the individual from God. Put another way, we might say that the violation of the Ten Commandments separates the individual from God, as sin is the transgression of God's law. Paul argues that we would not even know sin except by the law.

The ceremonial ordinances governed ritualistic festivities in Israel with all of their "holy convocations," "sabbaths," "new moons," and "sacrifices and offerings." God commanded Moses to write these laws *in a book* even though they were dictated to Moses by God (Deuteronomy 31:24-26; Leviticus 1:1-3).

Three great ordinances frequently called feasts had one or two ceremonial holy days celebrated annually by all males in Israel (Exodus 12:14-17; 43; 13:3-10; Deuteronomy 16:16). These feasts with their ceremonial sabbaths and the laws governing them were described for them (Leviticus 23). The laws governing sacrifices and offerings, for example, are detailed in Leviticus 6:8, 9, 14, 25; 7:1, 7, 11, 37, 38.

The first great feast was called Passover and alternately Feast of Unleavened Bread. This feast was celebrated on the fourteenth of the month Abid, which was the first month of the Hebrew religious calendar (Leviticus 24:4-8; Deuteronomy 16:1-3). The first and the last days of this week of celebrations were called holy convocation and no "servile work" was done. These convocations were *ceremonial sabbaths* of rest that fell on specific dates within the month, not on the seventh day of the week as do the weekly sabbaths. Moreover, specified sacrifices and offerings were required on each day of the convocations (Leviticus 23:4-8; 6:9-13).

The Passover was significant because it reminded Israel of its deliverance from bondage in Egypt, and it was a demonstration of the final deliverance of the people of God from the bondage of sin (Hebrews 8-10).

The second great festivity, which was called Pentecost, came on the sixth of Sivan during the time of the first spring harvest in Palestine. This day was a one-day ceremonial sabbath to remind Israel of its total dependence upon Jehovah for temporal and spiritual sustenance.

The Feast of Tabernacles, also called the Feast of Harvest and the Feast of Ingathering, was Israel's third great festive celebration. It was the most joyful occasion of the year because the year's fruits from the vineyard, orchard, and field were safely in storage for the families. Tribes would assemble outside their habitations and tabernacles in branch-covered booths to celebrate and rejoice because of the bountiful blessings of God during the year. On the first and last days of this feast, the fifteenth and twenty-second of the seventh month (Tishri), special ceremonial sabbaths of rest were kept, and specified sacrifices and offerings were presented to God. The significance of this ordinance was to memorialize Israel's life in the wilderness wandering during the exodus from Egypt. It also pointed to the final ingathering of people redeemed from sin in paradise (Leviticus 23:34-43).

The day of atonement was the most awesome of Israel's convocations, which fell on the tenth day of the seventh month. This solemn convocation is still celebrated by faithful Hebrews as Yom Kippur. It is regarded as sacred above all ceremonial sabbaths. The dramatic solemnities of this holiest of days reminded the Hebrews of the final judgment, when all mankind would be irrevocably consigned to eternal life or death. All Israelites participated in this sabbath celebration or were "cut off" from among God's people (Leviticus 23:27-32). A holy day of blowing of trumpets always preceded the day of atonement. This day was called Rosh Hashanah or New Year and regarded as a special ceremonial sabbath. It was a reminder of the approach of Yom Kippur and the beginning of the Hebrew civil year (Leviticus 23:24).

There were other festive ordinances during which Israelites celebrated ceremonial sabbaths (Numbers 10:10; 28:11-14; Ezekiel 46:1-6, 14; Leviticus 25:1-16). All of the laws and statutes governing the various festive ordinances, feasts, convocations, rites, ceremonies, and sacrifices were contained in the book of ceremonial laws that Moses wrote (Leviticus 7:37, 38; 9:3; Numbers 15:1-3, 15, 16). This book of laws was not kept in the inner chamber of God's Ark of the Covenant, where the law written by God on tables of stone was housed. The moral law of God was in the inner chamber of the ark and the ceremonial laws were in a side compartment of the ark. The rites and ceremonies practiced by the Hebrews in the religious festivities were intended to reveal various facets of Messiah's ministry as Priest and Sacrifice, Substitute and Saviour. The entire system of sacrifices and offerings foreshadowed Jesus' redemptive sacrifice on Calvary and dramatized His ministry for the salvation of mankind on earth and in Heaven (Hebrew 8:1-3, 6-8; 9:22-26; 10:1-22).

When the true sacrifice for man's redemption was made on the cross of Calvary, type met antitype and all shadows dissolved and faded into reality. Consequently, there was no longer any need for the ceremonial system. The ceremonial law contained in ordinance was nailed to the cross and came to an end (Exodus 12:43, 49; Numbers 15:14, 15; Colossians 2:14-17; Ephesians 2:14-16). The Ten Commandments containing its weekly seventh-day Sabbath of rest is meant to stand fast forever here on earth and eternally in the new earth (Psalms 111:7, 8; 119-44; Isaiah 66:22, 23).

The plan of salvation was dramatized to the Israelites in the handwriting of ordinances contained in commandments of rites and ceremonies. It was a foreshadow of the ultimate sacrifice of Jesus required to make salvation from sin a reality. The moral law of the Ten Commandments is eternal, showing the love relationship that is to exist between mankind and God and mankind and mankind, and revealing sin and the need of a Saviour.

The Judgment Process

Many black people believe that the judgment is a time after death when God will sit down in a big chair and have each person come before His throne in a line to argue his/her case for entrance into eternal life. The enemy of the souls of black people (Satan) is delighted to have the oppressed believe half-truths. Black preachers should be prepared to teach and preach the truth whether the congregation believes and practices it or not. The responsibility and obligation of the preacher is to deliver the truth to the people. It is the duty of the people to examine the truth and accept it, practice it, and share it with other oppressed peoples.

The Bible does speak of a judgment coming to all of us. Everyone who has ever lived in this world will stand trial at this judgment. In fact, this judgment is presently in session; and if black preachers are not teaching their congregations about the nature, character, and intent of such a process, they are denying and depriving the people of one of the most important biblical messages for these times. This judgment session will settle the question of ultimate liberation for the oppressed and downtrodden. The preliminary investigative stage of the judgment is going on presently, and thousands of black people are unaware of its purpose and significance. The Bible states, "It is appointed unto men once to die, but after this the judgment" (Hebrews 9:27). Thus, the most awe-inspiring event the human mind can contemplate is the setting of the Supreme Court of the Universe, where the eternal destiny of every soul is decided once and for all. II Corinthians 5:10 states, "For we must all appear before the judgment seat of Christ; that everyone may receive the things done in his body, according to that he hath done whether it be good or bad." This judgment session is of vital importance to every human being, because the judgment decides the case of every person for everlasting life or everlasting destruction. The judgment means life or destruction for everyone and should be discussed and understood by all persons in the community. The judgement settles once and for all the most important matter of life—that of the destiny of mankind. Black people need to learn about the judgment session and to understand what they might do that their cases may be decided for eternal happiness.

The judgment of the righteous precedes the second advent of Jesus. In I Peter 4:17 the Bible says, "For the time is come that judgment must begin at the house of God; And if it begin at us, what shall the end be of them that obey not the gospel of God." In this text, the house of God means the professed followers of God or the members of the church. The text also suggests that the cases of the professedly righteous are judged before the cases of the wicked. One of the important parts of the judgment of the righteous will take place in the court of heaven before Christ comes.

It is clear in I Corinthians 15:51-54 and I Thessalonians 4:16, 17, that at the very moment that Christ appears at His second advent, the faithful among those who have died will be instantly raised to immortality. The faithful ones among the living upon the earth will be changed in the twinkling of an eye to be immortal, or not subject to death. This fulfills the promise made by Jesus to his followers in John 14:3. This, however, shows conclusively that before Christ comes the second time, decisions will have been made as to who among the dead and the living are entitled to immortality. It also indicates that the cases of the professed righteous must be processed one by one, and judged during the closing era prior to the appearing of Christ, at the last days. From all indications, relative to the signs of the time, the last days are now.

The phase of the judgment would be known as the investigative phase or an examination of the evidence at the trial of each person now going on in the sanctuary in heaven. The executive phase of the judgment takes place when the decision is made effective for the righteous of "not guilty"— accepted/forgiven—at the second advent of Christ.

The people of the earth have been notified when the first part of the judgment began in Heaven as recorded in Revelation 14:6, 7. "And I saw another angel fly in the midst of Heaven having the everlasting gospel to preach unto them that dwell on the earth, and to every nation, and kindred and tongue and people, saying with a loud voice, Fear God, and give glory to Him; for the hour of His judgement is come." This prophecy indicates that in the last days God would raise up a people who would tell the world that the judgment *is* in session in heaven, and would show them how to prepare for it by fearing God and keeping *all* of His commandments and having faith in the imminent advent of Jesus. It is important to realize that the Bible does not say the judgment has come, or will come, but *is* come; meaning that the investigational judgment of reviewing every person is to be in session in heaven while individuals hear this message preached. The judgment-hour message, according to Revelation 14:6-12, has four special features of the truth for the last days that mankind must know. The first is the acknowledgement of God as Creator; the second is the call to God's people to come out of the false religious system of worship known as Babylon; the third is a warning against the reception of the Mark of the Beast or obedience to the anti-commandment power, and the fourth is the call to keep the commandments of God and the faith of Jesus. This message of the judgment began to be preached in the year 1844, or at the end of the longest-time prophecy of Daniel. "Until two thousand three hundred days (or years), then shall the sanctuary be cleansed" (Daniel 8:14). The only thing that defiles heaven at this moment is the record of the unconfessed sins of mankind; and this God began cleansing or cleaning up in the investigative judgment now going on in heaven. God told Daniel to count from the time His people got out of slavery, or October 22, 457 B.C., over 2300 years to October 22, 1844, and then God would start sweeping heaven clean of the record of sin.

To fully understand the cleaning session of the heavenly sanctuary, chapters 25 through 30 of Exodus should be carefully studied. During every day of the year but one, the service of the sanctuary had to do with the first apartment. The Ten Commandments law within the ark in the most holy place demanded the life of the sinner (I John 3:4; Romans 6:23). Thus the sinner, recognizing his guilt, brought his offering. Then laying his hands upon the head of the innocent victim representing the Christ to come, he confessed his sin, the animal was slain, and its blood put on the horns of the altar and poured at the foot of the altar. Thus the sins of all who confessed were pardoned, and in type transferred to the sanctuary. On the day of atonement the sanctuary was cleansed of the blood record of sins confessed during the year. The only ones passing the test of this yearly judgment day were those who had confessed every known sin. In a service strictly conforming to God's instructions, the high priest took the blood of the Lord's goat into the most holy place, where the visible presence of God appeared. The sprinkling of the blood there transferred the sins to the high priest in type, after which he cleansed the outer apartment and then transferred the guilt to the goat, representing the one responsible for all sin, Azazel or Satan. The goat was then loosed in a desert place, a "land of forgetfulness."

The heavenly sanctuary is to be cleansed of the record of sins before Jesus returns. The event that marked the beginning of this cleansing is recorded in Daniel 9:25 and Ezra 7:8-10.

In the seventh chapter of Ezra the decree is found in verses 12-26. In its completest form it was issued by Artaxerxes, King of Persia, 457 B.C. But in Ezra 6:14 the house of the Lord at Jerusalem is said to have been built "according to the commandment (decree, margin) of Cyrus, and Darius and Artaxerxes King of Persia." These three kings, in originating, reaffirming, and completing the decree, brought it to the perfection required by the prophecy to mark the beginning of the 2300 years (See Figure 5). Taking 457 B.C., the time when the decree was completed, as the date of the commandment, every specification of the prophecy concerning the seventy weeks was said to have been fulfilled.

From the going forth of the commandment to restore and to build Jerusalem unto the Messiah the Prince shall be seven weeks, and threescore and two weeks"—namely sixty-nine weeks, 483 years. The decree of Artaxerxes went into effect in the autumn

Figure 5. EARTHLY SANCTUARY

Unto 2,300 days; Then shall the Sanctuary be cleansed.

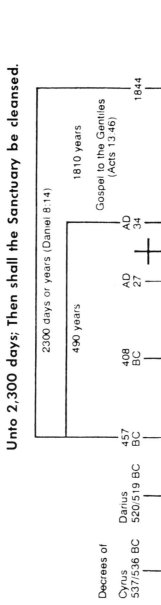

2300 days or years (Daniel 8:14)

1810 years

490 years

Gospel to the Gentiles
(Acts 13:46)

Decrees of

| Cyrus 537/536 BC | Darius 520/519 BC | 457 BC | 408 BC | AD 27 | AD 34 | 1844 |

| | | Decree of Artaxerxes for rebuilding city (Ezra 7:12) | Jerusalem finished and Jewish state restored (Ezra 7:26) | Baptism of Christ (Mt 3:15) | Church persecuted (Acts 8:4) | "The hour of his judgment is come" (Rev 14:7) | God's full message to go to all the world (Mt 24:14; Rev 14:6) |

These were for the building of the temple, which was finished March 12, 515 BC (Ezra 6:15) of 457 B.C. From this date, 483 years extend to the autumn of A.D. 27. At that time prophecy was fulfilled.[12]

The close of the 70 weeks or 490 years ended in A.D. 34, when the Jews officially rejected the gospel by stoning Stephen, and the gospel went to the Gentiles. The 490 years extended to A.D. 34, and only 1810 years were left. Adding the 1810 years left of the 2300 years brings the end of the prophecy in 1844. The angel Gabriel said that at the close of the 2300 years in 1844 the cleansing of the heavenly sanctuary, or day of judgment, will begin.

Just as the Ten Commandments were the measure by which judgment was executed in the earthly sanctuary, so is it the measure for judgment in the heavenly sanctuary. James says (2:8-12), "So speak ye, and so do, as they that shall be judged by the law of Liberty." The Ten Commandments is the test in the judgment in relation to the death of Jesus. The book of life will be opened "and the dead will be judged out of those things which were written in the books, according to their works" (Revelation 20:12).

The only lawyer who can practice before the bar of God in the Christian's behalf is Jesus. John 7:1 says, "If any man sin (transgress the Ten Commandments, the moral law) we have an advocate (lawyer) with the father, Jesus Christ the righteous."

Black people must know that the judgment process is in session and ultimate freedom and liberation can be assured them.

If black preachers would study and teach carefully the purpose and process of the earthly sanctuary, they would assist black people in understanding the purpose and process of the heavenly sanctuary and the work that Christ is presently engaged in. There are those who are convinced that Jesus is in heaven building mansions rather than believing that his work in the most holy place of the heavenly sanctuary is to assure that the sanctuary is cleansed of sins recorded in the book so that the names of the faithful might be recorded in the book of life. This assurance is secured when Christians confess and forsake, through forgiveness or pardon and power, their sins for which Christ died.

Conclusion

The religious experience of black people in America has enhanced the social, economic, and political survival and progress of black people and their community. The socioreligious significance of the gospel has sustained black people through times of bitter struggle against racism and oppression. In many instances, the distinction between the oppressor-racist and oppression-racism as behavior has been made. However, there is much work to be done to allow for the distinction between suffering and redemption. Suffering merely because of the economic, political, and legal acts of racism and oppression is not redemptive. Such acts should be fought, within the context of the distinction between the persons and their acts, for the purpose of liberation and freedom. Suffering for the sake of the gospel, and one's religious position, in relation to such suffering is redemptive.

The black church has played a significant role in assisting black people through the torture chambers of racism and oppression. It has preached a gospel that calls for humanizing individuals and defines each person as important and significant. The church has spoken to the situation of the disposed, the disinherited, and the powerless and has brought significance to the lives of the majority of black people. But the church's responsibility to black people extends to the promotion of truths that are now not taught or given little or no attention. Principles of health as taught in the Bible, the state of the dead, the moral and ceremonial laws, the judgment, and several other issues of religious significance to the ultimate liberation of black people should be dealt with in the church.

It is clear that black churchmen and black churches have involved themselves in one way or another in the struggle for black liberation in this present world situation. What is not clear is their commitment to teaching all of the truths of the Bible for the total and eternal freedom and liberation of black people.

The religious experience of black people must continue to embrace the task of challenging racism and oppression; and the church must continue to provide the institutional context for black people to struggle against injustices. Practices of racism, oppression, and injustice are condemned in the Bible as sinful, and the task of liberation is defined as sacred. While the church seeks to fulfill its responsibility to black liberation, it must also assume the responsibility for teaching the truth about the issues discussed in this chapter that are not now given much attention. The admonition is that blacks should fear Him who is able to kill body and soul, not him who can destroy only the body.

Notes

1. Carrie Hunter, *IFCO News*, Vol. 5 (September-October, 1974).

2. Robert Staples, *Introduction to Black Sociology* (New York: McGraw-Hill. 1976), p. 152.

3. Geoffrey Parrinder, *Religion in Africa*, pp. 21, 34, 40.

4. Ibid., p. 28.

5. W.E.B. Du Bois, "The Function of the Negro Church," in *he Black Church in America*, ed. Hart M. Nelson, Raytha L. Yokely, and Anne K. Nelson (New York: Basic Books, 1971), pp. 77-78.

6. Vincent Harding, "Black Power and the American Christ" in *The Black Power Revolt*, ed. Floyd B. Barbour (Boston: Porter Sargent Publishers, 1968), p. 90.

7. James H. Cone, *Black Theology and Black Power* (New York: Seabury Press, 1969), p. 34.

8. Ibid. p. 123.

9. Benjamin Chavis, et. al., "Message To The Black Church and Community," *Cross Current* 27, no. 2 (1977), p. 141.

10. Ibid., p. 145.

11. Ibid., p. 149. Cited in Lawrence W. Levine, *Black Culture and Black Consciousness* (New York: Oxford University Press, 1977), p. 207.

12. Ellen G. White, *Christ in His Sanctuary* (Mountain View, California: Pacific Publishing Co., 1969), 56. See also P. 54-58.

9

Political Participation and Economic Benefits

Kwame Nkrumah's famous saying is "Seek ye first the political Kingdom and all other things shall be added unto it," but Afro-Americans have come to realize that even in the face of some degree of political control of various institutions in their community, the neocolonial economic stranglehold that has forced an extralegal political subservience upon the community continues to exist.

Afro-Americans have come to view the political arena as the most powerful place to achieve political and economic equality for the masses of black people and their community. Soon after 1863 Afro-Americans sought to organize politically to bring economic value to their material condition, but the economic benefits from political participation have been slow and hard in coming. Certain gains have been identifiable since 1863, but political participation of blacks in the political arena of America has not significantly changed the oppressive conditions of the majority of blacks. The bargaining position of blacks has not been a national threat to those who control the political process and institutions, nor has significant national representation been voted in by blacks. Even those blacks elected by blacks have found it extremely difficult to translate political participation into economic benefits. The benefits derived from the Carter administration have not been encouraging, even when we compare the number of individual black appointments to federal jobs with the previous administrations of the Republican party. Black voters have to be encouraged to vote.

In local politics in many states during the mid-1860s, especially in Alabama, Florida, Mississippi, South Carolina, and Louisiana where blacks outnumbered white voters, black participation in politics achieved a number of benefits. Public schools were established, strong civil rights policies were adopted, and blacks were elected to the U.S. Senate and began to make the political process accountable to the masses of black people. However, by 1898 several measures were employed in several states to curtail the political and economic benefits that had come to blacks from their direct participation. The understanding clause, the poll tax, the good character clause, and the grandfather clause were measures designed to limit and control black participation in politics. Since this period and as early as 1870, blacks entered into heated debates regarding the right to vote and the most effective use of the votes of black people. Black officials elected between 1870 and 1901 were not only concerned with their racial and material conditions. These loyal Republicans supported such things as soldiers' pensions, internal improvements, and federal aid to education; they fought for the rights of Indians and defended them from unfair government laws. They defended the Chinese immigrants from the exclusion policies that many members of Congress were anxious to adopt. After 1901 blacks began to lose political ground.

It was a Republican Congress that in 1890 repudiated its campaign pledges by failing to pass the Lodge Federal Education Bill and the Blair Federal Aid to Education Bill, which would have protected Negro political rights and improved Negro schooling in the South. Republican Presidents grew increasingly silent on Negro rights, while the lily white faction of the party made its appearance. The success of the Democrats in 1884 and 1892, if anything hastened Republican desertion of the Negro's cause. Negroes were impressed by Cleveland's moderate policy in regard to colored office holders, and by the favorable actions of certain northern Democratic state machines like those in New York and Massachusetts. Consequently, Northern Negroes were brought to criticism and disillusionment, and in some cases even withdrawal from the Republican party.[1]

Debate regarding the effective use of the black vote resulted in the division of collective voting by blacks on issues and concerns that affected their quality of life. Some blacks remained in the Republican party, a significant number joined the Democratic party, and others went independent. This division shifted the emphasis and focus of blacks from those issues that were common to them as a group to identification of matters that concerned their respective party. Party loyalties became primary instead of racial solidarity in the political arena.

Peter Clark, a liberal Republican who occasionally supported the Democrats, urged a division and stated his reason in 1885.

I have never thought it wise for the colored vote to be concentrated in one party, thus antagonizing the other party and tempting it to do against us as Republicans what they would have hesitated to do against us as Negroes. Whenever colored men find themselves in accord with Democrats in local or national issues they should vote with them and thus disarm much of the malevolence that is born of political rather than racial antagonism. . . .The welfare of the Negro is my controlling political motive, and I supported Mr. Cleveland because I thought his election would promote this welfare.[2]

Between the end of Reconstruction and the beginning of World War I, black leaders, because of the failures of the Republican party, urged blacks on two occasions—one in the 1880s and the other between 1908 and 1912— to vote for the Democratic party. If it had not been for the loyal collective black vote on two occasions in the early days of Reconstruction, Republicans would have lost the presidency.[3]

Frederick Douglass broke with the Republican party in 1883 after he concluded that the Democratic leaders, particularly in the northern states, favored racial justice.[4] Douglas admonished black voters to follow no party blindly and to vote wisely. As the strategy was to gain support from all quarters, the parties sought to gain the support of black voters. Both parties cherished the hope of obtaining a greater portion of black votes than the other, a situation that created a spirited controversy over the issue across the country. There were those who argued that blacks should vote the Democratic ticket if they wanted more representation to effect their political, social, and economic betterment. Others urged loyalty to the Republican party. Du Bois, who was politically active during this period, traveled across the country advocating the defeat of Taft in the nominating convention and the uprooting of Rooseveltism. One of his primary points was that the Democratic party stood for strict regulation of corporate wealth. Du Bois also argued that the party advocated the freedom and independence of the brown and black men in the West Indies and the Philippines; better working conditions; the rights of labor; striving for higher wages; efforts in favor of a low tariff; and the end of special privileges. Black support for the Democratic party was advocated by Du Bois not for racial considerations but for the reason that blacks as consumers and laborers could benefit more as a group from the Democratic party.[5]

Depending largely on the issue and how the leaders addressed themselves to the issues, blacks identified with the different political parties. However, the factionalism in the black vote (between 1905 and 1910) greatly reduced blacks' influence and power as a group in the political arena.

The economic and political benefits of the political arrangements have always been distributed unequally to blacks in the American social order. On July 4, 1852, Frederick Douglass declared in a speech to an audience in New York:

Are the great principles of political freedom and of natural justice, embodied in that Declaration of Independence, extended to us?. . .What to the American slave is your Fourth of July? I answer, a day that reveals to him more than all days of the years, the gross injustice and cruelty to which he is the constant victim. To him your celebration is a sham; your boasted liberty an wholy license; your national greatness swelling vanity; your sounds of rejoicing are empty and heartless; your denunciation of tyrants, brass-fronted impudence, your shouts of liberty and equality hollow mockery; your prayers and hymns, your sermons and thanksgivings, with all your religious parade and solemnity; are to him mere bombast, fraud, deception, impiety, and hypocrisy—a thin veil to cover up crimes which would disgrace a nation of savages. There is not a nation of the earth guilty of practices more shocking and bloody than are the people of these United States at this very hour.[6]

Douglass reminded this audience and America of the racial contradiction implicit in the practice regarding black slaves and white America's proclamation of freedom from England. This blatant dichotomy continues to this day in the American social order. Gains from the political process, especially those of an economic nature or those touching power are not shared equally between blacks and whites. Even the political and economic benefits resulting from the brief alliance of blacks and poor southern whites were not shared equally, and the alliance did not last very long. The majority presence of blacks in various cities and the potential of a viable political coalition between blacks and poor whites threatened middle-class whites, who organized a systematic attempt to disfranchise blacks and render them powerless in the political arena. But what has happened since 1905, and especially today, is the attempt to give blacks the sense of participation in the political process and a control of their presence in powerless positions. This status gives the population of blacks the sense of change, thus regulating their collective efforts to organize and seek substantial and even radical change in the arrangements of the social order. Moreover, it allows the interpretation that success and progress are individually attained, rendering insignificant collective (group) effort to affect change and progress for the individual and the group.

Organized Efforts at Participation

Participation Through Conventions

In order to effectively address the issues of racial oppression, political domination, and economic exploitation, as early as 1830 blacks began to organize national conventions. All of the conventions were held in Philadelphia and Buffalo. On all occasions the free blacks who attended advocated the abolition of slavery and the improvement of the status and conditions of free blacks. These conventions were attempts at direct involvement in political action to challenge the various impediments, restrictions, and control of their direct participation in the political arrangements of the social order. It was through the organization of the conventions that free blacks felt they could influence policy issues effecting the group. These conventions or national and state conferences had no political power to establish policy and virtually no influence to impact policy. Nonetheless, the conventions provided a forum for blacks to effectively articulate the policy interest of the group, establish organized group activities, explore avenues to the liberation of black people, and facilitate an ongoing debate concerning the political, economic, and social problems faced by the group and their community. The conventions failed to achieve their stated goals primarily because of the nature and character of the social order. However, the conventions formed the basis for The National Equal Rights League that was organized in 1864 and The National Afro-American League that was founded in 1890. Their objectives were to achieve the right to vote and secure full privileges of citizenship in "every avocation of life" for black people. Hanes Walton, Jr., argues that these organizations were never strong. Plagued by personal jealousies and internal dissensions, they lapsed into dormancy after a couple of meetings. But like the national conventions of the 1830s and 1840s, they were later revived, on September 15, 1898, as the National Afro-American Council. The following year, this organization merged with the National Association of Colored Women and issued four strongly worded resolutions—two condemning the prevalence of anti-Negro mob violence and the lynching of Negroes, the third asserting that it was the duty of the federal government to protect Negroes from such harsh treatment, and the last indicating the convention's willingness to pursue its objectives through peaceful means.[7]

Even when the convention participants could adequately or correctly define the nature and character of the social order in relation to their economic and political position, it seemed difficult for them to achieve consensus on specific objectives, the priority of those objectives identified, and the ways—strategies, methods, and approaches—to achieve the objectives. Moreover, the methods employed have not matched their definition of the nature and character of the arrangements of the social order as capitalist and racist. Primarily, however, the failure of the conventions, as is the case with all organized efforts to date, is a function of the oppressive arrangements of the system, which were established to exclude power participation of Afro-Americans. Nothing short of rearrangement is necessary to assure power participation, the lack of which relegates blacks to the position where they have to request of whites that they initiate reform gestures on the blacks' behalf. Given this stance, blacks will continue to be powerless in the political arena.

Blacks were not discouraged that the convention movement failed to achieve all of their goals. Instead of conventions, organized group activity reappeared, including the Colored Farmers Alliance in Texas formed in 1886. By 1905 organized political protest group activity appeared with the founding of the Niagara Movement. The attempt of these political action organizations was to broaden the issue of civil rights from a regional issue to a national issue. While blacks were systematically denied full participation in electoral politics in the South, their electoral participation was diluted in the North. Moreover, the attempt was to keep before the minds of blacks that political participation was the basis for social and economic equality, contrary to the position taken by the Booker T. Washington machine, which advocated concentration on acquiring skills for economic self-improvement. With the formation of the NAACP, which became the legal arm of the civil rights movement, a measure of legal success was achieved. To what extent legal victories have translated into political power, economic value, and social mobility will be discussed in another chapter. The articulated objectives after 1909 were to:

Promote equality and eradicate caste or race prejudice among the citizens of the United States; to advance the interest of colored citizens; to secure for them impartial suffrage; and to increase their opportunities for securing justice in the courts, education for their children, employment according to their ability, and complete equality before the law.[8]

It is evident that the efforts of organized group activity were impeded by a variety of factors. Nonetheless, some progress could be identified. Even though blacks did not enter the political arena with more political power, there was evidence that the convention movement and the various organized group activities enhanced the mobilization of blacks for direct political action.

Party-Type Organization

Blacks organized political party-type organizations to facilitate direct political participation. The Negro National Democratic League, formed in 1900, and the National Liberty Party, formed in 1904, took the Democratic and the Republican parties to task on matters regarding racial justice. These two organizations were not directly engaged in electoral politics, but they constantly brought to the attention of blacks the contradictions and moral duplicities inherent in the system and in the organized political parties. By the 1960s there were several political party-type organizations claiming varying degrees of success. The Mississippi Freedom Democratic Party formed in 1964, the South Carolina Progressive Democratic Party in 1964, the Lowndes County Freedom Party in Alabama in 1966, the National Alabama Democratic Party in 1968, the Freedom Now Party of 1963, the Peace and Freedom Party in 1968, and the United Citizens' Party in 1969 in South Carolina are the party-type organizations that focused their attention, and that of their members, on local and national issues that affected black people and oppressed people in general. Prior to this period of the 1960s, blacks in Pennsylvania formed a state party in 1883 called the Colored

Independent Party. Blacks organized the Negro Protective Party in Ohio in 1897. In many parts of the Southern states during the 1920s and the 1930s blacks and browns formed alliances to protest or support issues and candidates of their choice. "In Texas in 1928 the Black and Tan groups nominated their own electors for President in order to protest the action of the Republican National Convention in seating the Lily White delegation."[9] Blacks in South Carolina formed in 1944 the South Carolina Progressive Democratic party. These organizations organized at the state, local, and national levels and protested, challenged, and revolted against many issues and political policies. Their efforts in running hundreds of candidates paid dividends in that there has been a significant increase over the past fifteen years in the number of black elected officials at the local, state, and national levels. Hanes Walton, Jr. argues that:

until recently the American black political party has for the most part been a by-product of the one-party system prevalent in many Southern states, just as national third parties have been by-products of the national two-party system. Black parties so far seem to be much more successful on the local and district levels than on the national and state levels. Mainly instruments for protest, black parties express the desire of Negroes to be included in the mainstream of American political life. Unique primarily in their almost totally ethnic composition, they are basically small third parties created because of the miscalculation or neglect of the major parties. Like other third parties, they will arise when the need presents itself, call attention to the difficulties and asperations and goals of the excluded, and then perhaps . . . if they fail to overcome internal or external organizational difficulties, fade from the political scene.[10]

Interest in establishing their own political machinery did not diminish black interest in meaningful involvement in the two party system. Blacks have always been involved in the Republican and Democratic parties. The question is the quality and significance of their involvement and the benefits derived therefrom.

Party Politics

Even though blacks have been participants in the Republican party since its formation, their attitudes have always been cautious and their involvement tentative. The party has never, until recently, attempted to attract black voters on a systematic basis, and its history is not one of advocacy for black causes. It did not advocate the abolition of slavery; it did not promote the extension of the franchise to blacks. In its attempt to compete with the Democratic party, it advocated the granting of suffrage to all regardless of race, but the Democratic party had succeeded in restricting suffrage rights to white males. The Republicans opposed the extension of slavery to nonslave states but would not interfere with its existence in slave states.

For a majority of black voters, the policy of the Republican party has always been ambivalent toward blacks and their participation in the political arena. In many instances blacks have viewed the Republican party as being antagonistic toward their full participation. The conclusion is that the relationship between blacks and the Republican party regarding political matters has been and is bad. While a few Republicans seem to be progressive on the issue, the majority of Republicans are viewed as conservatives and racists—overt and covert. This view has weakened the Republican image and position in the black community, and the policies and practices of the last two Republican administrations did nothing to enhance them. There are those in the black community and in the Republican community who call for the rebuilding of a new alliance and allegiance to the Republican party. Even though there is increased activity for political reasons among liberal Republicans in this direction, there is no real sign of increased acceptance of this allegiance by blacks. The Republican party has appointed a few blacks to bridge the gap between the party and the black community. For the most part, however, these blacks are unknown to the black community; they have no standing in the struggle for freedom and liberation among black people. All attempts to promote them through media, especially television, have failed.

When Carter got the overwhelming support of the black community in 1976, assuring his election to the presidency, it became very clear to Republicans that they could not win a national election without attracting a significant perentage of the black vote. Even though they had won in the past without a significant black vote, the percentage of black votes for the Democrats, primarily for Carter, was so great that the Republicans felt it politically necessary for effective party survival and progress purposes that a program be implemented to attract blacks and other "minorities" to its ranks. This effort was launched with no publicity or actual change in the basic philosophy and policy position on various issues important to black society. Without this change, no program to attract will be effective. It could be argued that the act of public interest by the Republican party is an indication of its shift in position and even its philosophy regarding blacks and their participation as partners in the political arena. However, the reading in the black community is that the efforts organized by the Republican party to attract more blacks to its ranks are designed to save the party rather than to assist the struggle of blacks for freedom and liberation. With the growing numbers of blacks, Mexicans and other ethnic groups defined as oppressed and powerless, no political party can afford to ignore them as insignificant in the election process. The relative success presently being experienced by the Republican party is not so much a function of its efforts as it is a function of the unwillingness and inability of the Democratic party to address the economic and racial issues as they affect oppressed people. Consequently, the increased number of black Republicans are coming primarily from the ranks of the Democrats. It is not true that blacks are attracted to the Republican party because of its history as a party or because of its change in political and economic perspectives. The Republican party still advocates special privileges to powerful groups, the absence of restrictions and regulations on corporate wealth, and other such policy issues that are oppressive and not in the best interest of powerless black people. Blacks are not in political positions within the party to change the policies, and they are not a powerful enough political threat to influence change. Those that are close to the leadership merely execute policies in accordance with instructions handed to them by the executive body of the party.

A significant amount of dollars was designated in the 1977-1978 budget of the Republican party to organize activities at the state and local levels to attract blacks to join the party. In Tennessee, Alabama, Georgia, and other southern states the activities were intense. The political materials organized for distribution did not identify any economic, educational, political, social or legal benefits accrued to black people or the black community as a result of the recent activities of the Republican party. The concern was to document the failures of the Democratic party and the promises not kept.

The persons distributing the materials in one city quickly note the appointments of previous Republican national administrations of blacks to positions in government. All administrations make such gestures to give the appearance of change and progress. However, the appointments are made to positions of apparent power, not to positions of real power. The leadership of the Republican party had publicly declared that there will be no change in philosophy and perspectives to attract the political participation of blacks to their party. Given this stand, they should not expect blacks to come running to their party even if their experiences as participants in the Democratic party were unfruitful. There is no doubt that the time is ripe for the Republicans to enhance their political position by taking advantage of the negative experiences of blacks in the Democratic party, but substantive changes must be made. Radical moves have to be made. Merely inviting some black leaders to speak at Republican conventions is not enough.

The record of the Democratic party has not been significantly different. At the psychological level, the experiences may have been more frustrating and stressful. Blacks have expected more from the Democratic party because of the support given the party over the years. However, it is only recently that blacks have had to redefine political success to put emphasis on economic benefit for the group. There has been a degree of public satisfaction among blacks to accept as success and progress the appointments of a few blacks to limited, powerless positions. As the economic situation of the nation became more acute, political appointments were no longer a measure of gains.

Even the most conservative black, if he/she has anything to conserve, tends to articulate positions that are left of center on the political continuum. An analysis of the political continuum from left to right will discover that both parties fall within the center, advocating policies and practices that maintain the status quo. Noting Figure 6, we can clearly understand the political situation of the parties. Both Democratic and Republican parties are in the center. The Democrats are left within the center and the Republicans are right within the center. There are occasions when policy and practice overlap, the reasons that many political participants find it difficult to make political distinctions between the two parties. A significant number of grass-root community members often exclaim, "they're all the same"—and they are correct. The shades of difference of two parties whose policies and practice are basically the same do not make a significant difference in the political arena relative to the economic benefits to oppressed people.

The power base, that is, the decision-making leaders of each party, occupy the center on the political continuum from far left to far right, even though the Democrats appear to be to the left of the Republicans in the center. Influential members and groups of each party might occupy positions to the left and right of their respective leaders hoping to persuade them that their positions are incorrect. There are those in each party also whose positions at times resemble each others'. Blacks tend to relate to some of the positions taken by many of the individuals and groups to the left mainly because they are seeking to change the system, while groups on the right seek to maintain the status quo or to advocate, in the case of the far right, a return to a prior national posture. However, the basic power position and center posture of both parties remain the same, with Democrats attempting small and insignificant changes and promoting the appearance of change and Republicans attempting to keep things the way they are and promoting a conservative national posture. In both cases, blacks as a powerless group suffer. Consequently, the debate regarding the best use of the black vote relative to the Republican and Democratic parties is not really politically profitable.

Whatever gains were experienced by blacks during the 1960s are not a function of the goodness of the Democratic party or its leadership. The cumulative pressure from sustained and systematic protest explains the apparent gains. The courts and the Democratic administrations were forced to make certain progressive gestures, again giving the appearance of change. An examination of the outcome reveals two negative results. The first is that those blacks appointed to powerless positions, especially those with visibility and contacts in the community, could not deliver economic benefits as a part of the system and lost their credibility in the community and were

Figure 6.   THE POLITICAL SPECTRUM

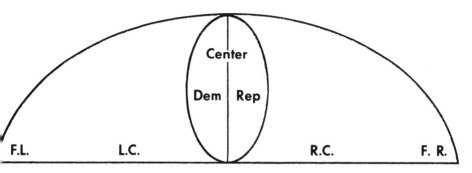

Political Spectrum (Continuum)

viewed as useless. Some resigned; others became less vocal and visible and were too embarrassed to admit their failure. A few even became defensive, saying, "a few of us can't do everything." One was even heard to admit, "Our hands are tied." In full view of the community, these leaders were being discredited, occupying powerless positions and not being able to translate political participation into economic benefits for the group they represented.

The other negative result is associated with the various social programs institutionalized during the 1960s and as early as the "New Deal." Chuck Stone argues that "by 1936, Negroes, economically benefited by the employment and Welfare policies of the New Deal, began to shift their votes to the Democrats."[11] It is this point that political scientists have identified as the beginning of the shift of the Democratic party from conservatism to liberalism. At the same time, the Republican party shifted from liberalism to extreme conservatism. This shift in political position found blacks shifting party loyalties. However, blacks have come to be viewed as a group looking for handouts from political parties in exchange for their votes.

Samuel Lubell also argues that "the economical appeal of the New Deal . . . broke the Negro's Republicanism and moved him into the Democratic party."[12] The move of blacks from the Republican party to the Democratic party was primarily in response to their interpretation of the programs of the party in relation to their needs.

Leslie Fishel, Jr., points out that "by midway through his term, Franklin D. Roosevelt had captured the admiration and affection of the Negro people and with that, their votes. . . . During the campaign of 1936 . . . the second Roosevelt . . . weaned the Negro away from the Republican party."[13]

Gunnar Myrdal has also argued that "when the New Deal relieved the economic plight of the Negro during the depression . . . Negroes began shifting to the Democratic party in large numbers."[14]

It is very evident that blacks were responding to the economic difficulties they experienced during the late 1920s and through the 1930s. This shift was therefore a gradual one that found a climax in 1936. Hanes Walton has argued that "this shift began at first in northern cities, slowly moved to the national level, and reached a climax in 1936. In short, blacks did not become Democrats because of the New Deal; they became "national" Democrats during the New Deal."[15] As early as the late 1800s we notice a dissatisfaction among blacks, as was stated earlier, with the Republican party and black leaders breaking with the party and encouraging blacks to shift political allegiance.

Whether because of the New Deal or during the New Deal that the shift was made, blacks have come to be viewed as a people interested primarily in social welfare programs established by white leaders that benefit black people. Consequently, even if poor whites are benefiting more from such programs, blacks bear the negative public image as welfare recipients over-anxious to become freeloaders selling their votes to the highest bidder. However, the political articulation of the masses of powerless blacks suggest that they are primarily interested in a system that is equal, fair, and just. Consequently, they are the ones that have advocated the change in the present capitalist-colonial nature of the social order. For the most part, however, middle-class blacks saw individual benefits from a capitalist-colonial system that controlled for individual progress, that advocated not a change in the social order but an inclusion in the system. What has resulted is that a few have had such inclusion experiences and have found themselves handicapped in attempts at bringing benefits to the group resulting from their inclusion in the system. They have had to go along with and even support policies that were not in the best interest of the group to keep their jobs. This has been the experience of even the most vocal representatives of the black community who believed that the best position to be of benefit was to be in a position within the arrangements of the system. The power of the arrangement, in the absence of change, forces compliance and conformity to the point of active indentification and support. As more and more blacks gain economic middle-class status and enjoy a degree of security through inclusion in the system, they will be content to support the Democratic party or the Republican party as the parties appear to shift from left to right within the center on the political continuum. Black participation in the two-party system is defined by interest and depends upon the interpretation of blacks relative to the degree of liberalism identified in the policies and practices of the parties. This stance is not liberating. Oppressed people need to do more. Following a liberal attitude in an oppressed condition in a capitalist-colonial society relegates the group to political domination, economic exploitation, and sociocultural control. In a capitalist-colonial society an oppressed group has to be radical in its advocacy and must seek transformations in the arrangements of the social order. Reforms are not useful to the group.

National Black Agenda

A radical agenda is required that would give direction to national, state, and local groups. This agenda should be the result of a series of conferences that would allow for debate on the content of such an agenda. The agenda should include mechanisms for achieving the ends of the agenda and a time frame for the process. The agenda would be a source of direction for black people through time and would be discarded once the objectives are achieved. The content items should be dealt with in terms of priority and used to measure and determine the political move of the black community relative to platforms of political parties, groups, and individuals seeking support. With no agenda issues, the community is left to the political whims of those who, at election periods, attempt to manipulate the participation of oppressed people. The agenda should also assess the economic, sociocultural and political benefits of each agenda item to the black community. In other words, black people should be able to measure, know, and observe the benefits resulting from political participation. The right to vote is of no real value if it is not organized to change the oppressive arangements of the social order and achieve real benefits to the participants.

No real progress is possible until "A Black Political Community Agenda" is established and in place for blacks to follow in making political decisions. The agenda should be based on two things:

1. The nature and character of the general society and its relation to the black community
2. The nature and needs of the black community within the context of the general society

The process of establishing the agenda will highlight the kind of relationship that exists between the oppressed black community and the established political economy of a capitalist-colonial system. It will also help to determine the kind of action that is necessary and the collective response that would achieve the objectives of the agenda.

The establishment of an agenda to be followed at the national, state, and local levels will require devotion, hard work, and serious commitments. Long hours must be spent doing practical research, pulling on every available resource in the community, with dedication to such a task.

It is true that at this point in the history of black struggle it appears difficult to organize black people around issues. Nonetheless, this is the important or primary point of struggle. Black people cannot be significant in political matters nor will their vote make any difference if it is not organized around issues that would mean more and make a difference in their collective objective conditions. Blacks cannot afford to vote for individuals merely because they are nice or because they seem to be good persons. They should vote for men and women with plans—plans that approximate the plans outlined in the agenda; plans that are easily translated into practical solutions to the conditions of black people; plans that include black people as subjects and objects of the process of change.

Candidates, black or white, who request or otherwise seek black support in political elections will be required to meet with the community to explain and outline their agendas to the community members. The community will also have an opportunity to measure their agenda against the plans of those that seek their support. To the extent to which there is agreement relative to the comparability of a candidate's agenda with that of the Community Agenda, an agreement should be read an signed by the candidate and the community representatives that would commit the candidate to seek to operationalize the agenda once in office. If the candidate's efforts are contrary to the signed agreement, the community should bring suit against the official as outlined in the agreement for breach of contract.

It is clear that the black community must begin to act as a collective force to bring about freedom and liberation to the community and its people. It could be that the establishment of an agenda is only a first step, given the nature and character of the oppressive arrangements of the American social order.

The Democratic and Republican parties reflect and reinforce the political culture of a given system, and the political culture of the American system has long been a major force in subjugating blacks by such mechanisms as exclusion, nonenforcement of laws, and co-optation. If fact, every black is co-opted into the system insofar as that person votes for candidates who will not or cannot work for the things that black people and oppressed people in general need.

If the system is unwilling and/or unable to change to satisfy the fundamental needs of blacks and other oppressed groups, their duty, as articulated in the Declaration of Independence, is to change and destroy the government.

Loss of Economic Infusion

One of the most perplexing problems of Afro-Americans is the inability of thousands of their young black adults and teenagers to secure productive work. The growth of unemployment among black youth has persisted through recession and prosperity for over a decade during the establishment of "minority job programs" and civil rights enforcement. The unemployment among black youth and other "minority" youth is what it was for the entire nation in the depths of the Great Depression. The economic policy of the Carter administration of cutting the federal budget to help cure inflation has caused unemployment to disproportionately affect blacks and other oppressed youth. As white youth unemployment decreased in 1979, black youth unemployment increased.

The causes for the unemployment situation are listed as follows: Racism in the marketplace; the failure of the federal government to establish effective programs to reach the most needy; the inability and unwillingness of many youths to accept the jobs that are available; the movement of jobs out of the central cities where many blacks live; the rise of an underground economy of alternatives that provide easy, quick, and more money for less effort; the large influx of aliens, legal and illegal, who are taking jobs once held by blacks; and the entry of white women into the labor market in great numbers. Acording to the Bureau of Labor Statistics, the work force grew by three million in 1978, and 1.9 million were women. However, only 400,000 of them were black women. The other cause is identified as a fractured society in which various groups militantly defined their own interests, creating a new political climate that makes assimilation of blacks and other poor minorities more difficult.

The fact that $13 billion more would go into the black community each year if there were no racial discrimination in employment, according to the Council of Economic Advisors, suggests very clearly that racism, in spite of class differences in the black community, accounts for much of the economic problems faced by the black community. Further, this estimation also suggests that economic policies and practices are still based on race and do control and dominate the economic and social position of black people and the nature and quality of their survival and progress. Although the Civil Rights Act of 1964 made illegal racial discrimination in employment, from the above indication of the amount that is denied the black community through acts of racial discrimination in a single year, it is evident that the act is ineffective. The law, therefore, has an inability in addressing the practice of racism.

Court decisions have upheld the right to equal access to jobs, but the activity of racial discrimination has become a covert operation and very subtle. This is the reason that racial discrimination in job opportunities continues to exist.

The black community is on the brink of economic disaster with no effective solutions to their economic problems. There is chronic youth unemployment and a growing permanent black underclass that has developed therefrom. There are thousands of black youth that have no hope of entering the labor force.

Herbert Hill concludes "that a large part of the young black urban population will remain in a condition of hopelessness and despair and that the social and psychological cost in wasted lives continues a major tragedy in American life."

The billions of dollars spent on vocational education and federal jobs are not helping in any significant way. The history of racism; being systematically barred from construction and other jobs by unions; company preference for white workers; white seniority in employment; and inappropriate preparation and, in many cases, no preparation are now having their effects on the black community and black youth.

Because old racial practices and patterns have continued, even in the face of the absence of relative policies to support such patterns and practices, the political economy has changed along with the social climate to combine with old racial patterns and practices, with the effect of keeping the unemployment of blacks approximately twice that of whites. The gap is widening.

According to data from the Bureau of Labor Statistics, in 1954 the unemployment rate for blacks 16 to 19 years old was 16.5 percent. The same age group of whites registered a 12.1 percent rate. In 1978, the rate for blacks of ages 16 to 19 was 36.3 percent, as against 13.9 percent for whites. In early 1979, the black teenage unemployment rate had dropped to 32.7 percent, but by March it began to climb and reached 35.5 percent by April. The rate for whites, however, has fluctuated between 13.9 percent and 13.6 percent.

In 1978, the unemployment rate for blacks 20 to 24 years old was 20.7 percent as against 9.5 percent for whites. In 1968 the unemployment rate for blacks was 10 percent. The rate had doubled in ten years and has tripled in eleven years, The creation of 450,000 jobs will ease the situation among black youth between the ages 16 to 24. However, equalization of job opportunity does not address the quality of employment and the economic benefits that accrue to the black community from the quality of employment. In many cities where city governments have created jobs for their "minorities," the jobs are at the bottom of the pay scale with tenuous status because they are usually maintained on "soft" money. The numbers are increased, but job stability is usually absent.

There are many more youth than those represented in the statistics that are legitimately unemployed. Many have stopped looking and have joined the underground economic system. In many large cities and growing cities, the employment-population ratio is declining while the factories are becoming white-collar operations. Apathy among the youth and a growing indifference to the poor, with the attitude that they are poor because they want to be poor, plus the political and economic climate in the social order, will make it more difficult to sort out the needs and priorities and address them adequately. The attitude of businesses and even state and local governments that they will hire the best qualified will not help the situation. However, they do not seem to be doing anything about the poorly qualified whites they presently have employed.

The attempt in a growing posture of explanation is to inform the public and create conflict between the oppressed that jobs once held by blacks are being held by others, such as the Asians and South Americans who are serving in restaurants, the Iranians who drive taxis, the Hispanics who are picking vegetables and citrus fruits in fields and orchards. This is true, but unemployment is high for all poor "minorities," who control few jobs. Blacks control fewer jobs and have less job-creating power than any other group. This means that those who enjoy job advantages and income mobility have an inability to help those who are unemployed to any significant degree.

In a capitalist-colonial system the gap between the would-be black capitalists and the poor and working-class blacks can be explained in terms of the need of the social order to sustain itself by creating a sense of change and the possibility of economic mobility among the oppressed. However, by the very nature of the economic structure and political process of the order, the economic and political position of the would-be black capitalist remains in doubt. Consequently, this group is controlled by decisions made by those who own and control the means of production, causing them to suffer, in many cases, to a greater extent than poor and working-class blacks. Those indications of a conflict between would-be black capitalists and poor and working-class blacks surrounding busing and inner-city schools are the function of the nature of the social order and the combination of the impact of the class and racial position of the blackness and what it has come to mean in a capitalist-colonial society.

When would-be black capitalists attempt to protect their achieved position by believing that they are secured, they are defending something that is important to them as an indication of hard work, education, patience, and struggle. There are also indications that their attack on the system is a strike against oppression, possible failure, and the relative economic position they hold in the society. It is still true that blacks with equal education to whites are expected to earn about half as much. This is part of the reason that $13 billion are denied blacks each year because of racial discrimination in employment.

When the Congressional Black Caucus came into existence and began to raise certain issues, the group presented a powerful set of political possibilities for black people. One possibility was the development of a framework to increase the number of black representatives in Congress to oppose the practice of gerrymandering against black people, and the other was the possible development of a framework of a national black political movement.

The presence and the existence of this group with these possibilities provided an effective mechanism for the black community based on its own creativity and needs. The white majority simply used the black community during the election period, playing the game of American politricks. They do not speak to the pressing issues. They are unreliable, and whenever it comes to a show-down on democratic principles as applied to black people, the tradition of white politicians has always been to change the rules of the game.

Black people remain a captive electorate taken for granted by political parties unresponsive to their needs and demands. The approach should be that, as Congressman William L. Clay of St. Louis said, "We have no permanent friends . . . just permanent interests."[16]

The national black political movement organized and led by the Black Caucus must fight for power to support the struggle of black people throughout America. An unabashed stand against the political arrangements must be articulated, and they must not continue to work for white-defined ends. They must establish a political agenda of issues around which blacks must struggle and use to measure those who seek to and those who now represent them. This is the leadership that is essential at this point, as their presence in Congress has not translated itself into real economic gains for the majority or masses of black people.

Notes

1. August Meier, "The Negro and the Democratic Party, 1875-1915," *Phylon* 17, no. 2 (1956):175.

2. *Washington Bee*, March 14, 1885.

3. Proceedings of the Colored National Convention . . .1869, (Washington, 1870), p. 3; *Washington News National Era* (July 13, 1871).

4. S.A.M. Washington, "George Thomas Dowing" (*Newport News* 1910), p. 19.

5. *Washington Bee*, March 14, 1885.

6. Charles V. Hamilton, *The Struggle For Political Equality* (New York: National Urban League, 1976), p. 23.

7. Hanes Walton, Jr., *Black Politics* (New York: Lippincott Co., 1972), pp. 144-46. See also Charles V. Hamilton, *The Struggle For Political Equality* (New York: National Urban League, 1976), p. 9.

8. Quoted in Freedom to the Free, Century of Emancipation (Washington, D.C.: Government Printing Office, 1963), p. 81.

9. Hanes Walton, Jr., *Black Politics*, p. 123.

10. Hanes Walton, Jr., *Black Political Parties* (New York: Free Press, 1972). See also Charles V. Hamilton, *The Struggle for Political Equality*, p. 10.

11. Chuck Stone, *Black Political Power in America* (Indianapolis: Bobbs-Merrill Co., 1968), p. 54.

12. Samuel Lubell, *Black and White: Test of a Nation* (New York: Harper and Row, 1964), p. 47.

13. Leslie Fishel, Jr., "The Negro in the New Deal," in Bernard Sternsher, ed., *The Negro in Depression and War* (Chicago: Quadrangle Books, 1969), p. 9.

14. Gunnar Myrdal, *An American Dilemma*, 2nd ed. (New York: Harper and Row, 1962), p. 494.

15. Hanes Walton, Jr. *Black Politics*, p. 100.

16. *New York Times*, March 11, 1979.

10

Survival and Progress of Black Colleges and Universities

Historical Context

Former slaves were greatly assisted by the Freedmen's Bureau in organizing education for themselves. However, former slaves had built schools, churches, and meeting halls before the government had thought of a Freedmen's Bureau to assist. In its five years of existence, the Bureau built 4,300 schools, including Howard Fisk, Stover, and Hampton universities. Black and white teachers who had been educated in the North went south to teach, and many became targets for anti-black violence. Seemingly, it was the growing competence and knowledge of blacks that southern whites feared. This fear arose not simply because many southern whites felt that educating blacks would create an "uppity" group but primarily because educated blacks were viewed as a threat to their positions in the social, political, and economic system.[1]

In spite of threatening attempts by white mobs to destroy many of the schools where "freedmen" learned, blacks continued to assemble for instruction, and many formed defense groups to protect their schools and teachers.

Black voters and legislators insisted on a public free-school system in the South. Although there were a few schools before the Civil War, the established public school system can be traced to the time that blacks obtained political power.

It was not, however, until 1868 that encouragement was given to any general system of public schools meant to enhance the whole youthful population. The Constitution of 1868 made it the duty of the legislature to establish "a uniform system of free public schools, by taxation or otherwise, for all children between the ages of five and twenty-one years." In Alabama the Reconstruction Constitution of 1868 provided that "It shall be the duty of the Board of Education to establish throughout the state, in each township or other school district which it may have created, one or more schools at which all the children of the state between the ages of five and twenty-one years may attend free of charge." Arkansas in 1868, Florida in 1869, Louisiana in 1868, North Carolina in 1869, South Carolina in 1868, and Virginia in 1870, established school systems. The Constitution of 1868 in Louisiana required the general assembly to establish "at least one free public school in every parish," and that the schools should make no "distinction of race, color or previous condition." Georgia's system was not fully established until 1873.[2]

Colleges established to serve black people in former slave states developed after the Civil War. However, Lincoln University in Pennsylvania, founded by the Methodists, and Wilberforce University in Ohio, established by the Presbyterians, were developed from mission schools in "free territory" prior to 1860. Although the black colleges were entirely a missionary enterprise, the federal government gave them grants, which were comparatively meager.

From these initial efforts there emerged a class of schools engaged in providing the rudiments of learning to the freedmen and bearing titles which were usually the expression of distant hopes rather than descriptions. This is particularly true of those institutions which were designated as colleges and universities, but which naturally were compelled for some years to spend their major energies in work at the secondary level.[3]

After 1885, however, though inadequately equipped and supported, the schools began to show changes in curricula, with the entrance of black teachers and a few white teachers who had been trained in the North and who attempted to teach black students many of the things they had been taught in northern universities. Many black students were prepared by their teachers to go north to study. Over a period of time, many of them did; most of these students prepared themselves for the ministry and for teaching—both sources of black leadership for several generations.

As a result of teachers' demands for more facilities in black schools, church boards, who had borne the responsibilities of black schools, began to seek help from organized philanthropy as well as from the states. It was during this period (1885-1915) that philanthropic foundations such as the Julius Rosenwald Fund, the John F. Salter Fund, the General Education Board, and the Phelps-Stoke Fund began to involve themselves seriously and directly with the matter of education for blacks. An extensive study of the seventeen state-supported land-grant colleges for blacks conducted by the Phelps-Stoke Fund revealed grave discrepancies in standards and distribution of funds and equipment between white and black colleges. As a result of this study, additional financial aid came from the state governments.

From the very inception of education for blacks, violence and threats of violence plagued their school operations. However, the demoralization of black students came from within, when many white teachers with a "missionary spirit" who now had control of the system sought to "acculturate" black students. Little mention was made of Africa, except to suggest that it was a backward country with savages who ate one another. All the colleges founded by the states under the terms of the First and Second Morrill Acts of July 2, 1862 and 1890 respectively, trained the physical rather than the mental faculties of the black students. The notion was that it was best to prepare young blacks for practical life, that is, to prepare them to enter the labor force to be manipulated and exploited by corporate capitalists and would-be-capitalists.

It was thought that the individual learned by doing and gained the best benefits from labor by being taught how to do it right. Lessons were learned best by working under the leadership of competent christian teachers. Students in the schools of the Society were constantly reminded that work was the great mission of life. It was a mandate of heaven that through the sweat of the brow they were to eat bread all their lives, a statement implying not to work was to fail in the mission of life. Industrial training, therefore, was elevated and ranked along with the scholarly and necessary attainments of life.[4]

Much controversy revolved around the issues regarding the philosophy, methods, and content of the education of black students. Issues such as the extent to which freed blacks could be educated; what kind or kinds of education they should receive; for what ends they should be educated and what should be the content, devices, and methods to be employed in the process occupied those who planned curricula.

Bond points out that:

At Fisk University, Eractus Milo Cravath instituted a curriculum taken bodily from the classical course of study at Oberlin where he had studied. At Atlanta University, Edmund Asa Ware and Horace Bumstead adopted with change the curricula which they had studied at Yale. General O.O. Howard, head of the Freedmen's Bureau, was a graduate of Bowdoin College; in inviting Armstrong to establish a school, he doubtless had in mind the same sort of institution which his New England agents had set up elsewhere in the South.[5]

Horace Bumstead's argument was that "in terms of higher education for blacks, they should get such as the white boy gets when he goes to college."[6] He continued by saying:

I mean a curriculum in which the humanities are prominent and in which intercourse with books and personal contact with highly educated teachers constitute the chief source of power. . . .A very practical service which college education renders to the individual Negro is to teach him to think. The power of rational thought is one which the past history of the race has not tended to cultivate. . . .It is the lack of this power which constitutes one of the chief weaknesses in the Negro today. The studies of the usual college curriculum are especially fitted to develop it.[7]

Training black students to think—that is, to develop their mental faculties —was the philosophy of such schools as Atlanta University, Fisk, Howard, Morehouse, Talledega, and a few others from which black leaders continued to emerge. However, like the controversy between Du Bois and Washington, the debate concerning the role of the black college, its objectives and aims, revolved around what was best for blacks. The primary aim of many college administrations was the character building of black students, which was supposed to be effected through manual labor. Very closely related to character building were wage-earning and occupational skills, evidenced by the establishment of farms, sawmills, soap-making shops, boom-making shops, carpet-making shops, and other industries whose profits went to organized capitalism. Many of these students—despite the fact that they labored consistently in the firms—had to stay out of the classroom for a length of time until they had saved sufficient money from their meager earnings to pay their college expenses.[8]

Although many administrators of black colleges talked about the training of the "head, heart and hand," they received funds to establish trade courses. Between 1886 and 1892, many colleges received monetary gifts from Slater Fund and other philanthropic organizations to establish shops for technical training in the use of carpenter's tools.[9]

Around 1904, black students subjected to manual and technical training became more aware of academic work with its attendant recognition and social prestige. The academic students was the "aristocrat," and black students' attitudes began to change toward hand work.[10]

Administrators must have sensed the change early, for they set about to "dignify" the trades by requiring an entrance examination as a prerequisite for studying the trade. So strong was the "philosophy of the hands" ex-pounded by Samuel Chapman Armstrong, Hollis Burke Frissell, and Booker T. Washington,[11] that support for other types of black education (particularly academic) suffered greatly.

Profile and Problems

There are approximately 100 traditionally black colleges and universities in America. These institutions have a majority black student body and the administration officials are black. In most cases, especially among private black institutions, the board members are mostly black. Sixty percent of these institutions are public and 40 percent are private institutions. Private colleges and universities do not receive direct state funding as do public institutions, but many receive some public funding for a few of their academic or special programs. The majority of the 100 institutions were established between 1854 and 1925. However, a few were established between 1935 and 1972. Most of these colleges and universities are located in a black community. Yet not too far away is a public or private white college or university, the context for some of the difficulties black institutions are facing today.

Black colleges and universities are now faced with the burden of justifying their existence. The mission of black colleges identified by W.E.B. Du Bois was to:

Establish the principle that higher education should be available to blacks;
Defend the principle of racial equality by combating national and international doctrines to the contrary;
Establish freedom for black Colleges to decide what they should teach and to whom it would be taught;
Promote democracy and social power for black people by working for enfranchisement and gradual acquisition of political power.[12]

In spite of efforts to resurrect them in one form or another, doctrines of racial inferiority have been debunked. It is firmly been established that blacks are educable; consequently, higher education has been made available. To a great extent, many of the overt impediments to the franchise and formal political participation have been overcome. Black colleges have also defended the principle of racial equality. However, the realization of the goals has not resulted in substantive changes in the conditions of the black community and in the lives of black people. The realization of these objectives renders the traditional mission obsolete. A few social scientists have argued that this realization has ushered in a new mission with new responsibilities and different objectives. The intensity of the black struggle, the demands of students, and oppressive and repressive responses from American society have all contributed to the call for a new mission.

In light of the heightening of white oppression, and black colleges' failure to bring about equality of status as many blacks had expected, "it is now their task to create a new political consciousness among blacks that will lead to a commonly shared ideological network or world view which, in turn will facilitate an understanding of the black predicament in an international context."[13]

Criticism of black colleges and universities has come from various quarters. There are those who have argued that these institutions on the whole have been too elitist, not giving much attention to the demands and needs of the masses of black people, especially those in the community in which they find themselves. There are others who suggest that black colleges have failed to take the initiative in giving direction and leadership to the black community. This lack of leadership, it is argued, has led to misuse of the colleges' resources and the continued oppression and poor quality of life of community members. Others have argued that black colleges have not assumed the role attributed to major white colleges in the American society and that they should. On the other hand, there are critics who denounce them for "slavishly aping" white institutions.[14]

All of these criticisms have some basis in fact. However, the political and economic positions of black colleges and universities are not fully understood in the criticisms. What seems lacking is an analysis that puts sufficient attention on the societal context within which these institutions are obliged to function. Those who manage these institutions have responded that it is precisely this context that impedes, dominates, controls, and renders their institutions incapable of being more than producers of undergraduates and some graduate students for the labor market or to continue graduate and professional studies at white schools. Beyond the fact that there are not very many black colleges and universities offering doctoral programs and only a few offering professional training, some administrators believe that blacks are more comfortable with terminal graduate and professional degrees from white institutions. The powerless position that black colleges have occupied in the American social order has strained the relationship of these institutions and the black community. Most black people perceive these institutions as a place simply to obtain a degree. This view is shared by most administrators, who say that to expect more is to strain the already limited resources of the institutions. However, when black colleges were founded in the aftermath of emancipation their major objectives were grounded in the conditions of the black community.

It is no secret that institutions of higher learning are systems that tend to reinforce the legitimacy of the prevailing social order as defined by those with power and wealth. Within the constraints imposed by the regime, black educational institutions have to function. Consequently, the performing of functions deemed essential to the survival and progress of an oppressed group could be sacrificed. In the process, the institutions find themselves performing secondary functions involving secondary matters that are in many cases inconsequential and at times counterproductive. This is the reason that many black colleges and universities have had to repeatedly justify their existence in an educational environment that allows for the assumption that other institutions can do just as good a job educating blacks—or even a better job.

As universities, black institutions are not a community of individuals at various levels of development seeking solutions to the problems that confront the black community or the society at large and considering those problems that the communities are likely to face in the future. For the most part, they are communities of teaching systems that attempt to educate a majority of students for whom there might not be any other real opportunity for success. Black colleges and universities educate a large number of students that a large number of white universities would not accept, and would not know how to educate if they did. It is amazing how well black colleges do what they do with the resources they have or how well the resources they have are managed to educate black students. A significant percentage of those who graduate do well in graduate and professional schools and/or perform satisfactorily on the job. Many have been confronted with situations in which they were more qualified than their white supervisors and in some cases more knowledgeable about their jobs. In this regard, black colleges and universities are outstanding educational systems that have developed an approach for educating black students, developing an educational national resource that originally had little or no potential for educational success.

White universities don't graduate the majority of black students they accept. However, the majority of these white educational institutions have a variety of resources that allow for the development of a community of individuals at various levels of development who are engaged in finding solutions to the problems that face the society and those that are likely to face the society. This is the role that guarantees local, national, and international recognition and at the same time establishes accountability to the social order.

During the late 1960s scholars advocated a black curriculum for black colleges.[15] Very little argument was made for conducting basic research to answer some of the questions relative to the fundamental oppressive conditions of black people and the reasons for the status and position of the communities. Black teachers argued that their institutions were teaching institutions and that they had no time to do research. It is not felt that any more research into the conditions of black people would increase if teachers were given reduced loads.

Private black colleges with small faculties might have been in a better position to facilitate such research activity. Most of the basic research that has taken place has been conducted at Fisk, Atlanta University, Tuskegee, and Howard. However, Daniel C. Thompson reports that at private black colleges, the faculty are generally weak, with below-average students, inadequate academic programs, and substandard libraries; there is an unnaturally easy, relaxed, nonchalant academic atmosphere in which even their most capable students make no sustained effort to succeed beyond the mere passing of a required program of courses. Even those students planning to go on to graduate school feel no urgency about being prepared, because they feel that certain rules would simply be set aside for them.[16]

Thompson also reports that the faculty suffer from poor qualifications and a high turnover and that only 4 percent have ever published in scholarly journals. The administration is authoritarian, and all power is concentrated in the college president, who is typically authoritarian, arbitrary, and capricious and surround himself with weak and incompetent subordinates. Thompson concludes that the authoritarian administration, the confused or belligerent students, and the general anti-intellectual atmosphere cannot be bought out with money.

Of the trustees, Thompson concludes that they are out of touch with educational and social reality and fail to raise any substantial money for improvement. The theme of the work, however, is that black colleges have made a unique contribution to the education of blacks in America and indirectly to American society as a whole and that they have done this with grossly inadequate financial support while drawing upon a pool of under-prepared students from inferior southern schools. These colleges, he observes, are now faced with severe financial problems threatening their survival, largely as a result of increased competition from white institutions and from public black institutions, but still have an important role to play and need to redirect themselves and to receive additional funds.[17]

The fact is that private and public institutions that served black students are threatened by white private and public colleges and universities, especially since the claim of cuts in financial support to educational institutions. Serious questions have been raised regarding their usefulness in light of concerns for funding. In terms of costs and benefits, black colleges are less expensive to operate than white colleges. They pay their faculty less to teach more courses, their administrative budgets are less than those of white schools, and they have a lower overhead. They have less equipment and fewer facilities, especially recreational and research facilities. The controls placed on black colleges and universities over the years have created a role for these institutions that has excluded them from active participation in the creation of knowledge. This is an important role for educational institutions. For the most part, therefore, white educational institutions have dominated this role; if black institutions participate, it is as reactors to knowledge pertaining to black people. News media in major cities and even the major newspapers and television stations with national coverage seek the advice, commentary, and opinions of white scholars on economic, political, social, legal, educational, and religious matters as if black scholars do not exist. If, however, the matters are of a racial nature, a black scholar might be found at a white educational institution to participate and make comment.

Money-raising activities by the United Negro College Fund and other organizations have tried to enhance the role performance of black colleges, yet these colleges continue to struggle to survive. The very traditional role of producing black leaders on which fund-raising advertisement is based is being questioned. The argument is that these colleges simply provide the initial step in the process of education. It is this foundation at black colleges that is critical to black students for coping purposes at white universities where they continue their graduate and professional training.[18]

Responses to the advertisement by the United Negro College Fund have not been overwhelming, not even from blacks, especially those who have graduated from UNCF supported schools. Consequently, the role of the historically black colleges and universities has been controlled by policies and practices that are based on race for the purpose of domination and the lack of adequate economic support from those sources that fund white colleges and universities and from the black community. Between 1977 and 1978 enrollment was up at black schools; new courses were being offered, and these institutions were steadily looking for the federal government to assist in their struggle to survive. However, the Secretary of Health, Education and Welfare has given notice to black colleges that if they do not bolster their programs, they will be deprived of substantial amounts of money. The Secretary developed rules that would channel government grants to schools that show they are using federal funds to strengthen their curricula and to improve their academic programs. If there is no discernable improvement these institutions will lose millions of dollars set aside for "developing institutions" that serve large numbers of economically deprived students. The rules are tough and put these institutions at a disadvantage as they struggle to compete with white institutions for students, funds, and recognition in the academic world. There is evidence that the threat of losing federal funds has caused many black colleges to develop expanded curricula and remedial programs at relatively low tuition. The definition imposed by those who have reason to observe what is happening at the colleges is that the programs are not rigorous enough. If this were to be changed, black colleges would have to redefine their clientele. Presently, the majority of students at black colleges are poor and not initially very well prepared academically for rigorous academic programs. To change significantly would mean further competition with white institutions for the better and best-prepared students and an abandonment of the traditional student population that the historically white institution would not accept. Many black colleges have responded to the funding pressure by developing more challenging and contemporary courses in such areas as criminal justice, engineering, telecommunications, architecture, and nursing. Some black colleges have also established cooperative programs with predominantly white colleges. A few have also developed student-faculty exchanges with white institutions. There are those officials at white institutions who realize that black schools serve a function, that is, educating a large number of black students that they are not sensitive to and have no experience in successfully helping. Privately, black officials know this to be a fact and see a greater role for their institutions as a result of the Supreme Court's decision in the Bakke case.

Even though many black students are lured by good scholarships from white institutions attempting to increase their "minority" enrollment, about 90 percent of the students attending black colleges simply wanted to attend a black college. Some students lured by scholarships fail along the way, giving black colleges an outstanding record of student completion compared with white institutions. Aside from feeling more comfortable at black colleges, black students want to take advantage of the low tuition at black colleges. Black students have accepted the argument that if they are to participate in the mainstream of society they are to qualify themselves by obtaining a college degree and a graduate or professional degree. If the number of blacks going to college increases, and the income of their families stays below $10,000, black colleges will have to be cautious about raising tuition. They will have to appeal to the federal government for assistance. However, as the enrollment of black students increases at white colleges, more federal funds would be diverted from black colleges. Appeals have been made to the President of the United States articulating the great need to preserve the integrity and strength of black colleges and universities. Several of these schools, however, are under severe pressure in their attempt to maintain their racial and ethnic identity and comply with desegregation guidelines.

Mergers and Desegregation of Black Colleges

The federal government has in recent years intensified its efforts to de-segregate state systems of higher education. It is rather clear what the intent is and what the results have brought, especially when we note the elimination of predominantly black junior and senior high schools and their replace-ment by predominantly white junior and senior high schools. Tennessee State University is in the process of carrying out a court-ordered merger with the University of Tennessee at Nashville. Arkansas A&M was merged into the University of Arkansas system and, many feel, lost its character as a black school because it now has to conform to the policies and practices of a white system. Moreover, the presence of a significant number of white students and key white administrators also means change away from those values and practices peculiar to black students. The fact is that once merger occurs, these institutions do not remain the same. The shift in numbers is accompanied by a shift in purpose, meaning, hope, direction, academic perspective, norms, and culture. The view of students and many black administrators is that desegregation is the process of dismantling traditionally black educational institutions and disrupting the sociocultural foundation and tradition of black people for the purpose of control and educational domination. Some students argued that at the level of higher education it is the control of future collective protest and demonstration of an oppressive arrangement, including the oppressive nature and character of the educational arrangements. Some administrators argue that it is not so much the physical shift that should concern black people as the destruction of an educational mechanism that promoted and provided for the expressions and growth of a cultural tradition.

Since the passage of the Civil Rights Act of 1964, HEW has assumed the responsibility of enforcing state compliance with the provisions of Title IV of the act. Initially the states were encouraged to voluntarily develop desegregation plans. Title IV forbids any institution receiving federal support from discriminating on the basis of race, creed, color, or national origin. Most black institutions had complied with the provisions and had desegregated their faculties and students bodies. In fact, most black institutions had always had nonblack faculty members. White students were never discouraged from attending. The decision not to attend was primarily the function of the negative perceptions held by the white social order and the importance and credibility of black institutions to legitimize white students. White institutions had policies and practices that denied and controlled the presence and participation of blacks on their campuses. Most of these institutions were reluctant to do anything about compliance and the NAACP and HEW applied pressure for state compliance. Some state legislatures responded by proposing the merger of black and white institutions and the creation of white institutions near established operating black colleges. These institutions competed with black colleges for black students to achieve desegregation. Between 1964 and 1977, Maryland State College merged to become The University of Maryland-Eastern Shore and West Virginia State and Lincoln University at Missouri have desegregated to the point that whites now constitute a majority of the student body. Mention was made of the merger of Arkansas A&M with the University of Arkansas, losing its black identity. Delaware State, Kentucky State, and Bowie State are struggling to maintain their identity as black institutions, with more than a third of the student body nonblack. In 1972, students at Fort Valley State successfully fought an attack on their institution to convert the college into a white school. Blacks constitute a majority in the city and became politically active as voters to fight the attack. Florida A&M University (FAMU) has been fighting merger with the nonblack Florida State University (FSU) since 1967. Attempts were made to simply abolish FAMU; to make it a satellite of FSU; or to change it into an undergraduate school concentrating on specialities not offered at FSU. The pattern of all of the proposals to merge indicates the intent of states to desegregate the institutions where the racial identity of the white institution is maintained and to radically alter the racial identity of the former predominantly black institution.

John Engerton says that "there is a blueprint to get rid of Black institutions. We're not talking about integration but disintegration, not about merger but submerger, not about equity but inequity.'' Many black local leaders predicted this trend because they observed the closing and in some cases the takeover of almost all primary and secondary schools in the South by nonblacks. In the process, the principals and other persons of authority were forced to retire, transfer, or be demoted. In an effort to achieve equity and justice, the NAACP has argued in court that plans for desegregation should include specific "proposals to enhance predominantly Black colleges.'' The guidelines of July 1977 developed by HEW include requirements for states to establish timetables and goals for upgrading the status of black institutions. Furthermore, the guidelines allow for specific steps to be taken to strengthen the role of traditionally black institutions in the state system. Commitments for improving physical plants, program offerings, research equipment, and the like are indicated.

The case of Tennessee State University and the attempts to have it absorbed by the University of Tennessee at Nashville will have far-reaching implications for the survival of those black colleges and universities that now remain. District Judge Frank Gray, Jr., ruled that Tennessee had "an affirmative duty" under the Fourteenth Amendment to the constitution "to dismantle the dual system of higher education which presently exists in Tennessee.'' Many blacks and whites assumed that TSU would merge with UT at Nashville with administrative control at UT. The judge took most by surprise in his last ruling by declaring that Tennessee State University should absorb the University of Tennessee at Nashville, by July 1, 1980. The judge noted the "reluctance of the powerful University of Tennessee to take significant steps to eradicate dualism in Nashville.'' The only alternative, he concluded, "is the merger of TSU and UTN into a single institution under a single governing board.'' This board is to be the state board of regents. The decision had never been made before for a black takeover of a predominantly nonblack institution of higher learning.

Savannah State College and Armstrong State College are still trying to work out plans acceptable to all parties. An attempt to lean heavily on the decision in the TSU-UTN case is advantageous because the case is similar in several respects. TSU was established in 1912, and the University of Tennessee at Nashville was established in the mid-1960s. Savannah State was established in 1890, while Armstrong State was founded in the 1960's. In both cases the white institutions were new constructions, attempts at such times to avoid having nonblacks attend black institutions and possibly dominating higher education in the cities and states. In both cases the institutions have made attempts at developing strategies to limit competition. They proposed a combination of joint and cooperative degree programs and exclusive assignment of certain other programs to one or the other institution. Duplication and competition continued as the judge found in the TSU-UTN case, placing the blame on the UTN officials. Savannah and

Armstrong are following specific proposals for cooperative degree programs and the desegregation of specific academic programs for each of the institutions to avoid duplication. It is felt that competition will continue in light of the designation of more attractive programs at one or the other institution.

In Louisiana the situation might be different. Even though the federal government is intensifying its efforts to desegregate state systems of higher education, predominantly black Grambling State University seems likely to stay that way. Grambling has had a tumultuous period in recent years. Acute financial difficulties with huge deficits, severe management and accounting problems, and faculty dissatisfaciton created a turnover in the presidency after forty-one years and the establishment of a new administration. The new administration struggled and politicized to gain state officials' support and managed to get the situation under control. State officials, who are mainly white, have voiced their commitment to the institution and have joined forces with the new administration and black leaders to assure a place for Grambling in the academic affairs of the state. Nonetheless, it is evident that if Grambling's identity as a historically black institution of higher learning is not tampered with significantly, the university will not be appropriated the kind of money required to make it a competitive institution. One thing is sure: It will not get the amount of money its white counterparts receive.

Louisiana officials want the system to remain the same, not willing to admit that there is a dual system operating in the state. The suit filed by the Justice Department to force compliance with desegregation guidelines in 1974 is still at the "discovery stage." Grambling University is older than Louisiana Tech University and only five miles away. Racial distinctions are also indicative of the governing structure of the Louisiana state college and university system with Southern University, a predominantly black institution, under a different governing board from that of Louisiana State University, a predominantly white institution.

Special appropriations have been made to Grambling because the state legislature believes that the institution is "uniquely suited to educating their special clientele of impoverished and often academically deficient black students." Officials at Grambling understand their special position in the state and argue that the students they serve might never get a college education if Grambling were not around. Furthermore, they note that Grambling is very sensitive to what their students require to survive and make progress. Therefore, Grambling is dedicated to "teaching unpolished gems in the rough." The survival of Grambling is based on this fact. However, there is another realization that legislatures respond to—and that is the fact that blacks in Louisiana are very political. Even though they exercise no real power in the state in terms of making policy, their political influence is growing, and legislatures understand that they have to reckon with such influence.

Most blacks who have graduated from a black college or university perceive their institutions as important systems for enhancing vertical social and economic mobility and support their retention as black institutions, but most alumni do not really support their colleges financially.

Grambling State University is not the only black institution experiencing financial difficulties. The case at most of these institutions is that new and more appropriate management systems are installed and organized efforts are being institutionalized for raising funds, but other problems threaten the survival and progress of black institutions serving the black community.

Langston University is being attacked and is not expected to survive, and others are being attacked through a proliferation of lawsuits that charge discrimination against whites. Alabama State University in Alabama was sued by Charles R. Craig, a white professor who was dismissed in 1973 and called the administration racist for dismissing him. Not only was he reinstated, he was promoted to full professor and awarded $22,500 in back pay. The judge ruled that Craig's dismissal was part of a "pattern and practice of racial discrimination against white persons" at the university. The university had denied the practice, but feeling powerless to fight "the system" agreed to rehire or promote nine other whites who joined Craig's lawsuit. A total of $209,000 back-pay awards were made to about fifty-seven persons who were either former employees or applicants invited to file a claim against the university after the court had ruled. This is the first time a federal court has found a black institution guilty of discriminating against whites. This is a strange racial phenomenon, as it was only fourteen years ago that various white institutions in Alabama, including the educational, systematically excluded blacks as buyers, consumers, participants, and employees.

The argument since the 1974 ruling is that there is racism on both sides. This, however, is the argument of whites who have come to feel guilty of racism and want blacks to share such guilt with them. Moreover, it is believed that this attack is another attempt of whites to control the progress of black people and the institutions established to meet their needs. What should be made clear is that racism and discrimination are not the same concepts. Racism is the establishment of policies and practices by one racial group on the consideration of race for the purposes of domination and control of another racial group. In a capitalist-colonial society the racially oppressed do not have the power to establish such policies. Practices that do not have the benefit of prior policy are not legitimate and have no power of control. Behavior that appears to be discriminatory, especially as perceived by the oppressors or representatives of that racial group, is behavior that is a response to domination and control. Most whites who use the term racism, even white sociologists, psychologists, and other such professionals, do not know the meaning of the concept and confuse it with acts of discrimination. Those practices that appear to be discriminatory are patterns of response to white society and its representatives who would like to have their cake and eat it also.

Social institutions form the foundation of a people. The church, the school, and the family constitute the basic institutions in the black community. It is no wonder that they have been under constant and severe attack from whites and their social order. As long as these institutions are weak and barely surviving, the people will be weak and unable to make progress.

Most black faculty and students usually raise questions as to the real reason white faculty elect to teach at black colleges. Most black students tend to avoid them if possible. Some chairpersons have had difficult times convincing students to take their courses. Some had to impose teachers on students by assigning required courses to white professors. One student remarked at a private black college, "It's not enough that we have to read their textbooks, they got to have them teaching required courses! The reason I came here was to get away from these white folks. They make me sick." A faculty member at a private black school identified white faculty and classified them as conservative racists and liberal racists. Conservative racists are those who perceive black students as being difficult to teach and distribute a large number of D's and F's with a sprinkling of C's to ease their racist conscience. Liberal racists are those who give students the impression that they don't really have to study or read the material in order to pass their courses. Consequently, students do very little and end up with D's and F's. These professors are somewhat popular on the campuses and have their regular get-over students register for their courses. Those students who attempt to learn may succeed in getting B's and C's. For the students the results are the same. A majority are not motivated to learn and are not expected to learn, and their grades tell the academic story of ignorance and failure. Those students who are aware of the situation, along with many black faculty, develop negative attitudes toward white faculty, and white faculty interpret their presence as intruders. The contempt and hatred that most black faculty and students have for the conservative and liberal racists do not allow whites to feel welcome on black campuses.

Although there is evidence of contempt and hatred toward most white faculty at black college campuses, there is little or no evidence that there are policies and practices established by these colleges on the consideration of race for the purpose of domination and control of white faculty members. To the contrary, there are black faculty who have been silenced and even fired who articulated concepts and views that made white faculty uncomfortable. Most black college administrations have always acted as if there was something special in having a significant number of whites on campus.

Some colleges paid them more and gave them special attention in faculty meetings and committees. When we observe the entire picture, the treatment of white faculty on black college campuses is significantly better than the treatment of black faculty at white institutions.

Black people are always the losers. Black colleges are now under attack, being charged with reverse discrimination by a white system that established the rules of segregation and racism. Why should black people and black institutions have the burden of correcting a practice that they had no part in establishing? Black colleges have never been guilty of segregation. Whites made the rules that prohibited whites from attending or mixing with blacks in educational settings and other social settings. The system has not corrected its institutions, but sees fit to exert pressure to make black colleges comply with rules that white institutions pay little or no attention to. Black faculty are dismissed from black schools each year. That a white faculty member is the only one in a department, an experience blacks have had for years, does not mean that he or she cannot or should not be terminated if it is the decision of those whose responsibility it is to make such decisions. This is a common practice towards blacks at white college campuses, especially if the professor is not tenured. Blacks were the victims for whom the laws against discrimination were established and are now the victims against whom the laws are being applied.

White faculty make up 24 percent of the full-time faculty at black colleges in the South. Only a very small percentage of the 54 percent who hold doctorates obtained them from outstanding or strong universities. The majority of their degrees were obtained from good colleges and colleges rated as adequate. On the other hand, the majority of the 35 percent of blacks who hold doctorates obtained their degrees from outstanding and strong universities.

Those majority of whites on the black college campuses came out of the civil rights movement and have missionary attitudes of helping an underdeveloped people and their institutions gain status by their presence. They soon shifted their focus from the traditional objects and subjects for reform to the black underdeveloped institutions as objects for reform. This attitude has antagonized faculty, students, and administrators. Most white faculty at black institutions have a takeover complex with a strong desire for recognition and domination. Their aggressive disposition is usually interpreted as wanting to have their way to sense that they have some power even in a black situation.

If a white professor sees his future tied up in being reinstated in a permanent position at a black school, it is usually because that person has not published or has not done much more than teach classes and could not obtain a comparable position at a white institution. Very few white faculty at black institutions bring in research and grant monies. Very few of them publish. Many of them have come to feel very secure financially; and when evaluated and dismissed, they are shocked that blacks have standards to apply to their presence and performance. The realization is that the oppressed rejected the presence of a member of the oppressor group. This is a psychological blow to white faculty, and no doubt they would seek redress from their fellow whites who control the legal system. Rejection and disapproval are difficult to deal with normally, but when whites are subject to such from blacks, it is more difficult to accept, especially when professional positions provide the context for rejection and disapproval. Usually they expect to be promoted for just being there, as if that were sufficient. The same question raised by white faculty at black colleges as to whether it is possible under the law for black institutions to remain black-controlled should be raised by white institutions. Those concerns are dangerous to the survival and progress of black colleges and universities in light of the fact that there is no possible way for whites to lose their control over white-dominated and white-controlled educational institutions. It is evident that whites who share the thought that they don't know whether it's possible any more, under the law, for blacks to continue control of traditionally black institutions are dangerous to the black colleges, especially if they are not advocating Indian, Mexican, or black control over traditionally white institutions.

Most white teachers at black institutions are cookie-cutter teachers. They are anxious to have their students internalize values that advocate conformity. Students are made to feel that it is not necessary to raise critical and radical questions about the American system for purposes of change. Black professors who raise such questions are labeled classroom radicals. In many cases, they are even ridiculed by white faculty with no challenge heard from black faculty or students in whose presence the ridicule is made. Most white teachers are afraid of serious critical questions raised in the classroom about the social order, the content of the course, or the selection of the textbook. Taking the teacher to task, as is the interpretation and perception of white teachers, is an indication of loss of control of the classroom, and in turn, a powerless position in the thinking of other students. As a result, their classroom performance is weakened and they fail to teach adequately because they constantly try to manage the perceptions held of them by black students.[19]

Teaching Black Students

In an attempt to pay attention to the political and economic factors that threaten the identity, survival, and progress of black institutions, black faculty and administrators have not given the attention to the teaching process, content, and academic climate in the classroom as a place for gripe sessions or as a rapping room where they talk about irrelevant issues that could easily be dealt with on the corner or at the student center. This is the case, especially in classrooms where there are no podiums for teachers to place their notes. Instead of preparing appropriate notes and placing them on the table where they would be very obvious to students, they avoid dealing directly with the subject or being very specific about the subject for fear their students would develop a low esteem of them as they read or otherwise follow their prepared notes. Some courses lend themselves, by virtue of the content, to rapping; others do not. Most students are frustrated during the exam period because they are usually faced with specific questions taken from the assigned book or study guide for teachers. A majority of black teachers are dedicated to the teaching process at black colleges. These are the ones who see teaching black students as an art and a challenge. There are those teachers who have published widely and do so regularly. However, there are those who are so lazy that they have never written anything for publication and are just as lazy regarding matters related to the teaching process. These faculty do very little if any critical thinking, writing, and research. Basic and applied research and critical writing complement teaching and critical thinking and are important to the creation of knowledge, which the majority of black colleges and universities have not been involved in, which explains in part their low visibility and academic power.

Black students must be allowed to gain small degrees of success that will motivate them to continue trying and building on that initial success. Moreover, black students, as is the case with most persons, must experience a degree of success to enhance self-reliance and self-worth.

The struggle of black people for the right to gain quality liberating education must be instilled into black students. If this is fully understood, students will take the process much more seriously. Those who come to this realization tend to value the development of the mind, which is essential to the progress and creation of knowledge about a people. In the process of creating thinkers, well-trained, concerned, aware, dedicated, and committed teachers are crucial. With such faculty the atmosphere in the classroom is enhanced and the motivation to know, or to learn, becomes greater.

Black faculty must invite their students to promise to study. A commitment to that end is the buying of the book assigned to the course. Many students reason, especially in cases where required books are expensive, that they might as well get something out of their investment. Many students make an effort to study and read if they know the books were carefully and especially selected with them in mind. They develop a sense of concern and tend to enter into a trust relationship with their teachers. Material, to be relevant to black students, must not only stimulate intellectual thought but must answer certain questions and offer solutions to problems.

Many black teachers complain about the high number of failures and low scores in their classes. They hasten to assign blame by noting the kind of students attending black colleges today and the intellectual attitude students tend to embrace. Some have been heard to remark that students of the 1970s have a don't-care attitude toward the educational process. Many even complain that students do not listen and that they are preoccupied with trivial matters. Even if this were true, the responsibility and challenge of the teacher is to break their preoccupation and enter their minds.

Most teachers are one-method professors. They simply lecture or discuss; they give false-and-true, multiple-choice, essay, or oral exams; and so on. Those students for whom the method is suited succeed, and those to whom the method is not suited fail. Failure in this sense is not the function of the inability of the students. Rather, it is the lack of understanding of the academic position of the students and the method most suited to promote intellectual action. Black teachers should accept students where they are and start there and take them where they ought to go in order to influence their will to take intellectual action. Once teachers determine what motivates or influences the free will, mental force can be employed to induce intellectual and academic action. Students will take action when they think they can get a value they do not yet have, or when they think they can save a value they may lose. Black teachers must know how to deal judiciously with them.

To break preoccupation in any situation, teachers have to use words, action, or emotional gestures to get most students to listen. As students differ in strength in terms of what appeals to them, a variety of these approaches may be employed. The material will reach students when the right preoccupation-breaking approach is used. What stands between many students and their teachers is not a lack of knowledge of the subject matter by the teacher, but a lack of an understanding of what motivates students and the attitudes that preoccupy them. Consequently, they do not know what emotional and intellectual approaches to use to arouse or persuade them. Teachers must learn to observe action so as to discern motives and interpret actions. Listening carefully to students allows teachers to determine what preoccupies their thoughts. If farmers want to have a successful season of crops, they do not simply throw seeds all over the ground. They study their soil. Effective teaching requires the choice of the right approach or a combination of approaches. Personal enjoyment; a desire for reward, pleasure, riches, money, possessions; a desire for novelty, originality and new experiences; a desire for popularity, reassurance, and appreciation are motives that can be employed to arouse students to intellectual and academic action.

When black teachers know their subject matter and the motivational and emotional character of their students, they can become most powerful teachers. Teachers expect students to come with a high level of intellectual motivation to the classroom. But there are several levels at which they come: high, neutral, and low. Teachers should begin where they are and not where they ought to be.

All teaching must be persuasive. Teachers must persuade students to take some intellectual, academic, and/or practical action or to believe some fact, information, or ideas. Therefore, teachers must build into their teaching expectations for students that are clear and precise. The fact is, however, there are many teachers in higher education who are not persuasive, nor do they have any expectations of their students. The importance of being persuasive and having expectations is that it demands an intelligent and purposive structuring of materials and ideas for presentation, discussion, and analysis. In the process, there must be unity, coherence, and emphasis. Effective teaching requires arresting the attention of students, creating an interest, arousing a desire to study and learn, and implanting conviction and commitment in the minds and wills of black students.

At the beginning of each class, teachers should seek to relax the students. They must create an atmospherre that will help the students release the tension they bring to the learning experience. Attempts must be made to stress the importance of the developed mind and that the development of the thinking faculties is one of the most important endeavors students could be involved with. If this message is understood, the questions of attention, interest, and motivation will be answered. Teachers can use themselves or other persons they know as reference and examples. John Hope Franklin, W.E.B. Du Bois, E. Franklin Frazier, Eric Lincoln, Oliver Cox, Nathan Hare, Joyce Ladner, J.J. Johnson, Henry Bullock, Lee Brown, Al Pinkney, Francis Wesling, Hanes Walton, Jr., and many others are excellent examples for purposes of identification. It is more significant if those referred to attended the particular institution or are present as teachers at the college or univeristy. Students must come to realize that it is liberating to know and that knowledge plus action is power.

Students are dynamic beings with intellect and emotions. Therefore, teachers must address the intellect and the emotions of students in the classroom. They must present their material in the most attractive way to excite a desire in students to possess it.

There are times when teachers teach for a whole semester and deal with questions students have already answered in other classes or with questions they are not asking or interested in. They sometimes spend an entire semester offering solutions students already have or solutions to problems they are not facing.

Teachers need to convince black students that their presence is valuable and important in the classroom. They should be made to feel as though they are partners in the business of education. The benefit of attendance must be stressed in terms of announcements that are made, a danger of getting information secondhand, the technique and process of note-taking, the art and process of developing the ability to think, the intellectual exchange of ideas, and the value of getting to know the views and sharing the aspirations of other developing human beings. What teachers and students get out of their classes is what they collectively put into them. The context of this process is the kind of classroom environment that is created and maintained.

Teachers should use books, articles, and other materials authored by blacks or having a black perspective. Somehow the use of works by blacks promotes a sense of the possible and a reassessment of capabilities and promise among black students.

The story is told of a black student who waited until his last year as an undergraduate to take a required statistics course. He walked into the classroom filled with fear and apprehension. His hands trembled from spells of nervousness. As the time approached for the class to begin, the silence became more apparent and stressful. His heartbeat was louder and a little faster as the time neared for the professor to enter. In he came, a medium-sized black man with an Afro haircut that was not especially neat. He had a full beard that he stroked as he walked to the desk. He greeted the class as he pulled off an old jacket and threw it across the chair and introduced himself as the professor of the class. Suddenly, the black student reported that his fear began to take flight. The teacher handed out an outline for the course on which appeared works of the professor. The student said later that he almost said out loud, "If he can teach and write in this area, I can learn the material." The student made a B in the class and never had a conference with the professor. This is the importance and significance of the prepared black professor.

Teaching Methodology

While issues of content, course outlines, textbooks, theories, and the like are important to the process of education in the classroom, some discussion must be given to the issue of teaching methodology. Traditional teaching methodology is authoritarian and dominating, which promotes class and intellectual snobbery. To avoid this bourgeois style of teaching some teachers are tempted to employ the "do your own thing" style of teaching. The class flows at the express wishes of the student as the structure and content of the course is developed. Both methods of teaching are inappropriate in the classroom at black colleges.

Effective teaching is providing the social context of the content and ideas, which do not exist in a vacuum. Special attention must be given to the social context of the subject matter for most students to fully understand and put the content in proper perspective.

Although lectures cover more materials, they should be short. Long lectures may not allow for the learning of more material. Therefore, short lectures, think-and-listen discussion groups with focused questions on the material, question-and-answer sessions, after coming together again on questions that arose from the short lecture, or questions assigned by the teacher related to the lecture and a report to the whole class from each group may increase the amount of material that is actually covered and learned. Reinforcement of the material may be achieved by having two or three students present short summaries of the essential points of the previous class. Teachers can organize this activity so that every student who is willing will have an opportunity to make oral presentations, especially in small classes. This process allows the teacher to know each student better. In the process the teacher has the opportunity to point out the strengths of students. This does not preclude making supportive criticisms. If teachers recognize the potential for growth and development they can create confidence in the students as they seek to learn. Black students do not need to feel invalidated in the process of learning. In a society that seeks to invalidate black people, strong criticism is destructive and renders the students helpless and reinforces pessimism.

Black students are human beings who are inherently characterized by the possession of enormous intelligence. Most of the problem of learning in the classroom is not the lack of inherent intelligence; rather, the problems stem from the suppression of intelligence in a class-stratified society. This suppression does not allow for clear and critical thinking and analysis. In a society that needs an easily disciplined labor force, rigid and indoctrinated forms of thought are usually promoted in the classroom.

The fear and anxiety associated with the learning process create stressful situations and provide for the control of critical thinking in the classroom. When information is received in a stressful context it gets locked into the mind without being analyzed or sorted out. Any other information is blocked out, ignored, or distorted. It becomes difficult to correct false information and argue for the acceptance of correct views. Moreover, stressful situations distort thinking and enhance indoctrination. Certain teachers in the classroom create and generate stressful situations by their very presence and attitudes or as a result of the definitions and interpretations by students of the teachers' presence and attitudes. Some teachers create feelings in many students of being worthless, inferior, and unimportant. These feelings are painful to black students, especially when generated by black teachers. Such feelings do not allow for the development of self-respect, which is crucial to the development of and the utilization of intellectual abilities and inherent intelligence. It is difficult to study effectively, think clearly, and take appropriate action when students are depressed, and especially about themselves. The stressful situation interferes with the process of thinking and creates a certain amount of defeatism and cynicism in students.

Many students come into the classroom depressed, anxious, fearful, and expecting the worst. Black teachers must establish a positive class environment by spelling out clearly what the course is all about and the hopes for the student. Following this, teachers may ask each student to introduce himself/herself to the class and make a statement about his/her hopes and how the classmates may assist in the realization of these hopes. This may relax the members of the class and create a collective spirit among the group. It could also break the doldrums of the beginning of class and deal with the isolation students tend to experience in the classroom environment.

The black community has always attempted to survive and make progress as a collective. Collective actions to survive as a people indicate the African philosophical/behavioral principle of the survival of the tribe and the oneness of their being. The Euro-American philosophical/behavioral principle is the survival of the fittest. This philosophy breeds extreme individualism and competition in the process of educating black students, contrary to the basic principle of their survival. Supportive situations where students work together in the classroom enormously increase the learning and thinking process in the classroom. There must be a serious effort to increase the abilities of students to participate in teamwork. Collective effort will enhance a sense of caring, friendliness, and concern, which is lacking among college students today. This may be achieved by breaking the class into small units of work groups with specific tasks. Students must also be encouraged to think and listen. Teachers must allow students time to speak without interruption. This helps the student speaking to focus on what he/she is saying and forces the other students to listen if they are to be responsive. Some teachers have a small committee elected by the class who would bring anonymous criticisms, grievances, complaints, and compliments to them. Although doing it directly is best, too many sociopolitical problems may result. Many teachers are afraid of critical comments from students, especially teachers with identity problems and those who may have feelings of being inadequate.

With so many obstacles, including dominating teachers and finances, learning is a difficult process. Many of these obstacles are painful and impede the process of thinking and the development of other vital skills for survival and progress. There are many contradictions in the classrooms and in the society that black people must deal with.

As teachers, blacks must attempt to reduce the obstacles and to provide the social and political context for the materials and content that must be discussed in the classroom environment. Teachers must also assist students in the development of a perspective on the several fundamental contradictions in society and the classroom process. Teachers may accomplish this task only by embracing new methods of teaching that are not dominating, invalidating, irrelevant, isolating, authoritative, and repressive.

Notes

1. See Office of the Adjutant, Letters Received, vol. I (Washington & National Archives, War Records Office), 1866.

2. Melvin Dremmer, ed., *Black History: A Reappraisal* (New York: Doubleday, 1968), p. 290.

3. D.O.W. Holmes, "Seventy Years of the Negro College—1860 to 1930," *Phylon*, 10, no. 4 (1949): 307.

4. A.A. McPheeters, "Interest of the Methodist Church in the Education of Negroes," *Phylon*, 10, no. 4 (1949): 343.

5. Horace M. Bond, *Negro Education in Alabama* (New York: Associated Publishers, Inc., 1969), p. 196.

6. Horace Bumstead, "Higher Education of the Negro—Its Practical Values," Report of the Commissioner of Education for the Year 1902, Vol. I, 1903, pp. 225-26.

7. Ibid.

8. M.F. Armstrong and Helen W. Ludlow, *Hampton and Its Students*, p. 23; Samuel C. Armstrong, *Twenty-two Years' Work of Hampton Normal and Agricultural Institute*, p. 1. Samuel C. Armstrong, *Annual Report*, 1878, p. 5. See also other annual reports on both Armstrong and Trissell, and Samuel C. Armstrong in *Report upon Hampton Normal and Agricultural Institute* (Hampton, Virginia, 1869), p. 8.

9. Samuel C. Armstrong, *Annual Report* (Hampton Normal & Agricultural Institute, Hampton, Virginia), 1886, pp. 3-4.

10. William A. Avery in *Hampton Normal and Agricultural Institute: Its Evolution and Contribution to Education as a Federal Land-Grant College*, Bulletin, 1923, U.S. Bureau of Education, p. 72.

11. Hollis Burk, *Tressell Report*, 1904; Edith A. Talbot, Samuel C. Armstrong, *A Biographical Study* (New York: Doubleday, 1904), p. 209; Booker T. Washington, *Working with the Hands* (New York: Arno Press, 1904), p. 58.

12. Mack H. Jones, "The Responsibility of the Black College to the Black Community: Then and Now," *Daedalus*, p. 737.

13. Ibid.

14. Gerald McWorter, "The Nature and Needs of the Black University." *Negro Digest*, March 1968, pp. 4-13. Darwin T. Turner, "The Black University: A Practical Approach," *Negro Digest*, March 1968, pp. 14-20. Christopher Jencks and David Riesman, "The American Negro College," *Harvard Educational Review* 37 (November 1, 1967): 53. Mack H. Jones, "The Responsibility of the Black College," p. 738. Henry Allen Bullock, "The Black College and the New Black Awareness," *Daedalus*, p. 573-602. Nathan Hare, "Legacy of Paternalism," *Saturday Review*, July 20, 1968; "Behind Black College Revolt," *Ebony*, August 1967; and "Final Reflection on a Negro College: A Case Study," *Negro Digest*, March 1968. Bernard Haletson, "Higher Education for Negroes," *Atlantic Monthly*, November 1965.

15. Jencks and Riesman, *American Negro College*, p. 53; Turner, *Black University*; McWorter, *Nature and Needs*.

16. Daniel C. Thompson. *Private Black Colleges at the Crossroads*. Westport, Conn: Greenwood Press, Inc., 1973.

17. Ibid.

18. Douglas Davidson, "The Furious Passage of the Black Graduate Student," *Berkeley Journal of Sociology*, 1970-71.

19. See Lorenco Middleton, "Black College Guilty of Racism: Some of their Whites Charge," *Chronicle of Higher Education*, December 11, 1978; also L. Alex Swan, "White Professors at Black Colleges and Universities," unpublished study, Department of Sociology, Fisk University, 1976-77; Donnie D. Bellamy, "Whites Sue for Desegregation in Georgia: The Fort Valley State College Case," *The Journal of Negro History*, 64, no. 4 (Fall, 1979): 316.

11

Forty Acres and a Mule: Restitutive Justice

Introduction

In discussing the political presence of blacks in the American social order and their relative economic and political position, it must be borne in mind that, unlike all the other inhabitants of America, blacks came to America against their will and without their own consent. Blacks originally were compelled to leave their country of origin through physical force. It must also be kept in mind that once in America blacks were forced to labor for approximately 250 years under circumstances that were cruel, harsh, inhumane, and exploitive. That is, they were laboring not for their own economic benefit but for the benefit of those who owned their labor and their persons. In 1619 the Dutch brought twenty slaves to America. By 1890 the census taken showed that the number had increased to 7,638,360. Approximately 6,353,341 of this number resided in the southern states, and the rest (1,283,029) were scattered throughout the western and northern states. By the 1900s the number of blacks was about ten million. Whether they were in New England or the southern states, they were owned. As slave labor was not as remunerative in the northern states as it was in the southern states the greater portion of slaves were held in the southern states, where they were used in raising cotton, rice, and sugarcane. From 1619 to about 1876, the white man had organized his slave property, his farms, and other industries—his whole industrial and economic system—on the basis of the production capabilities of black labor. Since that time he has developed and established policies grounded in certain practices on the consideration of race and social position for the purpose of maintaining those economic and political benefits accrued and derived during the period of slavery through oppressive and exploitive measures. Although technically, slavery (physical control and ownership) began on the shores of Africa, the appropriate place to begin the discussion of restitution and the process of victimization of Afro-Americans is at the historical point of entry in America.

Many groups may argue that they have experienced economic exploitation, but black people are the only group in America who have experienced both economic and physical ownership, victimization, and racial oppression resulting from the construction of the political, economic, educational, and legal arrangements of the system. The specific focus here is black people as victims of these arrangements. Further, the basis of their victimization, the dynamics of victimization, the purposes and consequences of victimization, and the necessary restitutive measures to restore black people to a whole position as a means for equal economic and political power are general concerns.

Although black people as individuals and as groups have been victims of political, racial, and economic crimes at the hands of white people, such as lynchings, beatings, and other killings, there have never been any legislative measures to prevent or restore their families to a whole position or even to compensate them in any substantial manner for such crimes. The state has also been party to such crimes either by commission or omission and by maintaining a set of legal arrangements restrictive to the economic and political advancement and progress of black people. The concept of victim does not only include victims of crimes defined by the law, but also victims harmed by certain racial policies and practices and legal regulations determining economic and political positions. No wonder racism and oppression have not been defined by law as crimes.

Sidney M. Willhelm[1] and others, including Eric Williams[2] argue that slavery came into being for economic reasons that were used to rationalize the enslavements of blacks. Because the English settlers brought with them certain racial prejudices and beliefs, it is concluded that economic forces plus racial prejudices explain the origin and continuation of slavery and its effect. After America had established its economic foundation through commercial racism by reason of slavery and free and cheap labor, (oppression and monopoly) industrial capitalism was created, which eliminated the kind of labor provided by slaves and the entire black population. Once the political, economic, and educational arrangements were established and controlled, legal equality achieved through certain constitutional measures functioned to give the black population a sense that things would improve. However, the fact is that the situation of black Americans has not substantially changed since the days of slavery. In fact, the idea of legal and constitutional equality placed the burden for black success on the backs of blacks. The victims are blamed not so much for the origin of their victimization but for their continued victimization. Consequently, blacks are seen as themselves responsible for their lack of progress. Profit-making is the main concern of America and it is achieved by any means at the expense of anyone or any group, especially former slaves and the descendants of slaves.

If the situation gets worse, which some predict will be the case, and blacks are no longer useful to the profit-making motive of America, black America will experience genocide, as in the case of the Indians, who were no longer economically useful to Europeans. When the Indians became useless and their labor was no longer needed, racism took the more complete form of extermination rather than exploitation. Some thinkers are of the opinion, based on their observation of history, that black people are faced with the probability of the same treatment from governmental programs focused on control of the black population.[3]

There is a discrepancy between the poverty of the majority of black people and that of white people. This discrepancy is a function of the systematic historical exclusion of blacks from entrepreneurial activity in the American society. It can also be explained in terms of the historical relegation of blacks to functionally menial positions in the economic life of America. The present economic condition of blacks, therefore, has a historical basis and has manifested itself in the same manner throughout every period in American history.

Because whites as a group and as the keepers of the system did not want black people to control and own substantial financial resources, blacks have not been free or have not been allowed to invest in any significant way in profit-making enterprises. In fact, they have not had the economics to make substantial investments. Comparatively, only a token number of blacks own businesses in America, and most of those that are black-oriented are not owned by blacks. A few blacks own a small number of banks with capital so small that they are not particularly significant in the community and lives of black people. There are a few black-owned life insurance companies and a few federally insured savings and loan associations. These businesses are not increasing for blacks but are in fact decreasing. The problem is that the capital outlay is so small that they cannot compete. Moreover, the colonial nature of the oppressed black communities and the historical presence of racism have caused blacks to lose faith in the possibility of progress. Therefore, the progressive competition by blacks is inadequate. Credit standards, the lack of adequate credit, and the lack of available collateral have also influenced, and in many cases determined, the economic and political progress of black people. Aside from the fact that blacks have little or no property or investments to use as collateral, because insurance companies are reluctant to cover property in the black community, insurance costs are almost three times higher for blacks than for whites. The result is that those small businesses in the community that cannot pay these high costs to operate and compete are eliminated by big businesses and large corporations that continue to dominate the American economy. Small businesses in the community cannot continue to function with the proliferation of chain supermarkets because they do not have the economic capacity to compete. As blacks are historically assigned to unskilled labor while unskilled labor is not the primary factor in the American technological economy, it is difficult to forecast political and economic equality for black people. With the lack of large black-owned businesses and blacks at a high national level of corporate management, the colonial and oppressive role of dependency of the black community on the system and on white people who control the economy will continue to exist. This is really the position that the system wants blacks to assume and maintain. This is the reason that the promises to restore black people to a whole position for the crimes resulting from racism and oppression have not been made good. This is also the reason that blacks as victims of the police force, state violence, oppression, exploitation, domination, and racism have not been included in the popular conception of the victim. However, as Quinney argues, "The victim is a social construction. We all deal in conventional wisdom that influences our perception of the world around us. This wisdom allows for us just who the victim is in any situation. What this also means is that alternative victims can be constructed."[4] Consequently, an "alternative world view" may be assumed to conceive of alternative victims.

Blacks as Victims

Implicit in the social construction of the law is the conception of the victim. Every crime has a victim. Eugene Perkins argues that crime is "any social harm defined and punishable by law."[5] Crime is derived from the Latin word *crimen*, which means "an accusation," a tort or wrong done by one individual against another or by a group against another group. However, as Quinney notes:

all conduct which could conceivably result in social harm is not regulated by law. Only those acts which cause harm to those who are able to make and enforce the law become crimes. And similiarly when the social harms that are a part of the written law cease to be regarded by those in power as a harm to their interests, these laws are no longer enforced. While every act may conceivably involve a victim, only those acts that threaten the welfare of the ruling class become crimes. Social harm, no matter how abstract, is a reality decided upon by those in power.[6]

Because our conception of the victim is influenced and in some cases determined by the law, it is difficult to conceive of the victim outside of the crimes of rape, fraud, homicide, stolen property, and the like. Whites as well as blacks conceive of blacks as victims of an oppressive and racist set of arrangements (the system), but the conceptions that regulate the lives of us all and establish public policy are those held by those who rule the system. Some criminologists have influenced public policy and the ability of the ruling segments of society by arguing that in certain crimes the victim plays a significant role. What is argued is that the victim makes a contribution to his own victimization.[7] Others have argued that there are crimes without victims.[8] The arguments in both cases do not speak to the case of black people. Black people have never consented to racism and oppression and have not been willing to suffer such crimes. The protest, resistance, and struggle by black people have primarily been directed at liberating and freeing themselves from such crimes, and secondarily at gaining equality. Somehow, black people have privately realized that equality would not be achieved unless something drastic were done. To the extent that they have not resisted, they have been part of their own victimization, but black people have not made any contribution in this regard except, however, in those instances where they were forced to do so or sensed a requirement or a pressure to do so.

Forty Acres and a Mule

"Forty Acres and a Mule" is a slogan that stands for the promise once made to black people that was never fulfilled. The promise was made to address the issue of restitution. The slogan became popular in the 1860s and expressed the compensation the slaves expected to receive from the federal government when they were emancipated after the Union victory.[9]

With regard to the case of black people, America has always had a conception of the nature and extent of the groups' victimization. Because black people suffered from the historical effects of criminal racism and oppression, the world view of reality has changed to exclude blacks as victims who have a right to restitution. Black people's world view of reality has to include their case as one of victimization for which the system and those instances where they were forced to do so or sensed a requirement or Without this reality we are bound to be exterminated. Black people are becoming more and more superfluous economically; and although there is little overt activity to indicate the extreme racial hostility that exists, the system and those who own, rule, and benefit from it make profit out of repression and oppression. This is a result of the loss of economic value on the part of black people. This is a serious problem as we face the future, because the related problem is that of who has value in the society and whose lives must be sacrificed when we run out of space, good air, clean water, and the like. The world view of reality that includes blacks as victims of crimes of racism and oppression at the hands of the system and those who own, rule, and benefit from such crimes has rendered the victims powerless, with no value that needs to be considered or addressed. The mule and forty acres have accrued interest and dividends to which black people have a claim as one means of establishing economic value for their situation.

In 1974 a white Iowa farmer by the name of Joe Dorgan at the age of 79 willed all of his fortune ($400,000) to black people. Dorgan seemed to have understood the presence of black people in the American society. He watched the riots during the 1960s, and they told him something. He got a message that many white people did not get. He interpreted the riots and the reasons for them as the greatest national disgrace of America. He said, "We (whites) stole them (blacks) from their land, crammed them into ships like animals and we've been treating them like animals ever since." This is the reason he left his fortune to blacks. Dorgan's niece was bitter, as were other whites, who said that the money "had always been handed down through the family, and now this. If he had given it to the church, a hospital, a university or something like that—but this, giving it to blacks, is so far out. It doesn't sound like him at all. He had good days and he had bad days. He must have decided this on one of his bad days."[10] Dorgan must have remembered the promise America made to blacks to supply them with land and mules. As the promise was not kept and there was no successful way of redressing the issue, he made a gesture of restitution. This was not a compensation, for Dorgan recognized and realized his role and the benefits he and his family had derived from the historical presence of blacks in America. He included himself as an offender against blacks and pronounced guilt on all white people when he said "we." All white people have benefited, by definition, from the crimes of racism and racial oppression. The land and the mules were willed and bequeathed to them, and they have developed economic and political power as a result. For those who do not now have such power, the system provides the potential for such power.

Many black people, especially our youth, may not know anything about the "forty acres and a mule." However, every black person, especially the youth, knows that something is wrong, but has no answer to the functionally powerless positions that are ascribed blacks in the system. Moreover, older people have no power, economically or politically, to will and bequeath to black youth. To argue and advocate equality and equal opportunity does not correct the historical situation and compensate the victims. It simply asks the victims to continue to struggle under grave odds assisted by legal equality, which has not and seemingly does not have the capacity to be translated into corrective economic and political gains.

Most people, black and white, who do not fully understand the problem argue against compensation or restitution. In the early 1970s there were blacks who refused to be promoted on the basis of being black. There are those today whose argument is the same. Those who make decisions to hire, promote, and give advances have never taken very seriously a concern for quality or qualification. This is the reason there are so many ill-prepared and unqualified whites holding significant and not too significant jobs today. Whiteness and what it has come to mean in the American society in relation to blackness and what it has come to mean in economic and political terms has always been an element in the various economic and political decisions made in the society. In light of the fact that many matters have been decided on the basis of race that resulted in crimes of racism and oppression, it is not liberating to advocate equality of opportunity when these matters have not been corrected. It is also a mistake to deny promotions and the like because the consideration is apparently based on race. It really is not based on race; rather, the corrective decisions are based on what race has come to mean and the effects of those meanings in terms of policies and practices that oppress, control, and dominate black people.

There are those who say that while it is true that blacks have been treated badly as slaves and as freed people with few political, economic, or civil rights, others have suffered and overcome. However, over 200 years of slavery and continued oppression and racism with the visibility as blacks and the historical meaning of blackness defined in economic, political, and at times legal terms that accompany the experiences and presence of black people, have not been significantly challenged to offset the neglect and exploitation that cripple black people today.

There have been massive expenditures to improve the employment, housing, and education of blacks to make up for centuries of racism and exploitation; but this apparent special treatment has not done anything substantial to the economic and political power position of black people. The reason is that by definition of the economic and political order most of the expenditures went into the pockets of those who own, rule, and benefit from the system. The victims of the system have not benefited from these massive expenditures. On the back of a book written by Charles V. Willie entitled *A New Look at Black Families*, Willie notes an estimate by The Council of Economic Advisors that during a single year, $13 billion more would have been placed in the hands of blacks had there not been any racial discrimination in employment.[11] If we were to multiply this figure by ten, twenty, thirty, or fifty years, the economic situation that black people now face would substantially change if these billions of dollars were in the hands of black people circulating in the black community.

During the 1960s, the late Whitney M. Young (1963) of the National Urban League declared that

the nation must undertake an immediate and tangible "crash program"—a domestic Marshall Plan—to close the "intolerable" economic, social and educational gap, which separates the vast majority of black citizens from other Americans. . . . the scales of equal opportunity are now heavily weighted against blacks and cannot be corrected in today's technological society simply by applying equal weights. For more than 300 years the White American has received special consideration, or "preferential treatment," if you will, over blacks. What we ask now is that for a *brief period* there be a deliberate and massive effort to include the black citizen in the mainstream of American life. Furthermore, we are not asking for equal time, a major effort, honestly applied, need last only some ten years. . . .the crash programs that we propose are not an effort to impose the guilt and sins of a past generation on our present white community. This is an appeal for all Americans, working together to rid present-day America of its sickening disease and its moral shame."[12]

Years have passed, and the situation is graver. However, compensation is not what black people are seeking. This society owes black people a debt that has never been paid. Paying this debt brings justice to the position of black people; it will correct historical wrongs and place blacks in an economic position to really compete if that is what is required to make progress. Equality of opportunity, which really does not exist, and massive economic programs where the monies return quickly to those who own and rule society, have not changed the situation. The paying of a debt acknowledged by the offenders and the beneficiaries of the original offenders is the only means for justice and equality. Paying the debt is not penalizing the living to collect a debt owed by the dead. The living beneficiaries owe the debt also by virtue of the fact that the benefits and the political and economic potential to those benefits were willed and bequeathed to them. It is a common legal practice and principle that the property and benefits of a deceased owner can be used to pay his debts. The benefactors become responsible to the victims and the victims' social group. It is just to recognize the rights of the victim to be restored by the offender and the humanitarian concern for the restoration of the victim. The victims do not seek pity but justice.

Blacks as victims of America's historical crimes of racism and exploitation seek restitutive justice because the offenders are solvent and have the ability to make monetary payments. Forty acres and a mule are not sufficient. What blacks seek is economic and political justice, which will cost much less than the programs already proposed and acted upon. However, the benefits will go directly to the victims.

The slave economy in which black human beings were treated as property and denied the fruits of their labor is the start for the analysis and discussion of restitution. Black people have not been rewarded for their labor and upward mobility has not been theoretically or actually unlimited. It was through the utilization and exploitation of this labor that the United States was able to lay the foundation of what has come to be a powerful economy. Malcolm X described the origins of the American economic strength in this manner:

Our mothers and fathers invested sweat and blood. Three hundred and ten years we worked in this country without a dime in return—I mean without a dime in return. You let the white man walk around here talking about how rich this country is, but you never stop to think how it got rich so quick. It got rich because blacks made it rich.[13]

Martin Luther King, Jr., subscribed to this notion by saying: "Few people consider the fact that in addition to being enslaved for two centuries, the Negro was during all those years robbed of the wages of his toil."[14]

Understanding the economic plight of Afro-Americans, which has persisted since 1619, there have been demands from the Urban League and A. Philip Randolph for a $10,000,000,000 "Freedom Budget." The Nation of Islam asked for the exclusive possession of six or seven southern states (land and its resources). There have been similar demands from various other groups within the black social movement. The consensus is that restitution in the manner defined here is the only way for blacks to achieve economic and political equality and justice.

Restitutive Justice

The concept of restitution suggests a sense of sociopolitical responsibility on the part of those who commit crimes against individuals and groups. It also offers the possibility for the restoration of the rights and interests of those individuals and groups who have been victims of crimes.

The idea of restitution is not a new notion. It had its place in primitive and ancient societies. Its concern, however, focused on the rehabilitation of the offender's social group in addition to the rehabilitation of the offender's tution of the victim and the implications restitution has for the offender and the offenders' social group in addition to the rehabilitation of the offenders' social group.

Benefits made to the victim of crimes by the community and not by the offender were defined as compensation. Benefits paid to the victim by the offender were regarded as restitution. The distinction made by contemporary thinkers on the subject is not particularly useful to this discussion, as our definition is rooted in nullifying the effects and damage to the victim. It is therefore not very important who provides or pays the benefits to the victims. Moreover, for us the offender is not simply an individual, but rather the society and individuals as beneficiaries of the victimization.

The crimes committed by the society are crimes committed through a set of political, economic, educational, and legal arrangements that brought benefits to some and victimization to others. For local restitution, as when an offender steals a television from a victim, it might be significant to have the offender directly involved in the process of restitution. However, when the offender cannot be identified except through a series of collective criminal acts, benefits from collective crimes, and the present position of the beneficiaries of a history of victimization, it is not useful to identify the exact individual as offender except to identify the individual as a beneficiary of political and economic victimization. Power through the arrangements was willed and bequeathed from the actual and real offenders to the offenders' social group. The responsibility for restitution is the collective unit that guaranteed benefits to the offenders' social group on whose behalf the arrangements were established and maintained. The present beneficiaries are responsible as beneficiaries of a collective unit and have a direct responsibility to the victims. The role of the individual beneficiary is simply the recognition of his/her historical position relative to the arrangements that made him/her a beneficiary in relation to the victims. Restitution, therefore, embraces the notion of the offender as a collective unit. As a collective unit, whites have benefited from the victimization of blacks as a collective unit.

Historical Perspective

As societies developed, punishment of the offender shifted from retaliation and revenge by the victim or private vengeance to vengeance regulated by the collective order.[15] Acts of crimes and violence committed against a group or a member of a kinship group by outsiders met with the retaliation of the entire group. Retaliation and vengeance by the kinship group was not without certain regulations and rules.

The ancient scheme did not require the identification of the offender as a member of the social group for the payments of benefits to the victims. The code of Hammurabi provided that "if a robber has not been caught . . . the city and governor in whose territory and district the robbery was committed, shall replace for him his lost property." The code further provided that "if it was a life that was lost, the city and governor shall pay one mina of silver to his heirs." In many ancient societies statutory schemes incorporated restitutive provisions within their penalty structure establishing not only individual responsibility but also communal responsibility.[16] Redress was achieved through economic means, and in many cases the offender was required to compensate the victim beyond the value of the damage. For assistance in the process of restitution the king or lord was paid a commission. This fee was also for protection of the offender against further acts of retaliation by the victim and/or the victim's group. It was the victim's behavior that was called into question, as the concern was for the control of the victim who could pursue private vendettas in response to wrongs perpetrated against him.

However, the fee of restitution decreased for the victim as power became centralized in society even to the point where the state replaced the victim as the offended party. In the process, the state assessed fines against the offender and assumed the right to punish and received compensation from the offender. Evidently, the increasing need of the state to exercise political control over the members of society accounts in part for this shift. The punitive power of the state supplanted the direct relationship between the victim and the offender. Damages claimed by victims became less and less appropriate to the penal process as the state assumed the moral and political power to exact punishment from offenders.[17] This move by the state was to strengthen central authority and reduce the fear of vengeance by victims of crimes of personal violence.[18] The police were used to note the behavior of the victim, who was believed to be desirous of seeking private punitive actions against the offender. Furthermore, as the victim's claims became burdensome and prejudicial to the process of criminal prosecution, the mechanism by which assets could be transferred from the offender to the victim was relegated to a civil forum, with the state assuming a neutral role.[19] However, restitution in some form has never disappeared from society, but the increasing greed and power of the state provided the basis for the shift of restitution to the victim to restitution to the state defined as the victim. It was this shift in the process that set the stage for the development of restitution in civil law rather than its significant role in the administration of the criminal law. The consequence is that the victim became responsible for initiating civil action against the offender. In many instances the victim was financially incapable of seeking remedies. In many of those cases adjudicated, the offenders were poor and insolvent and found it difficult to comply with the judgments against them. Therefore, this process of civil remedy was not an effective restitutive measure for the victim.

In the evolutionary process where political power became concentrated in the state and the state became stronger, the interests of the state overshadowed the interests of the victim. Schafer puts it this way: "As the state monopolized the institution of punishment, so the rights of the injured were slowly separated from the penal law: Compensation as the obligation to pay damages became separated from the criminal law and became a special field in civil law."[20] In the process the state became more concerned with its power to punish the offender than with the sufferings and claims of the victim. Although the emphasis of restitution decreased in the criminal law, the notion that the victim is entitled to restitution remains unchanged among criminologists and the general public. It is even argued that the duty to impose restitution upon the offender is one that society should advance. In the event that the offender is not known or otherwise not actually identifiable, the society should assume the responsibility for restitution and compensation.

Restitution is argued here as a corrective and correctional device to redress the injury of the victim and to provide an educative value and liberating experience for the offender. As a matter of policy, those who rule and own the society must be made to be responsible, as beneficiaries, for the restitution of the victims. Payments should be made from restitutive funds to victims by the offenders as indemnification for the harm caused by their crimes.

The American social order has not protected black people from crimes of racism and exploitation. Because the state has failed to protect black people, which is its duty, it has incurred an obligation to indemnify blacks who have been victimized by the collective criminal acts of racism and exploitation. A restitutive scheme should be established and administered through a community agency.

The reawakening interest in the victims of crime has developed in many states. For the most part, there have been compensation schemes rather than restitutive schemes involving payments by the state to the victim. The offender is not involved in the programs. However, in the case of black people, the state is the offender along with those who own, rule, and benefit from its arrangements. Therefore, the offender would be involved in the program and the program would be restitutive.

The society passed sentence on itself for the acts of violence and crime against black people by promising forty acres and a mule and again by admitting that the society is racist because it has made political, economic, and legal decisions on the consideration of race for the purpose of control, domination, oppression, and exploitation of black people. As black people have not yet received forty acres and a mule and as the crimes continued over the years have resulted in physical injuries, the loss of property, physical pain, and mental anguish, the state is responsible for restitution as an offender of black people as victims. The state is aware of the harm it has caused. The question is how we determine how much is owed the victims. Massive programs in which vast amounts of monetary expenditures are made have not worked because the programs are designed to defend the beneficiaries. They are not usually designed to really benefit blacks as victims. More importantly, blacks are not merely interested in being compensated for the crimes of the past, but the crimes of the past have established the crimes of the present and the inability of blacks to achieve equality and justice. The power to be beneficiaries of historical crimes was willed and bequeathed in the set of arrangements that have come to be defined as the system.

Calculating the Debt

There are approximately twenty-five million black people of African descent in the American social order whose parents and grandparents have suffered physical and mental pain from the crimes of racism and oppression at the hands of those who now own and have owned and ruled the system. For those crimes those who own, rule, and benefit have not paid the victims even though they have acknowleged their crimes and have been convicted by the victims and by themselves. It is time that payment is made to the victims. Until such debt is paid there will be tension in the society and the sense that justice has never been achieved. This will result in conflict at various periods in the future of the society.

Most black persons in America can trace their existence to a great-great-grandfather and mother who were taken into slavery. Many blacks have ancestors of royal lineage and have suffered socially and psychologically from many of our names, that speak to our oppression rather than to our pride.

If we were to calculate from twenty years of hard slave labor for each slave ancestor, we could estimate the number of slave labor hours on which to collect monetary value from those who rule, own, and benefit from such labor. Twenty years multiplied by twelve months per year equals two-hundred and forty months; multiplying by four weeks per month equals nine-hundred and sixty weeks. Nine-hundred and sixty weeks multiplied by six days per week equals 5,460 days. When we multiply this figure by fifteen, which represents the numbers of hours worked each day, we get 81,900 hours of slave labor. Because slave labor was the basis for economic development of America and because the millions of dollars made as a result of the labor of black people were never shared with blacks as partners or skilled workers, the charge for such labor per hour is a minimum of one dollar. When we multiply the number of hours of slave labor by one we arrive at $81,900 to be collected by each black person on behalf of each great-great-grandparent. If we were to multiply the amount of money due each Afro-American by the twenty-five million blacks in America we would arrive at the amount of $2,047,500,000,000 that now has accrued to black people. This debt does not include the payment for the lives of millions of blacks who died during the passage from Africa to the New World and to the United States of America.

This debt that we must collect, if justice and equality are to be obtained and achieved, is for work done from which we never benefited and for the crimes of racism and oppression from which black people continue to suffer economic damage at the hands of those who were willed and bequeathed economic and political power through the operation and mechanisms of racism and oppression. As we seek to apply the notion of restitutive justice to the cases of those who have been victimized by offenders, we must also define blacks as victims of a racist and oppressive society by which they have not been compensated even though forty acres and a mule were promised as a restitutive gesture. Now dividends and interest have accrued, and justice demands that the debt be paid. We call for a "Community Restitutive Justice Committee" to handle the procedures for determining those who are eligible and the manner in which distribution will be made to the black victims of crimes and violence. This committee should meet with the political leaders of the nation, along with the leaders and owners of the major giant industries and corporations, to work out the monetary details. This is not money for programs and the like but money to be paid directly to each black victim. Restitution is being advocated.

The black caucus should take a leadership role in the process of restitution, and the details of distribution should be worked out at the state level. Once this debt is paid the offender would be free and may be assured that the victim will no longer, expect, demand, or struggle for equality of opportunity. Until this debt is paid black people will continue to struggle to survive without making any real progress. Moreover, we will continue to be deceived by White America, the owners, rulers, and potential owners and rulers who display individual members of the black community as examples of black progress, creating the sense that the lack of progress among us is related to racial (group) inability. The burden then rests with the victim to experience progress against defeating odds.

The good news of restitutive justice should be spread throughout the black community, and an organized political effort should be staged to demand the restitution of blacks as a social group to a whole position. The promulgation of a sense of change and progress among black people is defeating and stagnating. Restitution is not a new practice in the political and economic affairs of the American system. After each war with Korea, Germany, and Viet Nam, America engaged in forms of restitution that required the expenditure of billions of dollars to assist victim nations in reestablishing themselves to their whole position. The Marshall Plan is one example of the restitution efforts of the American social order. There were a few congressmen who argued against such efforts, but the Congress and the system approved billions of dollars to restore the economy of these governments and to reestablish America's imperialist position in the affairs of other nations.

The Indians are beginning to have some success with their restitution efforts. They have won legal actions in the court that have gained them money and land. Presently, their activities are confined to a few states. No doubt they are contemplating expanding such efforts to include other states, and even the federal government.

Legal action is required on behalf of black people. Every black legislator should introduce a restitution bill for discussion and action by the various legislatures. The Congressional Black Caucus should also introduce a restitution bill for discussion by the Congress. This bill could establish the basis for a Black National Agenda around which black voters should be organized. The president's support should be sought, and the consequences of lack of support should be clear. Some of the present problems of stress and those related to the economic and political position of black people will be solved. Most of the survival crimes of robbery, mugging, burglary, auto theft, and other such thievery will be solved if restitution is realized by the black community. No economic issue is as important to black people at this time as the question of restitution. To ignore the issue as some whites have indicated, admitting to the claim for restitution, is to kindle additional and continued conflict and racial hostility. The debt is legitimate and should be paid so that black people might be restored.

Notes

1. Sidney Willhelm, *Who Needs The Negro* (New York: Doubleday, 1971).

2. Eric Williams, *Capitalism and Slavery* (New York: Capricorn Books, 1966).

3. Samuel F. Yette, *The Choice: The Issue of Black Survival in America* (New York: Berkeley Publishing Corporation, 1971).

4. Richard Quinney, "Who is the Victim?" *Criminology* 10 (November 1972): 314-23.

5. Eugene Perkins, *Home is a Dirty Street: The Social Oppression of Black Children* (Chicago: Third World Press, 1975).

6. Richard Quinney, *The Problem of Crime* (New York: Dodd, Mead and Co., 1970), pp. 29-42.

7. Stephen Schafer, *The Victim and His Criminal* (New York: Random House, 1968); Marvin Wolfgang, *Patterns of Criminal Homicide*, Philadelphia: University of Pennsylvania Press, 1958.

8. Edwin M. Schur, *Crime Without Victims* (Englewood, N.J.: Prentice-Hall, 1965).

9. Claude F. Qubre, *Forty Acres and a Mule* (Baton Rouge, Louisiana: Louisiana State University Press, 1978).

10. *Ebony*, March 1974, p. 58.

11. Charles Willie, *A New Look at Black Families* (New York: General Hall, Inc., 1976).

12. Whitney M. Young, Jr., "Domestic Marshall Plan," *The New York Times Magazine*, October 1963, p. 43.

13. Malcolm X, quoted in George Breitman, ed., *Malcolm X Speaks* (New York: Grove Press, 1965), p. 32.

14. Martin Luther King, Jr., *Why We Can't Wait* (New York: New American Library, 1964), pp. 81-82.

15. Marvin Wolfgang, "Victims' Compensation in Crimes of Personal Violence," *Minnesota Law Review* 50 (1965): 223, 229; Stephen Schafer, "The Victim and His Criminal," *President's Commission of Law Enforcement and Administration of Justice*, Ref. Doc. 5.

16. Richard L. Worsnop, "Compensation for Victims of Crime," *Editorial Research Reports* 11 (September 22, 1965), p. 693.

17. Leroy L. Lamborn, "Remedies for the Victims of Crimes," *Southern California Law Review* 43, no. 1 (1970): 28-29.

18. I.O.W. Mueller, "Compensation for Victims of Criminal Violence," *Journal of Public Law* 8 (1959): 228; Dogan D. Akman, "Compensation for Victims of Crimes of Personal Violence: Idea and Realization," unpublished paper, March 1966, pp. 3-6.

19. Leroy L. Lamborn, "Remedies for the Victims of Crimes."

20. Stephen Schafer, "Victim Compensation and Responsibility," *Southern California Law Review* 43, no. 1 (1970): 66-67; *Compensation and Restitution of Victims of Crime* (Montclair, New York: Patterson Smith, 1970).

AFRO-AMERICAN RESPONSE

12

The Black Social Movement: Response to a Racist-Capitalist System

Black students of the black social movement and the black experience are raising critical questions about the ability of the movement to achieve liberation and freedom for black people and to give incentive and direction to other oppressed peoples. The questions have come at a time when it is evident that black people have temporarily withdrawn from activism and when the reformist mood of America has changed to more rigid oppression, covert racism, and control of black progress. However, it is also evident that the political consciousness of black people has been raised regarding their economic and political position in America. As a consequence, blacks will again become very active in the struggle for liberation and freedom, in spite of the posture they now assume. Before such time, however, there are a number of issues about the movement itself and the nature of the American social order that students of the black experience must understand.

The American society is a reformist society, and gradual change or gradualism is its philosophical and pragmatic posture. Gradual change takes place over a long period of time, and power shifts from a few individuals to another few individuals within the same racial group. Power and control are bequeathed and willed within one racial group. Representatives of oppressed groups might assume apparent power with no real power to make policy to influence and change oppressive practices that affect the groups they represent. This posture of change does not have the potential for the liberation of black people. More importantly, the very nature of the American social order is in contradiction to the liberating efforts of black people. The mode of production in the black community is the exploitation of black people in industries and other economic enterprises owned by and operated for the profit motives and social well-being of racist-capitalists. Consequently, the property that blacks possess is the legal property of racist-capitalists who have title to such property. Therefore, the majority of the money earned by blacks find itself in the hand of those who dominate and control the political economy of the American social order. A number of individuals are involved in this process. Many whites and blacks identify with this oppressive process not fully understanding its dynamics.[1]

Organized and Unorganized Resistance

From the close of the eleventh century, when Europeans began to explore West Africa, and later, when Portuguese merchants realized that they could enrich themselves by selling captured black Africans to work as slaves, blacks resisted their domination and control. Moreover, as soon as Europeans realized that blacks possessed the color potential to annihilate them, they made rigid their institutional arrangements to control the economic, political, educational, and sociocultural progress of blacks. As a result, blacks have been regulated and relegated to token and thereby powerless positions within these arrangements. While blacks remain biologically superior, according to Dr. Francis Welsing, because of their color potential to annihilate whites, they remain functionally inferior, that is, they have functioned at an inferior level within the social system.[2]

There was resistance on the shores of West Africa and on the ships that brought captive blacks to the shores of the New World. It is believed that over half of the captured blacks died of various causes during the passage from West Africa. During the period of slavery in America there were over 250 slave revolts. Some are well known and others are not. Many were well organized, and others were not well planned. However, they collectively demonstrated the insistence of blacks on achieving freedom and liberation.[3] The revolts that are given much attention are those that occurred between 1800 and 1831. In 1800, Gabriel Prosser, a slave on a plantation in Virginia, organized a small group of slaves under divine mission to bring feedom and liberation to the oppressed. Slaveholders and their families were to be killed, and powerless and economically oppressed whites were to be recruited to join the fight against their wealthy oppressors. The revolt was well planned and organized, but a few blacks who had developed a sense of loyalty to their oppressors informed on Prosser and his plans to revolt. The revolt and the revolters were killed.

The revolt in Charleston, South Carolina, in 1822 was planned and organized by Denmark Vesey. Vesey was an ex-slave who had purchased his freedom. He became a preacher with a divine mission also to lead slaves to freedom and liberation. Again the plans of the revolt were disclosed to slaveholders by loyal slaves who felt the need to protect their oppressors. Vesey and his associates were killed along with many of their supporters. The revolts that are given much attention are those that occurred between had a degree of success, was led by Nat Turner. Like Prosser and Vesey,

Turner felt divinely called of God to lead black people out of bondage. Turner's revolt was subdued by armed militia, and he and many of his associates and followers were executed. It is evident that the executions of slaves who resisted their oppression influenced other slaves to employ more covert strategies for freedom and liberation. Stampp argues that:

no slave uprising ever had a chance of ultimate success, even though it might have cost the master class heavy casualties. The great majority of the disarmed and out-numbered slaves, knowing the futility of rebellion, refused to join in any of the numerous plots. Most slaves had to express their desire for freedom in less dramatic ways.[4]

Many black women who worked in the "big house" ground up glass and placed it in their masters' soup, causing many to bleed internally to death. Many field slaves set many plantations afire and acted as though something strange was taking place. There were thousands of slaves who ran away from the plantations. Freed blacks and white abolitionists assisted. The underground railroad, an organized effort to help slaves to escape, was very successful in organizing the escape of thousands of slaves in defiance of federal fugitive slave laws.[5] The constant and intense forms of oppression caused the resistence of blacks to be rather persistent. Between 1817 and the 1960s, the black social movement took many forms to bring about change in the powerless position of black people. The ideological positions of the various organizations within the movement must be clarified if an under-standing of the efforts of the movement toward black liberation is to be achieved.

The Black Social Movement

The black movement is a collectivity of people acting with some degree of continuity to promote or resist change in the social order and/or within a social group. The movement is, therefore, an aggregate of people and not a formal organization. The black movement has lasted over time and is goal-oriented. It is in existence to change the objective conditions of oppressed blacks.

The black movement has been outward-directed in that it has focused its efforts at change in the way in which whites have conducted their business against blacks, and at the negative values whites held of blacks. However, the black movement has also been inward-directed, focusing its efforts on change within the movement itself. Therefore, the black move-ment has been value-oriented and norm-oriented, but at various times since the slave revolts it has only made attempts at being power-oriented or control-oriented. The posture of this orientation allows blacks to advocate power for blacks to make the necessary changes themselves to control their situation and reduce significantly the domination and control of oppression. The value and norm-orientations simply appeal to those with power, those who dominate and control, and those with the potential to do so, on whose behalf the system was established and is maintained, to make adjustments of accommodation in their views about oppressed blacks and in the ways in which they conduct their educational, economic, and political business toward blacks. These orientations allow for power and control to remain in the hands of oppressors and would-be oppressors. The power-orientation or control-orientation advocates the assumption of power by the oppressed, which provides for the control of the territory of the oppressed and ownership and control of the various institutions and resources within the territory of the oppressed. It allows for some degree of control over external institutions that serve the needs of the people in the territory. It also allows for the reorganization of the oppressive arrangements of a racist-capitalist social order. The power and control attempts of the movement have been directed merely at the racist practices and policies and not at the combined and complementary dynamics of both a racist and capitalist social order. The free speech movement, for example, forced faculty and administrators to change their views of students. The civil rights movement forced many businesses to change their posture in conducting business toward blacks, but the civil rights movement was not a power-oriented movement.

To some degree the civil rights movement caused many whites to change the ways in which they viewed blacks. Theoretically, therefore, the civil rights movement and its various organizations were both value-oriented and norm-oriented. Their posture was to appeal to whites who exercised power and control over the lives of blacks and to those with potential power and control to change their views of blacks and the ways in which they interacted with them in political, educational, economic, and cultural matters. The posture was not to assume power to bring about the changes themselves. Very few individuals and organizations within the black movement advocated power or were control-oriented. Individuals and organizations that are value and/or norm-oriented come into conflict with those who are power/control-oriented even though they may share the need to advocate change. The change, however, is directed at individuals rather than at the social order.

Those of the value- and norm-oriented organizations within the movement do not share the same definition of society as those of the power/control-orientation. Their definition of those who control society and those with the potential, by virtue of their racial position in society, is different. Moreover, their perspective of the factors that motivate the oppressors and the possibility of change that would allow for the total power involvement of the oppressed in society is also different. These individuals and organizations operated simultaneously in society, even in the same community, because they shared the same historical experience of oppression and domination which produced their objective conditions and the sense that such conditions require change. Consequently, the nature of the conflict within the black social movement is a function of the beliefs about the nature and character of the social order, and the different definitions of the social order and of those who control society, held by various groups within the movement and brought to the struggle for change.

The varying definitions and associated meanings determined the methods employed to promote change and brought the various organizations into open conflict. The oppressor supported certain methods employed by certain organizations of the black movement to effect change and opposed and condemned others. While this action should have raised questions in the minds of leaders of those organizations, it validated, legitimized, and gave significance to such methods. In the process the degree and extent of change and progress was controlled by representatives of the oppressors who were in a racial position to benefit most from maintaining the status quo. Gradual change and reform do not benefit the oppressed, but rather they benefit those who dominate and control the political, economic, and educational arrangements of the society, allowing such power and domination, the several wars, and the killings, lynchings, and beatings during the group. The arrangements of the American social order have been established on behalf of whites and have been under their control ever since the territory was taken from the Indians through violence. It is also maintained through violence. This posture of control is evident in the American revolution, the several wars, and the killings, lynchings, and beatings during the 1940s, 1950s, and 1960s. Blacks, Indians, and other oppressed groups got the message that America was prepared to use any means necessary to maintain power and control over the arrangements that brought economic and political benefit to certain racial groups even though such arrangements oppress other racial groups. It's historically evident that many individuals and organizations within the black social movement did not develop a posture that promoted a struggle for liberation of the group. The posture has been for the reform of the social order that allows for the inclusion of "selected" and "safe" members of the oppressed groups, giving the rest of the members a sense of change and the representatives positions of apparent power. Even though there are hundreds of blacks and other members of oppressed racial groups in various political and economic positions in the society, they do not have real power to make policies and put into operation programs that would significantly benefit the masses of oppressed people and change their objective conditions. In the majority of cases, these individuals do not have the power to influence policies and programs. After all the struggle for several hundred years, the conditions of blacks and other oppressed racial groups in America are getting relatively worse. Black businesses are failing or merely surviving. Very few, if any, make real progress. Black schools and colleges are being taken over by the oppressor and their agents, not simply integrating individuals but destroying a collective history. Black politicians, judges, and others occupy powerless positions. The black community is still being exploited economically. Even though the earning capacity has increased in many cases, the earnings leave the black community for goods and services, leaving the community without an economic base for development. Very few, if any, industries are owned and operated by members of oppressed racial groups in their communities. Unemployment in these communities is record-high.

It seems clear that the failure of the black movement to bring liberation to oppressed blacks is a function of the nature and character of the social order. However, the black social movement has not organized itself in relation to the nature and character of the social order to achieve liberation. The Declaration of Independence argues, in its early paragraphs, that if a government and its arrangements have been oppressive to the experiences of a people over a long period of time, it is their duty to change and get rid of such arrangements. The basis for aggressive action against the system is established in this notion, but it was not intended to apply to oppressed blacks.

The Ideologies of the Black Social Movement

The black social movement has organized itself essentially around three ideals—the African Ideal, the American Ideal, and the Afro-American Ideal (see Table 9).

The African Ideal

The Back-to-Africa movement and its advocates represent the African Ideal. The early Back-to-Africa movement started at the turn of the nineteenth century when Paul Cuffee and many other freed blacks defined the social order as so oppressive that it was impossible for ex-slaves to obtain equality and justice in America.[6] The alternative was to return to Africa. The efforts of Cuffee and his associates received little financial support because there was still a need for the labor of slaves and ex-slaves. Nonetheless, by 1815, several blacks had returned to Sierra Leone.[7] Several blacks also emigrated to Canada.

Another advocate of the Back-to-Africa movement was Martin R. Delany, a physician, who was born "free" but the grandson of a slave. Delany opposed the Back-to-Africa movement initially but later shared the definition of the nature and character of the social order and the impossibility of blacks to gain equality and justice in America. He was convinced that

Table 9
TYPOLOGY OF ORGANIZATIONS WITHIN THE BLACK SOCIAL
MOVEMENT, 1880-1971

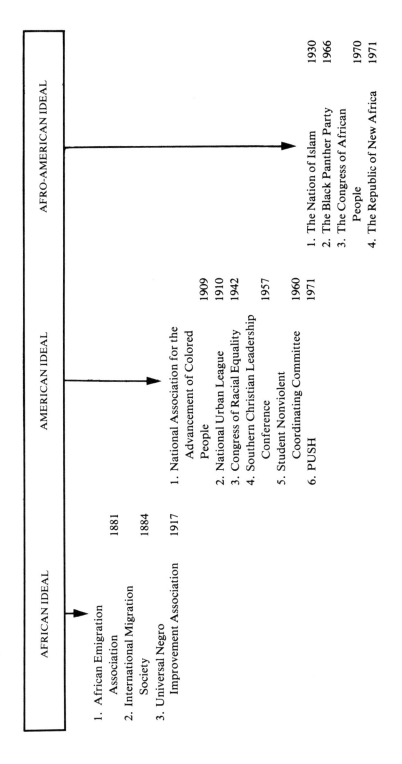

AFRICAN IDEAL		AMERICAN IDEAL		AFRO-AMERICAN IDEAL	
1. African Emigration Association	1881	1. National Association for the Advancement of Colored People	1909	1. The Nation of Islam	1930
2. International Migration Society	1884	2. National Urban League	1910	2. The Black Panther Party	1966
3. Universal Negro Improvement Association	1917	3. Congress of Racial Equality	1942	3. The Congress of African People	1970
		4. Southern Christian Leadership Conference	1957	4. The Republic of New Africa	1971
		5. Student Nonviolent Coordinating Committee	1960		
		6. PUSH	1971		

Africa was large enough and wealthy enough for blacks to establish a powerful nation in Africa. Delany remained committed to the idea of liberation for black people until he died in 1885, even though he modified his position regarding the African Ideal.

Before Garvey came to America in 1916 from Jamaica, Henry M. Turner, a bishop in the African Methodist Episcopal church, advocated the African Ideal. Turner believed and preached the resettlement of blacks in Africa. Turner organized the African Emigration Association in 1881, which failed in its efforts, but in 1884 he organized the International Migration Society. Through his efforts in this organization, severl hundred blacks were transported to Liberia. Turner's efforts in the Union army and blacks' assistance in defeating the Confederacy did not assure equality and justice for blacks. Turner's efforts were met with opposition and criticism from middle-class blacks, the black press, and leaders like Booker T. Washington who laid claim to the leadership of the poor masses. Turner died in 1915, the same year Washington died, convinced that all blacks should relocate to Liberia.

By the time Marcus Garvey got started in America, the masses of blacks had become disenchanted and disillusioned about the nature of their efforts to survive and make progress. Marcus Garvey sensed the mood of hopelessness and sought to speak to the issue. In 1917, he organized the Universal Negro Improvement Association, which was responsible for the development of business enterprises that were to build an economic base for the Back-to-Africa movement. Garvey was opposed by "elite" blacks who were advocating the American ideal. However, with the support of the black masses, Garvey was able to establish the Negro Factories Corporation, a chain of cooperative grocery stores and restaurants, and the Black Star Line Steamship Company. The Association is thought to have been infiltrated by persons employed to destroy the efforts of Garvey. The government seemed anxious to attack Garvey's efforts and hauled him into court for using some of the stock money for movement back to Africa. He was also convicted on a technicality in his advertisements of stocks. Upon his release, Garvey was deported, completing the design to crush the movement. The efforts of Garvey were destroyed because it was his personal charisma that had sparked the association. However, the African Ideal established itself as a viable alternative for change in the economic and political situation of blacks in America and other parts of the New World.

One of the problems the black social movement has had to cope with is the establishment of associations and organizations around the personality of one person. Whenever that person is removed, for whatever reasons, the movement tends to disentegrate. The Back-to-Africa movement was responsible for thousands of blacks who physically returned to Africa. However, it inspired thousands of blacks who remained physically in the New World to return culturally and spiritually to Africa. The Back-to-Africa movement was nourished by a consistent and persistent stream of African cultural survival.

The American Ideal

During part of the period between 1800 and 1917, the American Ideal (1905-1917) developed as an ideology and took root in the minds of many blacks. This ideal was supported mainly by black middle-class intellectuals and a significant number of whites who saw the economic and political importance of the black presence and began to define the Africans in America as American blacks. The notion that America was the home of blacks was being preached, and their rights within their homeland were being advocated. It was during this period that serious questions were being raised, especially after the Lincoln gesture in 1863, regarding the political, economic, educational, social, and legal rights of "former" slaves and blacks born "free." The white-organized American Colonization Society (1816-17) that promoted the African Ideal for racist reasons, organized efforts to establish laws that would restrict and even strip freed blacks of all the rights enjoyed by whites. Whites had opposed the convention movement that began in 1830 that sought to advocate and achieve social, political, economic, educational, and legal equality and justice for blacks, especially freed blacks. There was so much resistance to the efforts of those of the convention movement between 1830 and 1850 that the convention shifted its position from the American Ideal to the African Ideal. The African Ideal became attractive, especially after Liberia achieved independence in 1847.

Martin R. Delany was a leader of the conventions and an earlier advocate of the American Ideal. It was the efforts of the National Afro-American League in 1887 that again focused attention on the American Ideal. The Niagara Movement continued the focus in 1905; and the National Association for the Advancement of Colored People, which evolved from the Niagara Movement in 1909, pushed the ideal as its principle ideological position. All of the organizations were against the suppression of the voting rights of blacks, the unequal funding of black schools, the use of convict labor, the denial of public accommodation, and the racist lynch laws. To assure the continued struggle against these devices of control and oppression, the NAACP became the legal arm of the movement, using legal measures to guarantee the extension of all constitutional rights to blacks.[8] Through riots, lynchings, threats of violence, and assaults, whites persisted in their attempts to nullify the implementation of the Thirteenth, Fourteenth, and Fifteenth Amendments. Blacks received little or no protection from law enforcement because the police shared the political, social, economic, and racial ideas of their white group.

The NAACP established the goal of integration and pledged to end segregation in public accommodations and to provide protection from political assaults, violence, and murder. Furthermore, the association sought to employ its legal strength to obtain compliance and strict enforcement of the Thirteenth, Fourteenth and Fifteenth Amendments. By 1910 the Urban League was established, incorporated in 1913. As the NAACP had emerged from the NAAL and the Niagara Movement, the Urban League emerged from and represented the combination of the Commmittee on Urban Conditions among Negroes, the National League for the Protection of Colored Women, and the Committee on Industrial Conditions of Negroes in New York.[9] The League's primary concern focused on the improvement of the economic and social conditions of blacks living in cities. Both the League and the NAACP had significant financial support from white philanthropists, private charities, and business corporations. Furthermore, both boards of directors had a large number of white professionals and businessmen who secured support for the organizations. As a social-work agency the League has been active in finding jobs for blacks and other persons unemployed, promoting job-training programs, health education, open housing, vocational guidance, public welfare, day nurseries, clinics, and legal aid to those who needed it but could not afford it. The League's role has been enhanced by the litigation posture of the NAACP and the posture of direct action of the Congress of Racial Equality and the Southern Christian Leadership Conference.

The Congress of Racial Equality (CORE) was organized by James Farmer in 1942.[10] Farmer and a group of Chicago citizens who were a part of the Fellowship of Reconciliation, an interracial Christian pacifist organization, embraced the philosophy of nonviolent direct action. At first they confined their activities against residential segregation to the park areas and the privately owned roller-skating rink in Chicago. Restaurants that denied services to blacks were attacked. CORE launched an effective sit-in campaign in Chicago against discrimination in public and private places. By the early 1950s the organization began to organize nationally, with its focus on equality and justice in public-housing accommodation and employment. However, CORE gained national prominence during the 1960s when it organized the "freedom riders," forcing compliance with orders to desegregate interstate buses. CORE's efforts were very effective in the South even though their members were mobbed, beaten, arrested, and murdered. CORE secured compliance with the orders of the Interstate Commerce Commission issued to the bus companies in several states. Through the several chapters that were organized, the organization employed such tactics as picketing, boycotts, and sit-ins to desegregate public accommodations. Because desegregation efforts did not significantly bring substantive change in the objective conditions of blacks, CORE began to rethink its approach to change. By the middle of the 1960s the society that CORE hoped to open so that blacks might have free access to equality and justice was still closed. CORE began to reorganize the community for political action to change the racial policies and practices of the social order. The idea of organizing the community to harness its resources and potentials to bring about change on its own behalf paved the way for the leadership to embrace the notion of Black Power in 1966. Black Power is an ideological position represented economic, political, and consumer power. It also meant pride, self-determination, community control over institutions in the community, and some degree of control over those institutions external to the community that influence the lives of black people in their community. No longer was CORE interested in advocating integration. The leadership advocated black leadership and control under the notion of cultural pluralism.

In 1955, the Montgomery Bus Boycott was sparked by the arrest of Mrs. Rosa Parks in Montgomery, who refused to give her seat to a white man, thus attempting to break a custom. The boycott led to the formation of the Southern Christian Leadership Conference (SCLC) in 1957.[11] It was the Women's Political Council that advocated the boycotting of the bus after the arrest of Parks. After much planning and organizing the black community, led by the efforts of the local Montgomery Improvement Association, took to the streets. Martin Luther King, Jr., was selected as the leader of the Southwide organization, SCLC. The focus of this organization was full citizenship, total equality and justice, and complete integration of black Americans into the social order of America. SCLC became the major spearhead organization in the southern region for organizing civil-rights protests. SCLC, the Urban League, and the NAACP became the major advocates of the American Ideal. Black students on black college campuses in the South and in Washington, D.C., were significantly involved in the civil-rights protests and embraced the American Ideal. As a result, SCLC helped to organize and sponsor the Student Nonviolent Coordinating Committee.[12] By 1960, the African Ideal had little or no significant appeal among blacks in the black community because the major and most active organizations advocated and organized themselves around the American Ideal.

The collective efforts of the organizations that advocated the American Ideal produced several bills passed by the Congress of the United States. In 1964, there was the Civil Rights Act that forbade racial discrimination in public places, in labor unions, in employment, in state programs receiving federal aid, and in voting. A voter-registration campaign organized by SNCC and SCLC met with violent opposition from white citizens in the South, who attempted to continue to deny black citizens such rights. Blacks and several white marchers during the Selma-to-Montgomery march, which was to mark the end of the campaign, were attacked by whites. A voting-rights bill was being called for which would remove all obstacles to registration, eliminating all racist qualifying tests, and would give protection from white violence in the exercise of that voting right. In 1965, the Voting Rights Act was passed, giving the federal government, under the leadership of the attorney general, power to protect black citizens from physical violence.

The civil-rights organizations that advocated the American Ideal had organized hundreds of sit-ins, marches, and boycotts. There were even kneel-ins, wade-ins, stall-ins, walk-ins, stand-ins, and pray-ins. These non-violent tactics of disruption that were employed between 1960 and 1965 were met with violent opposition from whites and even the police who, under the law, were supposed to offer blacks protection. But because the police felt accountable to and identified with the white opposition, they in many instances joined the opposition in their protest against the exercise of the civil rights of black citizens.

Between 1963 and 1965 the conflict intensified as blacks increased their demands. The police arrested hundreds of demonstrators who picketed stores and called for the employment of and the upgrading of blacks in local business establishments operating in the black community and elsewhere. Local authorities used dogs, clubs, bullets, high-pressure water hoses, tear gas, electric prods, stones, and other weapons on women, children, and men to deter their nonviolent efforts for equality and justice. The federal government and also the local authorities were primarily concerned with the disruption of the operations of the local businesses, and not so much with the rights of black citizens and the racist practices of the business establishments. Federal and local intervention was to offer protection to these establishments, and there was public outcry about official brutality and racism.

The disenchantment with the advocates of the American Ideal who employed the nonviolent demonstration-legislation strategy intensified when in 1966 James Meredith attempted to walk through his home state of Mississippi to dramatize the problems of blacks resulting from racial and economic oppression. Meredith was shot in the back by a white man. This incident caused many blacks to reevaluate the American Ideal. The advocates assumed that the races are equal and that neither stands to gain from continued segregation. No significant or important value was placed on the particular characteristics of the black community. The position was that assimilation into the general American culture was desirable. The advocates intended only to force or persuade the system to live up to its own ideals and guarantee full equality and integration. They did not question the nature, character, and assumptions of the system or the objective of integration.

The Afro-American Ideal

By 1966, a significant number of blacks had come to realize that equality and justice would not be realized until black people developed a significant degree of political power. The issues of identity and dignity became very important to the majority of blacks. Consequently, the advocates of the Afro-American Ideal argued that strong emphasis must be placed on common identity and that before blacks integrate they must achieve power over viable alternatives. The desire and ability to exercise control over the community of black people as Americans was rooted in their ability to decide that their cultural heritage is African. The Afro-American Ideal is not only a cultural phenomenon connoting pride in one's race and racial group but is also a political and economic phenomenon advocating the rights of Americans of African heritage. The advocates of the Afro-American Ideal were committed to the goal of equality but came to believe that integration of the operations of the local businesses, and not so much with the rights face on the school board, for example.

The assumption that the society is worth entering has had disastrous effects because it leads to settling for a little now, with promises of more later. The social order is viewed as imperialistic with policies overseas that are racist and oppressive. There are also racial and economic policies and practices at home that are oppressive. Therefore, the advocates of the Afro-American Ideal argued that the society must be reformed before blacks can enter and expect to gain equality and justice. The integrationist approach was not working; and under the present set of arrangements, the white society was not worth entering. The advocates of the American Ideal asked for jobs, adequate housing, less police brutality; but the advocates of the Afro-American Ideal asked for, in addition, control over their own community and the resources. However, those who control the social order have been less willing to heed those who advocated the Afro-American Ideal than those who advocated the American Ideal. The primary concern of those supporting the Afro-American Ideal was the issue of black identity— encouraging blacks to take pride in blackness and their African cultural heritage and in black history, in addition to a struggle for the redistribution of power and wealth. The primary organizations that assumed this posture were the Black Panthers, the Black Muslims, the Congress of African Peoples, and the Republic of New Africa.

By 1966, many of the students who were involved in the civil rights struggle had come to define the system as being so racist and oppressive that it would require new tactics and strategies to achieve equality and justice. The achievements of the nonviolent demonstrations and the legislative efforts did not seem to change the objective conditions of the masses. Moreover, many of the young student leaders, inspired by the insights of Malcolm X, who spoke of the dissatisfaction with integrationists and with the reformists, advocated revolution and black nationalism. The rebellions between 1964 and 1966 were indicative of the fact that the civil rights activities had failed to help grass-root blacks.

When the Black Panthers were organized in 1966,[13] under the leadership of Huey P. Newton and Bobby Seale, they had a reformist posture seeking to change the political and social conditions of Black people. The physical security of community people was essential to their efforts. Therefore, they sought to protect blacks in the community from constant and unnecessary police brutality. They secured guns and patrolled the black community in self-defense against the oppressive activities of the police. As these students studied the society in relation to the black community, a political ideology developed that gave direction to their strategies and tactics. The community was defined as a powerless colony where the people were being exploited and controlled by internal and external forces, and where unemployment, ill-housing, and other oppressive conditions persisted. The Panthers defined the system as a capitalist-racist social order that should be overthrown and replaced with democratic socialism. They argued that it was impossible for the present system to address the issues of equality and justice for oppressed and exploited black people. They advocated revolutionary nationalism as a political approach to achieve the rights of blacks as Americans and the importance of the identity of blacks as Africans. The preached the overthrow of the American social order but did not seem to have any real revolutionary plans to do so. However, the Panthers made noble attempts to protect the black community from police brutality and to supply certain other basic needs of the poor.

The Congress of African Peoples consisted of cultural nationalists who advocated the Afro-American Ideal but did not preach revolution as a means to the end of liberation. In this regard, they differed from and in fact opposed the revolutionary tactics of the Panthers. The opposition is rooted in the belief that a cultural revolution that attempts to unify the black community must precede a violent revolution, otherwise a violent revolution could not take place in America. The cultural nationalists opposed alliances and coalitions with white revolutionary groups and preached the doctrine of Kawaida—traditional black values and customs—which embodies the following principles of a black value system: self-determination, collective work and responsibility, unity, purpose, co-operative economics, creativity, and faith.

When the Congress of African Peoples was founded in 1970[14] the primary goal of the organization was to promote pride and self-confidence through a new value system[15] among Afro-Americans. A secondary and complementary purpose was to develop among Afro-Americans some significant degree of political power. Their goal was to have political power transferred from whites to blacks, especially in local areas where the masses of blacks lived, so that progress toward liberation could be made. Because the condition of blacks got worse, Amiri Baraka, one of the leaders of the cultural nationalists, changed his ideology[16] and openly advocated the overthrow of capitalism. Although there is little organizational support given to cultural nationalism, the individual and group expression of cultural nationalism persist and give meaning to the historical experiences of peoplehood among Afro-Americans.

The Nation of Islam that was founded in 1930[17] also represents the Afro-American Ideal and combines religious, economic, and cultural nationalism. Unlike the Congress of African Peoples and somewhat like the Black Panthers, the Nation developed into an organization with chapters (temples) in every major city. Through its emphasis on economic security and development, self-reliance, self-respect, and self-pride, the Nation demonstrated that Afro-Americans can achieve a significant degree of independence and autonomy from white society. The members of the Nation are taught to obey the law but not to be subservient to white authority, especially to law enforcement officials. Nonetheless, many members have encountered police harassment and unfair treatment at the hands of police.

The fundamental argument of the Nation was that the black man was the original man and the white man is therefore inferior to the black man. Allah, the supreme of the black man, will one day reappear in America to establish freedom and liberation from oppression. The perspective on the white man shared by members of the Nation was that he was incapable of human emotion, compassion, and love. On the basis of this the Nation advocated the separation of the black man from the white man. In the mid-1970s this position was modified. The Nation established schools to teach its young people self-pride and the importance of pride in cultural heritage. However, the most impressive record of success is in the area of economics. The economic empire is considerable and is estimated to be worth over ninety million dollars. The Nation owns many acres of farmland where they grow vegetables and raise cattle and chickens. They have several factories where clothes are manufactured, as well as retail outlets for their clothing. The Nation also owns a fleet of jet cargo airplanes, apartment houses, and printing plants. From all accounts, the Nation is expanding and shows no signs of failing. The Nation advocates the cultural and religious importance of Afro-Americans and their economic rights as Americans. The nationalist sentiments in the black social movement of those who advocated the Afro-American Ideal have achieved a significant degree of unity among blacks, especially during the period of the 1960s, yet liberation has not been achieved and oppression still exists.

Conclusion

The black social movement has experienced a transition in ideal from the African to the American to a position that synthesizes the African and the American Ideals (see Table 10). Neither of these ideals has been suc-

Table 10

ORGANIZATIONS WITHIN THE BLACK SOCIAL MOVEMENT, 1800-1971

ORGANIZATIONS	DATES ORGANIZED
1. The Negro Convention Movement (NCM)	1830
2. The African Civilization Society (ACS)	1858
3. The African Emigration Society (AES)	1881
4. The International Migration Society (IMS)	1884
5. National Afro-American League (NAAL)	1887
6. Niagara Movement (NM)	1905
7. National Association for the Advancement of Colored People (NAACP)	1909
8. National Urban League (NUL)	1910
9. The Universal Negro Improvement Association (UNIA)	1917
10. The Nation of Islam (NOI)	1930
11. The National Negro Congress (NNC)	1935
12. The Congress of Racial Equality (CORE)	1942
13. The Southern Christian Leadership Conference (SCLC)	1957
14. The Student Nonviolent Coordinating Committee (SNCC)	1960
15. The Congress of African Peoples (CAP)	1970
16. People United to Save Humanity (PUSH)	1971
17. The Republic of New Africa (RNA)	1971

cessful in achieving freedom and liberation for oppressed blacks. While the society allowed for token expressions of integration, it controlled the creative demonstrations of reform and met revolutionary Black Power sentiments with violence. Organizations and individuals have shifted their ideology and strategies, but substantive changes in the objective conditions of oppressed people in the American social order have not been forthcoming. The African Idealists had hoped for a massive physical return to Africa, even though a cultural and spiritual return resulted. The American Idealists had hoped for meaningful integration to secure equality and justice, and they achieved tokenism and covert racism and control. A sense of change has been realized, creating a danger to continued creative struggle. Some of the Afro-American Idealists have sounded revolutionary but behaved like reformists, achieving very little by way of meaningful change. The rest of this group have given themselves to the struggle to create their own society (Republic of New Africa).

The black social movement had in many ways altered white consciousness for a while. Many whites came to believe that something was fundamentally wrong, but the efforts of these whites along with blacks failed. The failure is indicative of the fact that the barriers to the progress of oppressed blacks were not artificial. Leaving the social structure as it is and simply trying to get in does not achieve liberation. Once there is the recognition that racial and oppressive policies and practices are not just an epiphenomenal accident but are rooted in the nature of the social order, it would be understood that the failure to achieve liberation and freedom for the oppressed in America is a function of the very nature and character of the system and the inappropriate strategies employed by the movement in relation to that nature and character.

The American social order is inhumane; the problem is not only racism but also perpetual poverty, imperialism, and materialism. It seems a mistake to struggle for the dispersion of the oppressed throughout the system while leaving it fundamentally the same. Apart from the fact that such individuals are controlled in token numbers, they also occupy powerless positions with apparent power status, projecting a false sense of real power to those they represent. The other danger is the sense that they achieved their positions of apparent power solely on the basis of their qualifications, not recognizing the efforts of the movement in their behalf, thus denying all sense of accountability and responsibility to the movement and the struggle for liberation.

It is evident that the system is becoming less open for the oppressed and that the issue of racial justice and equality is seriously linked to economic and political equality. Blacks and other oppressed groups are trapped in a set of arrangements that are racist and capitalist; and those who benefit economically, politically, socially, and psychologically have steadily prepared to protect the arrangements so that the benefits might continue to be willed and bequeathed from one racial group to members of the same racial group. The next move, which is now being contemplated, is that of the oppressed.

Notes

1. See chapter 1.

2. Francis Cress Welsing, "The Cress Theory of Color-Confrontation," *Black Scholar* 5, no. 8 (May 1974): 32-40. See also N. Fuller, *Textbook for Victims of White Supremacy*, copyrighted, Library of Congress, 1969.

3. Marion D. deB Kilson, "Towards Freedom: An Analysis of Slave Revolts in the United States," *Phylon* 25 (Summer 1964): 175-87. See also Herbert Aptheker, *American Negro Slave Revolts* (New York: International Publishers, 1963), p. 162.

4. Kenneth M. Stampp, *The Peculiar Institution* (New York: Knopf, 1956), p. 140.

5. Wilbur H. Siebert, *The Underground Railroad from Slavery to Freedom*. (New York: Macmillan, 1898).

6. William Alexander, *Memoir of Captain Paul Cuffee, A Man of Colour*

(London: 1811). See also Sheldon Harris, *Paul Cuffee: Black America and the African Return*. (New York: Simon & Schuster, 1972).

7. Edwin Redkey, *Black Exodus: Black Nationalist and Back to Africa Movements, 1890-1910* (New Haven, Conn.: Yale University Press, 1969).

8. Langston Hughes, *Fight for Freedom: The Story of the NAACP* (New York: Norton, 1962); Robert C. Weaver, "The NAACP Today," *Journal of Negro Education* 29 (Fall, 1960): 421-25.

9. Whitney M. Young, Jr., *To Be Equal* (New York: McGraw-Hill, 1964); L. Hollings Worthwood, "The Urban League Movement," *Journal of Negro History* 11 (April 1924): 117-26; Kenneth Clark, "The Civil Rights Movement: Momentum and Organization," *Daedalus* 95 (Winter 1966): 239-267; National Urban League, *The Urban League Story, 1910* (New York: National Urban League, 1961).

10. James Farmer, *Freedom - When* (New York: Random House, 1966); August Meier and Elliott Rudwick, "How 'CORE' Began," *Social Science Quarterly* 49 (March 1969): 789-99; August Meier, "Negro Protest Movements and Organizations," *Journal of Negro Education* 32 (Winter 1963): 92-98; Elliott Rudwick and August Meier, "Organizational Structure and Goal Succession: A Comparative Analysis of the NAACP and CORE, 1964-1968," *Social Science Quarterly* 51 (June 1970): 0-41.

11. Martin Luther King, Jr., *Stride Toward Freedom: The Montgomery Story* (New York: Harper, 1964); Louis E. Lomax, *The Negro Revolt* (New York: Harper, 1962).

12. Charles Jones, "SNCC: Non-violence and Revolution," *New University Thought* 111 (September-October 1963): 8-19; Howard Zinn, *SNCC: The New Abolitionists* (Boston: Beacon Press, 1964); Gene Roberts, "The Story of Snick from Freedom High to 'Black Power.'" *New York Times Magazine*, September 25, 1966, p. 27.

13. Philip S. Foner, ed., *The Black Panthers Speak* (New York: Lippincott, 1970); Gene Marine, ed., *The Black Panthers* (New York: New American Library, 1969).

14. Amiri Baraka (Leroi Jones), *African Congress* (New York: William Morrow, 1972).

15. Leroi Jones, "A Black Value System," in Robert Chrisman and Nathan Hare, ed., *Contemporary Black Thought* (New York: The Bobbs-Merrill Co., Inc., 1973), pp. 71-79.

16. L. Alex Swan, "An Open Letter to Amiri Baraka," *Black World*, December 1975, p. 78.

17. Joseph Scott, *The Black Revolts: Racial Stratification in the USA* (Cambridge, Mass.: Schenkman Publishers, 1976). Alphonso Pinkney, *Red, Black and Green* (New York: Cambridge University Press, 1976).

Conclusion

The survival and progress of Afro-Americans have been of concern to black people since their forced entry into the new world. The struggle for liberation and freedom has taken many forms, and it has involved several generations of Afro-Americans. No doubt, black people hoped that their efforts during their history of struggle in America and particularly during the 1960s would achieve liberation for the group. However, as we enter the 1980s, racism and economic oppression, along with political domination, are issues and conditions that are still being addressed and are still negatively affecting Afro-Americans.

One of the great tragedies of emancipation and reconstruction was the failure of the government to provide economic security for Africans who were held in slavery. Their economic security could have been enhanced through the provision of land, which many have argued is the basis of liberation and freedom of a people.

The labor of African slaves was used to clear the wilderness of America to make it productive. They were a part of this production, but not as landowners. For over two hundred years, they were tied to the land and continued to realize the value of land to the survival and progress of a people. The denial to African people enslaved in America of land, for which they had supreme regard, was a clear sign that without such land of their own, they would forever be subject to the oppressive and racist will of their former owners and those to whom they had willed and bequeathed their ownership and power. Even though there were gestures and statements made by the government, over the years, that it shared an understanding of the plight of former slaves, it has not produced any substantial change in the oppressed conditions of Afro-Americans.

The decade of the 1970s has closed, and black unemployment at the beginning of the 1980s is over twice the figure it was at the end of the 1960s.

Black wages, when adjusted to the rate of inflation, are about 20 percent lower than they were a decade ago. The 1978 figures, however, showed a little rise in real income among black families. Again, adjusting for inflation, for black families, the median income increased from $9,563 in 1977 to $10,879, or 6 percent. The number of black families living below the poverty level changed very little from 1977, with more than 1.6 million families, or 27.5 percent, having incomes of less than $6,662. By comparison, the number of white families below the poverty level was 6.9 percent, or 3.5 million families. If the economic situation continues as it is, and the economy does not experience a significant recovery, than black families will suffer setbacks in attempts to survive and make progress.

The Black Power organizations that were very active during the 1960s and early 1970s, The League of Revolutionary Black Workers, SNCC, the African Liberation Support Committee, the Congress of African People, and others that did not have national attention, have self-destructed, disintegrated, or been destroyed by racist and oppressive acts of the police and the federal government. Black politicians have joined the black professional bureaucrats and many of the black educators and ministers in becoming even more conservative in their approach to economic and political change relative to the efforts of the masses for liberation and freedom. This shift in the approach to struggle is significant because these people make and influence political and economic decisions that affect issues that impact the lives of millions of black people.

There is a general consensus emerging among blacks that the Carter administration had demonstrated the most conservative and disastrous policies during its four years of rule. There are many who believe that the conservative policies of the racist administration of Woodrow Wilson were not so oppressive and restrictive of black progress and prosperity as those of the Carter administration. What must be borne in mind is that 93 percent of the black votes cast for president in 1976 went to Jimmy Carter, and blacks did not anticipate such policies and practices of the Carter administration. Since the depression, the objective material, economic, political, and social position of blacks in the American social order has not been worse. In fact, there is the realization that most of the achievements of the 1960s are being lost.

In March 1979, black historian Lerone Bennett described the period of the 1970s, especially the three-year period of the Carter administration, as the most serious since the Civil War. In the 1979 Annual Report of the Urban League, Vernon Jordon declared that Black America is currently at the "brink of disaster."

There is no doubt that there is a lull in the black social movement. The movement has reached a new nadir, a low point in the struggle for black liberation. The explanations are that the black liberation movement made too many errors, that the system has controlled the movement by allowing the absorption into the social order of a large number of key individuals of the mass movement, and that there has been a systematic and consistent attack on the movement by the agencies of the state such as the police, the FBI, and the CIA, along with other groups such as the Ku Klux Klan that have experienced, in the past three years, a resurgence even at the junior and senior high school levels and in other parts of America than in the southern states. All of these explanations are true and correct. It is also true that the organizations within the black liberation movement are operating as though in disarray. Many of the leaders seem confused as to their goals and objectives; some have been bought off because of their dependence on the economic support of whites; some are subtly silenced for other reasons; and many have been assassinated and imprisoned.

In Pensacola, Florida, black postal workers were threatened because of the gains they achieved; and in Greensboro, North Carolina, five people were killed on November 4, 1979, in conflict with the Ku Klux Klan. However, violence by anti-black groups were not confined to the South. In Boston, Michigan, and Illinois there was racial violence by the Klans. We have also witnessed the coming out of the closet of several police officers who declared themselves members of the Ku Klux Klan organization. In one conflict in Boston on April 6, 1976, white demonstrators protesting school busing grabbed and held a well-dressed black bystander, while two young white males beat him with an American flag pole. The man suffered a broken nose and bruises to his head and body.

In April 1979, before the Lawyers Committee for Civil Rights under Law, Attorney General Benjamin Civiletti warned that "the American public, lulled by past civil rights victories, should be kept aware that discrimination still is practiced as much as when segregation was the rule." He informed the group that "discrimination had been transferred from blatant, overt acts to today's more subtle, sophisticated and complex discriminatory practices." He further argued that "it is essential that we prevent the erosion of public awareness of the problems that persist and haunt the American dream."

There are many blacks who would like to believe that Civiletti's observation is incorrect. It is the subtle and covert nature of racism that has black leaders confused. They have no agenda for the solution of subtle/covert racism. The covert nature of racism has also caused many blacks to think that racism has disappeared from the American social order, and in many instances they do not want to discuss the issue. Ninety percent of the issues discussed at all of the black conferences and organizations that held meetings in 1979 had nothing to do with or to say about racism, and this has been the pattern over the last three years. However, the old problems persist and new problems constantly arise to make the situation for blacks more complex. In fact, the position might well be that blacks are stuck in the mud of racism and oppression with no real strategy for getting out. What has made the problem of being stuck in the mud more difficult is that there is a growing sense of individualism among blacks that seems to result from the belief that racism has disappeared and that liberation and freedom must now be achieved on the basis of individual merit and qualification. This notion of individualism will make it even harder, not easier, for blacks as oppressed and dominated people to survive and especially make progress. The commitment to the belief that an oppressed person can succeed through individual merit makes people blind to sociopolitical factors and traditional or historical conditions that hold the individual back and are beyond the control of the individual to change the situation. The belief and practice of individualism also causes other oppressed groups to be reluctant to form coalition efforts with black people. The struggle against individualism among oppressed blacks must consume their efforts during the 1980s if the group is to get out of the mud.

One of the pressing problems among blacks is the extraordinary growth in unemployment among black youth. This growth has persisted through a decade of civil rights enforcement and minority job programs and through periods of national prosperity, inflation, and recession. No strategy has been very effective in moving black adults and youth into more productive work. The psychological, social, and economic cost of unemployment to the black community and to the nation is enormous. It is obvious that black youth and adults suffer disproportionately from economic policies designed to curb inflation. One of the losses to the black community from the inability of over 60 percent of those black youths who want to work to find work is the loss of the potential economic infusions into the economy from the community that is essential to the survival and progress of its people. This is not to suggest that there has not been some degree of progress among blacks. However, the small progress is evident among middle-class professional blacks whose education and training placed them in positions that assured them of degrees of progress; yet their degree of prosperity was still less than that of their white counterparts. Moreover, when all classes among blacks are combined, one cannot convincingly speak about black progress. We must remember that we are more concerned with group progress than with individual gains.

When we compare black progress and gains over the past decade with that of whites, in terms of both the group and the individual, blacks have simply survived—and that not very well. What gains were made are circumscribed and limited. For the majority of blacks in America, little has changed, and the change for middle-class blacks has not been in terms of ownership and control of any of the means of production. Whites are still in control of the news media, the publishing houses, the government, the industries, the corporations, the major educational institutions, the land resources, and the lending institutions.

When we highlight those individuals who have made certain controlled gains in order to give credit to the efforts of the 1950s and the 1960s, we promote the notion that gains are made on an individual basis, not fully understanding that, in an oppressed and racist social order, gains are allowed on an individual basis to weaken the belief that the collective group was significant in such gains. Moreover, the individuals come to see their gains in individual terms, arguing that it was their qualifications and not the collective protest of the group that assured them of such gains.

During the late 1960s through the mid-1970s, white employers seemed very concerned with hiring qualified blacks. Their response to the pressure to hire and employ blacks was, "if the persons are qualified we will employ them." One brother was heard to say after one such statement in Nashville, Tennessee, "What are you going to do about the unqualified whites you have here?" The employer seemed puzzled, but he got the message.

The struggle for freedom and liberation of African people in the New World, and in the United States in particular, has historically taken a collective thrust. This is to suggest that black people in the United States defined their problems in collective terms that led them to take collective action against racism, oppression, repression, and exploitation. It was not too long ago that this collective spirit dominated the black community. However, there are indications and the sense that this experience that motivated blacks and gave direction to their every effort is disappearing and is being replaced by individualism. This attitude seems to be taking the sting out of the efforts of blacks to be free and is reducing their ability to struggle, survive, and make collective progress. This attitude also seems to indicate the absence of racism and oppression when in fact these two diseases are intensifying and the tentacles of the imperialist octopus are choking oppressed people to death.

Many factors have influenced this move to individualism. The period beginning in the 1970s was a peak period of a significant phase of the black struggle. Gradual changes and cumulative changes plus meaningless and insignificant reforms created a sense among struggling peoples that things were beginning to happen. But the most dangerous thing to happen to a people who are struggling is for the opposition (the oppressor and his agencies) to create a situation that promotes simply a sense of change. The period from 1969 to 1974 has also been a period of searching by white women for their individuality, which was historically lost in the interest of their white men. Although this situation was essentially a family problem, it influenced the black struggle in a way that has caused blacks to discuss and validate the philosophy of competition and the survival of the fittest, the ideological position of the American capitalist-colonial system.

Racism, oppression, and imperialism may be black people's principle enemies, but the enemy that renders blacks incapable and reduces their ability to deal with their principle enemies is individualism. Individualism is functional in the black struggle only as it is defined and operationalized within the context and concerns of the collective. Martin L. King, Jr., demonstrated and taught that in a struggle the collective entity is more important than the individual. The greatest leader of the poor, one who made successful attempts to organize the oppressed, one who was always on the side of the downtrodden, Jesus Christ, demonstrated that the individual was important within the context of the group. He also demonstrated that even the death of the individual within the struggle must be on behalf of the collective. Consequently, blacks must reject the philosophy of the survival of the fittest and reactivate and put into operation and demonstrate the African philosophical/behavioral principle of the survival of the tribe and the oneness of being.

The American system is forcing oppressed people to behave in individualistic terms. Once this individualism is assumed, a sense of alienation and social distance will develop among blacks. In the context of this behavior, no collective resistance is forthcoming because individualism plays its part in isolating, dividing, and fragmenting the struggling efforts of black people. Therefore, individualism is a dangerous tool promoted and used by oppressors to make ineffectual the collective struggle of oppressed peoples. The oppressor interacts with the oppressed on the basis of collective blackness but seeks to have the oppressed interact with him in individual terms. Continuous control and manipulation are implicit in this stance, and oppressed blacks must resist this every time and in every place.

Modern technology has also given support to the philosophy of the survival of the fittest and the rise of individualism. This philosophy demands a code of ethics that includes doing one's own thing; but in a struggle for liberation (a group concept), one cannot afford to do what one wants to do. Rather, one must do, within the context of the collective, what must be done. The identity of the individual is not a personal creation but the creation of a long historical process of unity, struggle, cooperative effort, reconciliation, mutual responsibility, and social accountability. These elements have shaped black identity as a people. For example, marriage was not simply the union of two individuals but a union of families, and the socioeconomic elements of the community were organized in support of the union. The rearing of children was not simply a matter for the parents alone. Again, the members of the extended family and other members of the community united their efforts to give direction to and discipline children. The black elderly were not institutionally cared for but were an integral part of the total family structure and the activities of the community. There was also close contact with their children whether the children were near (in the community) or far away (living in another city or state). In the event there were no children, there was a significant amount of interaction between the black elderly and other members of their neighborhood. There existed a sense of the interdependency of all human elements. This sense of interdependency played an important part in the survival efforts of black people. It helped members of the community to deal with psychological isolation, racism, economic oppression, social loneliness, and political domination and control. With the new generation of black youth the sense of these daily realities are not as vivid, and the sense that things are changing seems to eat at the heart of a hidden strength in the black community. Nothing should disrupt the traditional behavioral orientation wherein kinship and parakinship ties bind the lives and existence of the individual to that of the collective. "I" must become "we." The collective must define the individual, and the group identity must reinforce the ethos of the struggle, that of the survival of the tribe and the oneness of being. Every effort must be organized to maintain the psychological security and social solidarity that enable black people to struggle against their principle enemies.

Individualism is detrimental to the liberating efforts of any oppressed people. Its presence among such groups weakens the buffer that collectiveness provides against racism and the evils of capitalism. Individualism within the struggle destroys the individual, the group, and the movement, if it is not defined and operationalized within the context of the group struggle for freedom and liberation. It weakens the spirit and diminishes the ability to wage a successful struggle against oppression. Individualism also makes void the African philosophical/behavioral principle of the survival of the tribe and the oneness of being, forcing the adoption of the philosophy of the survival of the fittest, which heightens and intensifies competition and conflict among blacks within the struggle for liberation.

The greatest deterrent to racism and imperialism is national and international collective struggle rooted in this African principle. The principle must be translated into appropriate action to substantially change the objective conditions that oppress black people and render them powerless.

The rise of crime and suicide, whether among the black middle-class, the masses, black youth, black women, or the black elderly, is an indication of the reduction of kinship and parakinship ties in the community and the growth of individualism. In the light of no real change for the group, it is criminal and suicidal to go it alone. As Brother James Baldwin wrote to Sister Angela Davis, "If they come for you tonight, they will be for me in the morning." Not one black is safe when all are in danger.

The black social movement is losing its grip on the nation's conscience as the nation develops a dangerous form of conservatism in the face of covert racism and tolerated oppression. The real question of the future is whether, with the nation's growing conservatism, and the resurgence of right-wing organizations and groups, blacks are going to continue to believe that racism and oppression must be eliminated and that liberation and freedom are values and conditions to struggle collectively to achieve.

The greatest challenges Afro-Americans have faced since their forced entry into America will come during the 1980s. It will require collective aciton to meet the monumental tasks. The history of struggle and the heritage and ancient tradition of survival in the face of insurmountable odds suggest that it is possible. But the heritage of collectivism among Afro-Americans is slipping away, a heritage that is essential for black children if the group is to survive and achieve liberation. If collectivism is not enhanced, maintained, and promoted and individualism destroyed, then Afro-Americans will continue to be Stuck in the Mud.

Bibliography

Ackerman, Nathan. *Treating the Troubled Family*. New York: Basic Books, 1966.
_____. *The Psychodynamics of Family Life*. New York: Basic Books, 1958.
Bach, George R., and Wyden, Peter. *The Intimate Enemy: How to Fight Fair in Love and Marriage*. New York: William Morrow and Co., Inc., 1969.
Banks, L.J. "Black Suicide." *Ebony*, May 1970, pp. 76-84.
Baraka, Amiri. *African Congress*. New York: William Morrow, 1972.
Barbour, Floyd B., ed. *The Black Power Revolt*. Boston: Porter Sargen Publishers, 1968.
Becker, Howard S. *Outsiders: Studies in the Sociology of Deviance*. New York: Free Press, 1963.
Bell, John E., ed. *Family Therapy*. New York: Jason Aronson, 1975.
Bellamy, Donnie D. "Whites Sue for Desegregation in Georgia: The Fort Valley State College Case." *The Journal of Negro History* 64, no. 4 (Fall 1979).
Bennett, Lerone, Jr. "Clarity and Black Base." *Ebony*, October 1971.
Billingsley, Andrew. *The Evolution of the Black Family*. New York: National Urban League, 1976.
_____. *Black Families and the Struggle For Survival: Teaching Our Children to Walk Tall*. New York: Friendship Press, 1974.
Bloch, Donald A. *Techniques of Family Psychotherapy*. New York: Grune and Stratton, 1973.
Boggs, James. *Racism and the Class Struggle*. New York: Monthly Review Press, 1970.
Blumer, Herbert. *Symbolic Interactionism*. Englewood Cliffs, New Jersey: Prentice-Hall & Co., 1969.
Bohanon, P., ed. *African Homicide and Suicide*. Princeton: Princeton University Press, 1960.
Bond, Horace M. *Negro Education in Alabama*. New York: Associated Publishers, Inc., 1969.
Breed, W. "The Negro and Fatalistic Suicide." *Pacific Sociological Review* 13, no. 3 (1970): 156-62.
Breitman, George, ed. *Malcolm X Speaks*. New York: Grove Press, 1965.

Carmichael, Stokely, and Hamilton, Charles V. *Black Power: The Politics of Liberation in America*. New York: Random House, 1967.

Cavan, Ruth S. *Suicide*. New York: Russell and Russell, 1965.

Chambliss, William J., and Steele, Marion F. "Status Integration and Suicide: An Assessment." *American Sociological Review* 1 (1966): 524-32.

Chambliss, William J. "A Sociological Analysis of the Law of Vagrancy." *Social Problems* 12 (Summer 1964): 67-77.

Chrisman, Robert, and Hare, Nathan, eds. *Contemporary Black Thought*. New York: The Bobbs-Merrill Co., Inc., 1973.

Cone, James H. *Black Theology and Black Power*. New York: Seabury Press, 1969.

Davis, Angela Y. *If They Come in the Morning*. New York: New Library, Segret, 1971.

Dolbeare, Kenneth M., and Dolbeare, Patricia. *American Ideologies: The Competing Beliefs of the 1970's*. Chicago: Markham Publishing Co., 1971.

Drimmer, Melvin, ed. *Black History: A Reappraisal*. New York: Doubleday, 1968.

Durkheim, E. *Suicide*. Glencoe, Ill.: Free Press, 1951.

Edelson, Marshall. *The Practice of Sociotherapy*. New Haven, Conn.: Yale University Press, 1970.

_____. *Sociotherapy and Psychotherapy*. Chicago: University of Chicago Press, 1970.

Fanon, Frantz. *Black Skin, White Masks*. New York: Ronald Press, 1967.

Farmer, James. *Freedom - When*. New York: Random House, 1966.

Ferber, Andrew, et al. *The Book of Family Therapy*. Boston: Houghton Mifflin, 1973.

Foley, Vincent D. *An Introduction to Family Therapy*. New York: Grune and Stratton, 1974.

Foner, Philip S., ed. *The Black Panthers Speak*. New York: Lippincott, 1970.

Fuller, N. *Textbooks for Victims of White Supremacy*. Copyright, Library of Congress, 1969.

Gibbs, Jack, and Martin, Walter. *Suicide and Status Integration*. Eugene: University of Oregon Press, 1964.

Gilliam, Reginald E., Jr. *Black Development: An Advocacy Analysis*. New York: Dunellen Publishing Co., 1975.

Glick, Ira D., and Kessler, David R. *Marital and Family Therapy*. New York: Grune and Stratton, 1974.

Goffman, Erving. *Stigma*. Englewood Cliffs, N.J.: Prentice-Hall & Co., 1964.

Gold, Martin. *Status Forces in Delinquency*. Ann Arbor: University of Michigan, Institute for Social Research, 1963.

Goldenberg, Herbert. *Contemporary Clinical Psychology*. Monterey, Calif.: Book/Cole Publishing Co., 1973.

Gutman, Herbert G. *The Black Family in Slavery and Freedom, 1750-1925*. New York: Pantheon Books, 1976.

Hadden, Jeffrey K., and Borgatta, Marie L. *Marriage and the Family: A Comprehensive Reader*. Itasca, Ill.: F. E. Peacock Publishers, Inc., 1969.

Hamilton, Charles V. *The Struggle for Political Equality*. New York: National Urban League, 1976.

Harris, Sheldon. *Paul Cuffee: Black America and the African Return*. New York: Simon & Schuster, 1972.

Hendin, Herbert. *Black Suicide*. New York: Basic Publishers Books, 1969.

Holmes, D.O.W. "Seventy Years of the Negro College—1860 to 1930." *Phylon* 10, no. 4 (1949).

Hughes, Langston. *Fight for Freedom: The Story of the NAACP*. New York: Norton, 1962.

Irwin, John. *The Felon*. Englewood Cliffs, N.J.: Prentice-Hall, 1970.

Jackson, Don D., ed. *Communication, Family and Marriage*. Palo Alto, Calif.: Science and Behavior, 1968.

Jones, Mack H. "The Responsibility of the Black College to the Black Community: Then and Now." *Daedalus* 100, no. 3 (Spring 1971): 732-44.

King, Martin Luther, Jr. *Why We Can't Wait*. New York: New American Library, 1964.

_____. *Strike Toward Freedom: The Montgomery Story*. New York: Harper, 1964.

Levine, Lawrence W. *Black Culture and Black Consciousness*. New York: Oxford University Press, 1977.

Logan, Rayford W. *The Negro in the United States*. New York: Van Nostrand Reinhold Co., 1951.

Lomax, Louis E. *The Negro Revolt*. New York: Harper, 1962.

McLean, Helen Vincent. "Why Negroes Don't Commit Suicide." *Negro Digest*, February 1947, p. 6.

McPheeters, A.A. "Interest of the Methodist Church in the Education of Negroes." *Phylon* 10, no. 4 (1949).

McWorter, Gerald. "The Nature and Needs of the Black University." *Negro Digest*, March 1968, pp. 4-13.

Marine, Gene, ed. *The Story of the Black Panther Party*. San Francisco, Calif.: Peoples Press, 1970.

Meier, August. "The Negro and the Democratic Party, 1875-1915." *Phylon* 17, no. 2 (1956).

Mitford, Jessica. *Kind and Usual Punishment*. New York: Alfred A. Knopf, 1973.

Myrdal, Gunnar. *An American Dilemma*. New York: Harper and Row, 1962.

Napper, George. "Perception of Crime: Problems and Implications." In Robert Woodson, ed. *Black Perspectives on Crime and Criminal Justice*. Boston: G.K. Hall and Co., 1977.

Nelson, Hart M., Yorkely, Raytha L., and Nelson, Anne K. *The Black Church in America*. New York: Basic Books, 1971.

Nobles, Wade W. "Africanity: Its Role in Black Families." *The Black Scholar* 5, no. 9 (June 1974): 10-17.

Pelt, Nancy Van. *The Compleat Marriage*. Nashville: Southern Publishing Association, 1979.

Perkins, Eugene. *Home is a Dirty Street: The Social Oppression of Black Children*. Chicago: The Third World Press, 1975.

Pinkney, Alphonso. *Red, Black and Green*. New York: Cambridge University Press, 1976.

Platt, A.M. *The Child Savers: The Invention of Delinquency*. Chicago: University of Chicago Press, 1969.

_____. "The Triumph of Benevolence: The Origins of the Juvenile Justice System in the United States." In Richard Quinney, ed. *Criminal Justice in America: A Critical Understanding*. Boston: Little Brown, 1974.

Prudhomme, Charles. "The Problem of Suicide in the American Negro." *Psychoanalytic Review* 25, no. 2 (1938): 187-204, and 25 no. 3: 372-91.

Quarles, Benjamin. *Jet*, December 28, 1967, p. 32.

Qubre, Claude F. *Forty Acres and a Mule*. Baton Rouge, Louisiana: Louisiana State University Press, 1978.

Quinney, Richard. *Criminology*. Boston: Little Brown and Co., 1979.

_____. *The Problem of Crime*. New York: Dodd, Mead and Co., 1970.

_____. "Who is the Victim." *Criminology* 10 (November 1972): 314-23.

Redkey, Edwin. *Black Exodus: Black Nationalist and Back to Africa Movements, 1890-1910*. New Haven, Conn.: Yale University, 1969.

Rex, John, and Moore, Robert. *Race, Community and Conflict: A Study in Sparkbrook*. London: Oxford University Press, 1976.

Rusche, George, and Kirchheimer, Otto. *Punishment and Social Structure*. New York: Columbia University Press, 1939.

Sager, Clifford J., Brayboy, Thomas L., and Woxenberg, Barbara R. *Black Ghetto Family in Therapy: A Laboratory Experience*. New York: Grove Press, 1970.

Satir, Virginia. *Conjoint Family Therapy*. Palo Alto, Calif.: Science and Behavior Books, 1967.

Scanzoni, John H. *The Black Family in Modern Society*. Boston: Allyn and Bacon, Inc., 1971.

Schafer, Stephen. *The Victim and His Criminal*. New York: Random House, 1968.

_____. *Compensation and Restitution of Victims of Crime*. New York: Patterson Smith, 1970.

Schur, Edwin M. *Crime Without Victims*. Englewood, NJ.: Prentice-Hall, 1965.

Scoresby, A. Lynn. *The Marriage Dialogue*. Reading, Mass.: Addison-Wesley Publishing Co., 1977.

Scott, Joseph. *The Black Revolts: Racial Stratification in the USA*. Cambridge, Mass.: Schenkman Publishers, 1976.

Seiden, Richard H. "We're Driving Young Blacks to Suicide." *Psychology Today*, August 1970.

Siebert, Wilbur H. *The Underground Railroad from Slavery to Freedom*. New York: Macmillan, 1898.

Smith, Rebecca M. *Klemer's Marriage and Family Relations*. New York: Harper and Row, 1975.

Stampp, Kenneth M. *The Peculiar Institution*. New York: Knopf, 1956.

Staples, Robert. *Introduction to Black Sociology*. New York: McGraw-Hill, 1976.

Stein, Peter J., et al., eds. *The Family: Functions, Conflicts and Symbols*. Reading, Mass.: Addison-Wesley Publishing Co., 1977.

Stone, Chuck. *Black Political Power in America*. Indianapolis: Bobbs-Merrill Co., 1968.

Swan, L. Alex. "An Open Letter to Amiri Baraka." *Black World*, December 1975.

_____. "Diversion and Community-Based Corrections Programs." Department of Sociology, Texas Southern University, Houston, Texas, 1979.

_____. "Juvenile Delinquency, Juvenile Justice and Black Youth." In Robert Woodson, ed. *Black Perspectives on Crime and the Criminal Justice System*. Boston: G.K. Hall and Co., 1977.

_____. *Crime, Policing, Corrections and the Social Order*. (Forthcoming)

_____. "The Politics of Identification: A Perspective of Police Accountability." *Crime and Delinquency* 20, no. 2 (April 1974): 119-28.

_____."Research and Experimentation in Prison." *The Journal of Black Psychology* 6, no. 1 (August 1979): 47-51.

_____. *Families of Black Prisoners*. Boston: G.K. Hall & Co. (Forthcoming), 1981.

_____. "Reentry and the Black Parolee." *Journal of Social and Behavioral Sciences* 21, nos. 2 & 3 (Spring-Summer 1975): 104-16.

_____. "Clinical Sociologists: Coming Out of the Closet." *Mid-American Review of Sociology*, vol. 5, no. 1 (Spring 1980): 87-98.

_____. "The Content of the Image and the Development of Properties of the Self." Unpublished manuscript, 1978.

Thompson, Daniel C. *Private Black Colleges at the Crossroads*. Westport, Conn: Greenwood Press, Inc., 1973.

Turner, Darwin T. "The Black University: A Practical Approach." *Negro Digest*. March 1968, pp. 14-20.

Walton, Hanes, Jr. *Black Politics*. New York: Lippincott Co., 1972.

_____. *Black Political Parties*. New York: Free Press, 1972.

Welsing, Francis Cress. "The Cress Theory of Color-Confrontation." *The Black Scholar* 5, no. 8 (May 1974): 32-40.

Willhelm, Sidney. *Who Needs the Negro*. Cambridge, Mass.: Schenkman Publishing Co., Inc., 1970.

Williams, Carl E., and Crosby, John F. *Choice and Challenge*. Dubuque, Iowa: W. C. Brown, 1979.

Williams, Eric. *Capitalism and Slavery*. New York: Capricorn Books, 1966.

Willie, Charles. *A New Look at Black Families*. New York: General Hall, Inc., 1976.

Winters, W.D., and Ferriera, J. *Research in Family Interaction*. Palo Alto, Calif.: Science and Behavior Books, 1969.

White, Ellen G. *Christ in His Sanctuary*. Mountain View, Calif.: Pacific Publishing Co., 1969.

Woodford, John N. "Why Negro Suicides are Increasing." *Ebony*, July 1965, pp. 89-100.

Wolfgang, Marvin. *Patterns of Criminal Homicide*. Philadelphia: University of Pennsylvania, 1958.

Worsnop, Richard L. "Compensation for Victims of Crime." *Editorial Research Reports* 11 (September 22): 693.

Wright, Erik-Olin. *The Politics of Punishment: A Critical Analysis of Prisons in America*. New York: Harper and Row, 1973.

Yette, Samuel F. *The Choice: The Issue of Black Survival in America*. New York: Berkeley Publishing Corporation, 1971.

Young Whitney M. Young, Jr. "Domestic Marshall Plan." *The New York Times Magazine*, October 1963, p. 43.

_____. *To Be Equal*. New York: McGraw-Hill, 1964.

Index

Myrdal, Gunnar, 164, 171, 241

NAACP, 158, 182, 183, 219 (table), 221, 222, 223, 228, 230
Nacirema Society, 8-14
Napper, George, 79, 88, 93, 108, 241
Nashville, suicide in, 61-65
National Afro-American Council, 157
National Afro-American League, 157, 221, 222, 228
National Alabama Democratic Party, 158
National Association of Colored Women, 157
National Black Agenda, 165-166
National black conventions, 156-158
National Equal Rights League, 157
National League for the Protection of Colored Women, 222
National Liberty Party, 158
National Negro Congress, 228
National Urban League, 202, 219 (table), 222, 232
Nation of Islam, 219 (table), 227, 228
Negro Convention Movement, 228
Negro Democratic League, 158
Negro Factories Corporation, 220
Negro Protective Party in Ohio, 159
Nelson, Anne, K., 51, 241
Nelson, Elmer K., Jr., 108
Nelson, Hart M., 151, 241
New Deal, 163, 164
Newton, Huey, 226
Niagara Movement, 157, 221, 222, 228
Nixon, Richard (President), 5, 8, 45, 48
Nkrumah, Kwame, 153
Nobles, Wade W., 127, 241

Ogden, M. O., 59, 74

Paffenbarger, R. S., 70, 75
Parks, Rosa, 223
Parrinder, Geoffrey, 129, 151
Party-type organization, 158-159
Party politics, 159-165
Paul, 142, 144
Peace and Freedom Party, 158

Peck, M., 58, 61, 74
People United to Save Humanity (PUSH), 219 (table), 228
Pelt, Nancy Van, 126, 241
Perkins, Eugene, 199, 210, 241
Peter, 142
Pharoah, 130
Phelps-Stroke Fund, 173
Philip, 130
Piliavin, Irving, 108
Pinkney, A., 191, 230, 241
Plastics Corporation, 94
Platt, A. M., 77
Pokorny, Alex, 91
Poussaint, Alvin, 29
Prisons: blacks in, 89; blacks released from, 97-100. *See also* Crime
Prosser, Gabriel, 43, 46, 131, 214
Prudhomme, Charles, 55, 56, 71, 73, 74, 241
PUSH, 219, 228

Quarles, Benjamin, 55, 74, 79, 88, 241
Qubre, Claude F., 210, 242
Quinney, Richard, 90, 199, 210, 242

Raab, Selwyn, 107
Racism, institutional, 57
Randolph, Philip, 204
Reagan, Ronald (Governor of California), 11
Redkey, Edwin, 230, 242
Reisman, David, 195
Republican National Convention of 1928, 159
Republican Party, 154, 155, 160, 161, 162, 163, 164, 166
Republic of New Africa, 219 (table), 225, 228
Resistance, Organized and Unorganized, 214-215
Restitutive Justice, 204-205
Revere, Paul, 11
Revolutionary Black Workers, League of, 232
Rex, John, 107, 242
Roberts, Gene, 230

ABOUT THE AUTHOR

L. ALEX SWAN is Professor and Chairman of the Department of Sociology and Economics at Texas Southern University. His earlier books include *The Politics of Riot Behavior*, *Blacks and the U.S. Criminal Justice System*, *Issues in Marriage*, *Family and Therapy* and *Families of Black Prisoners*.